£1-99

THE FOUNTAINS
OF ROME

Endpapers The Trevi fountain, from an eighteenth century engraving

Frontispiece Maderno's fountain in the piazza of St Peter's

H. V. MORTON

THE FOUNTAINS OF ROME

WITH 49 COLOR PHOTOGRAPHS
BY MARIO CARRIERI
AND OTHER ILLUSTRATIONS

THE CONNOISSEUR
AND MICHAEL JOSEPH

First published under the title
The Waters of Rome 1966
This edition 1970

This book was designed and produced by
George Rainbird Ltd,
Marble Arch House,
44 Edgware Road, London W2
The text was phototypeset in ''Monophoto'' Bembo by
Oliver Burridge Filmsetting Ltd, Crawley
The colour plates were printed in Italy by
Amilcare Pizzi S.p.A., Milan
The text was printed and bound by
Butler & Tanner Ltd, Frome, Somerset

SBN 7181 5014 7

For Mary

CONTENTS

COLOUR PLATES

PREFACE

In preparing this account of the aqueducts of Rome and their principal fountains I was greatly assisted by the interest and goodwill of Dottore Ingegnere Mario Pediconi, Director General of the *Azienda Comunale Elettricità ed Acque*. I am particularly grateful to him for having selected Dottore Ingegnere Adriano Mazzarda, Chief of the Aqueduct Services, as my guide to underground Rome. In relation to the waters of Rome, Signor Mazzarda occupies much the same position as that held in the days of Nerva and Trajan by Sextus Julius Frontinus; indeed I sometimes thought, when listening to him, and when descending with him into the clammy depths where distant streams rushed onward to Rome, that I might have been in the presence of his remote predecessor.

Surprisingly, perhaps, it is not generally known that the water system of modern Rome is a reproduction of that of classical Rome. The relationship, partly deliberate and partly inevitable, began when the Renaissance and post-Renaissance popes restored three of the ruined aqueducts and, in sending onward to the capital, after a lapse of many centuries, powerful streams of water directed at certain areas, revived the same hydraulic problems as those created when the aqueducts were first constructed from 312 B.C. to A.D. 226.

The characteristic of Roman hydraulics is that the supply of water is a continuous one which passes from distant sources directly to the consumer without previous storage in reservoirs; and the water of the various aqueducts is never mixed. That was so in ancient Rome; each region, as today, possessed its local supply whose virtues, or the reverse, were constantly debated; indeed, the references in classical literature to the purity of the Aqua Virgo or the coolness of the Aqua Claudia are paralleled nowadays whenever Romans discuss their local waters, as they often do. This preoccupation with the quality of water, and the degree of connoisseurship devoted to this study by a nation of wine drinkers, often strikes those from cities served by reservoirs as distinctly eccentric.

Every visitor has noticed the symbol of the peculiar Roman system: the street

Roman street tap, symbol of a running water supply

tap that flows day and night, discharging a stream of water into the gutter. Frugally-minded strangers who have attempted to turn off the tap will know that this cannot be done: it is not intended to be turned off. Its job, when not refreshing carnations or small boys, is to provide water that completes its circle of usefulness in the drains. This sight, viewed so unsympathetically by the visitor if his hotel bathroom, owing to some fault in an aqueduct, happens to be dry, is one that was as familiar to Horace and Pliny as to the modern traveller. It was the theory of the ancient hydraulic engineers that the imported rivers of Rome should perform a dual function: having provided the city with the life-giving element, they should then pass on into the sewers and so ensure the health of the capital.

The present is an appropriate time to consider the waters and fountains of Rome. The increase in population in the last twenty years, and the growth of the city, have made necessary some reconstruction of the ancient system, and legislation now before the Italian Parliament is designed to increase the quantity of water by the building of two new aqueducts and by changing the traditional running supply to the more usual one of storage in reservoirs. The first reservoir has been built on Monte Mario and is partly in operation, and a second is to be constructed under the English-looking park of the Villa Pamphilj. The new aqueducts are not expected to be in operation until 1972, thus bringing the number to eight, the same number that poured water into Rome in A.D. 52, in the reign of the Emperor Claudius.

It is impossible to say how the changes which are to be made in the distribution of water will affect the fountains. At the moment they are, with some exceptions, still fed by the same papal aqueducts which created them in the sixteenth and seventeenth centuries, and it has seemed to me worth while to put on record that this papal dispensation has endured into the sixties of the twentieth century. I hope it may be as interesting to others, as it has been to me, to learn something about the relationship between aqueducts and fountains, and to be able to go round Rome knowing, at the Trevi, that one has cast a coin into the Acqua Vergine Antica, and that, in the Piazza Navona, one is in the presence not only of Bernini, but also of the Acqua Paola, which took its name from Pope Paul V.

The danger which I suspect may threaten the fountains comes not from any change from aqueduct to reservoir, but rather from an entirely different quarter. The motor traffic in Rome is now so appalling that it is already difficult, if not impossible, to approach some of the most delightful of the wall fountains because of parked cars. Many fountains are built into the walls of Renaissance

Rome at just the right height to be chipped and damaged, and some are already in poor condition. Once they become inaccessible and invisible they may be forgotten, and gradually fade from a scene which they have graced for so long. One guessed years ago that the petrol engine was the enemy of fountains when the sound of falling water which delighted our ancestors was no longer audible, but the present situation, when the bonnet of a car almost rests upon the basin of a fountain, is something that would not have been allowed in Rome even ten years ago. Already the car has abolished the innumerable *abbeveratoi* – the horse-troughs – which have departed almost unnoticed from the streets; and the lesser fountains, which include many delightful works of art and some superb classical and early Christian sarcophagi, may well follow them. A society should be created to care for and protect the fountains of Rome. It would find many friends in all parts of the world.

The colour photographs of Signor Mario Carrieri will be greatly admired. Of particular interest, perhaps, are those in which he has caught fountains in the romantic glow of floodlights. The difficulty encountered in Rome by any modern photographer who attempts to record fountains is that of excluding intrusive machinery; and in the art of isolating the fountains from their contemporary surroundings Signor Carrieri, at the expense of much patience exercised over a long period of time, has been brilliantly successful.

A word should be said about floodlit fountains. It is generally believed that the flood-lighting of classical monuments in Rome had to wait for electricity, but that is not so. The picking out of statuary by artificial light was already an old device of the "sightsman" when Goethe, in 1787, described the custom of paying a "torchlight visit" to the Vatican and Capitoline museums, "a visit desired alike by all strangers, artists, connoisseurs and laics". The eighteenth century guide, crouching behind the *Laocoön*, and other famous statues, knew exactly where to cast the light of his wax torch in order to reveal dramatic glimpses and unexpected beauties. The technique was also practised by Sir William Hamilton, who often held the light himself as his beautiful young Emma gave a display of those "attitudes" which achieved a European celebrity. Goethe was so interested in the possibilities of illuminated statues that he printed an essay on the subject by his friend, Heinrich Meyer, the Swiss artist, in *Travels in Italy*. Meyer believed that torchlight tours began during the eighties of the seventeenth century. The intention was that of modern flood-lighting: to isolate an object from its background and to reveal it in unusual lights; in this, the portable wax torch may have had some advantage over the unwinking flood-lamp of today.

A tour of the fountains by night will prove that some are more spectacular in artificial light, while others are best left to darkness or the moon. The most remarkable transformation is that of the central fountain, the *mostra* of the Acqua Pia Marcia, in the Piazza della Repubblica, which sheds its air of the naughty nineties and becomes a magical shower of golden water rising into the night against the background of Diocletian's Baths. The Moses Fountain is discreetly lit, emphasis being directed upon the three cascades, leaving the unfortunate figure of the Prophet to the mercy of darkness. The Trevi appears to be illuminated by a mysterious self-generated radiance which descends upon it from flood-lights cleverly mounted on the lamp standards, while nothing could be simpler or more effective than the lights sunk in the great basin of the Monte Cavallo fountain, which send a flickering glow over the two white horsemen and the obelisk. Some of the minor fountains achieve a dignity and importance denied to them by daylight, and owe more to the electricians of today than to the architects of past centuries. These, however, are few, and generally speaking the basin of travertine, or the marble bowl isolated and golden in the darkness, would have delighted such early amateurs of flood-lighting as Heinrich Meyer who was one of the first to observe how skilfully directed light revealed the proportions of a work of art and "brought out its tenderest *nuances*".

My warmest thanks are due to Professor T. J. Haarhoff for having turned Renaissance Latin into English for me, to Professor Ward Perkins for allowing me to use the library of the British School at Rome, and to Dr E. V. Rieu for having read the proofs of my first four chapters. Count Enrico Pietro Galeazzi, Director of the Technical Services of the Vatican City, Count Fago Golfarelli, and Signor Luigi Coppé have given much help in Rome. Among writers on this subject, I am most indebted to Signor Cesare d'Onofrio, whose *Le Fontane di Roma* is the most recent and scholarly account of the fountains.

H. V. MORTON

ACKNOWLEDGEMENTS

All the colour plates are from photographs by Mario Carrieri. Also by Mario Carrieri are the monochrome photographs on the following pages: 30 *top*, 48 *bottom*, 51, 76, 77, 89, 91, 94, 95, 98, 106, 116, 128, 129 *bottom*, 136 *bottom*, 137, 141, 145, 147, 152, 153, 157, 160, 161, 173, 182 *left*, 183, 193, 195, 198, 214, 229, 232, 233, 245, 255, 256, 257, 260, 264 *top left*, 283, 284, 289, 290.

The photographs on pages 196, 264 *top right*, and 264 *bottom* are by the author.

For permission to reproduce copyright illustrations, grateful acknowledgements are made to:

Administration des Monnaies et Médailles, Paris: pages 119 *left*, 165 *right*.

Alinari: page 39 (bust in the Uffizi Gallery, Florence).

American School of Classical Studies, Athens: page 22.

Anderson: page 107.

Azienda Comunale Elettricità ed Acque, Rome: page 10.

British Museum: pages 19, 48 *top* (from Robert Burn, *Rome and the Campagna*, London, 1871), 50 *top* (from Alo Giovannoli, *Vedute degli Antichi Vestigi di Roma*, Rome, ?1750), 50 *bottom*, 88 (from Giuseppe Vasi, *Delle magnificenze di Roma*, 1747), 93 (from Hermann Egger, *Die Römischen Skizzenbücher von Marten van Heemskerck*, two vols, Berlin, 1913-16), 97 (from Vasi, op. cit.), 111 *bottom* (from A. Lazzarini, *Raccolta delle vedute di Roma e Tivoli*, Rome, 1841), 122, 129 *top*, 136 *top*, 138, 171, 175 (from Vasi, op. cit.), 186 (ibid.), 203 (ibid.), 204 *left*, 210 (from Egger, op. cit.), 211, 243 (from Vasi, op. cit.), 244, 253, 270-71, 273, 286, 287, and endpapers.

J. Allan Cash: page 16.

Deutsches Museum, Munich: page 30 *bottom* (from a painting by Professor Zeno Diemer).

André Held: page 121.

Istituto Nazionale d'Archeologia e Storia dell'Arte, Rome: page 58 (from Giulio Ballino, *De' disegni delle piu illustri città e fortezze del mondo*, Venice, 1569).

Mansell Collection: pages 62 *bottom*, 165 *left* (bust by Bernini in the Borghese Gallery, Rome).

Foto Ann Münchow: page 204 *right*.

Radio Times Hulton Picture Library: page 223.

Edwin Smith: page 25 (fountain in the House of the Great Fountain, Pompeii).

Vatican Library: page 86 *right* (drawing by P. L. Ghezzi, 1744).

Victoria and Albert Museum, London: pages 86 *left* (from *Chronologia summorum romanorum pontificorum*, Rome, c. 1832), 119 *right* (bust, bronze, Italian, probably early seventeenth century), 146 (bust, copper, Italian, early seventeenth century), 182 *right* (medal in silvered bronze by C. J. F. Chéron, French, dated 1674).

The illustrations on the following pages are reproduced from the books cited.

26: Wilhelm Schmidt (ed.), *Herons von Alexandria – Druckwerke und Automatentheater*, Leipzig, 1899.

14

60: Étienne du Pérac, *Topographical Study in Rome in 1581*, ed. Thomas Ashby for the Rox-burghe Club, London, 1916.

62 *top*: Giovanni Battista Cavalieri, *Pontificum romanorum effigies*, Rome, 1580.

111 *top*: Giovanni Battista Falda, *Le Fontane di Roma*, Rome, ?1675.

272: Carlo Fontana, *Il Templo Vaticano e sua origine*, Rome, 1694.

The maps on pages 33, 66–7, and 69 were drawn by Audrey Frew; Father Stanley G. Luff in Rome and officials of ACEA gave valuable assistance.

The index was made by Myra Clark.

I

THE FOUNTAIN
IN ANTIQUITY

THE WORD "fountain" may be used to describe a natural spring or an artificial contrivance for the display of water: or even the water itself. It is derived from the Latin *fons*, a source – *fons et origo* – and is employed in that sense in such phrases as "The Fountain of Honour". When the word is used in ordinary conversation it usually means an architectural construction in a public place or a garden, from which water rises or into which it falls.

The fountain and the firework have the odd distinction of displaying elements of devastating possibilities in a mood of playful benevolence. Water, the giver of life, and also the taker of life in storm and tempest, achieves in the fountain an appearance of obedience to the will of man: and its apparent desire to please, as it springs into the air, or as it simulates a waterfall, or pours placidly from a bronze mouth, made a solemn impression upon the rustic mind. The countryman of remote ages who wandered into a city, and saw a fountain for the first time, felt that he was in the presence of some divine manifestation, a clear sign of good-will from the incalculable forces of Nature. The fountain has no enemies, even in cold countries: it is a device or invention which has given nothing but pleasure in the course of a long history. It has the ability to minister equally to joy and melancholy, to appeal to eye and to ear, to stand at a street corner ready to fill the water pots, or in a garden to assist the meditations of poet and philosopher.

It may appear difficult to classify fountains, so many are their decorative possibilities, but it is, in fact, quite simple. Limited, as fountains are, by the nature of water, there are only two kinds, rising jets or downward falls, and every fountain variation is played on that simple theme. "Fountains", wrote Bacon, "I intend to be of two natures: the one, that sprinkleth or spouteth water; the other a fair receipt of water, of some thirty or forty foot square, but without fish or slime or mud", a definition which accurately describes the duality of fountains, for displays even as complex as those of the Villa d'Este fall naturally into two groups: waters which rise and waters which fall.

The Castalian Spring at Delphi, which once fed a sacred fountain of the Oracle

Where did the architectural fountain begin? There must have been a first fountain and, as far as we know, it came, as so much beauty has come, from Greece. "No objects of the natural world", wrote Dr L. R. Farnell, "attracted the devotion of the primitive and late Greeks so much as rivers and springs, and no other obtained so general a recognition in the cults of the Greek states". Rivers, the sea itself, and particularly the springs that gushed so mysteriously from the volcanic soil, touched the imagination of that sensitive and inquisitive race. Those of us who are able to recall the moment in childhood when we looked for the first time into a natural spring will understand the awe such a strange sight inspired. We looked into water that appeared to be alive, shaken by a mysterious quivering different from the movement imparted to water by a passing breeze, since it originated, not on the surface, but in the depths. Glancing down to the bed of white sand at the bottom of the spring, we saw the "eyes" rhythmically tossing the sand here and there in little whirls and eddies, and even moving the pebbles as if invisible fingers were playing with them. It was an odd and hypnotic sight, and one can easily see how the Greek imagination fancied that springs were a gift of the gods and the abode of spirits.

In historic times it became necessary to enclose the springs in order to preserve their purity, and the first covered spring of which there is a record was the famous Callirrhoë of Athens, which was made into a fountain with nine outlets by Pisistratus and his sons (560–510 B.C.). The water fell from the mouths of nine bronze lion masks and the name was changed to Enneacrunus – "Nine-pipes". The veneration in which Callirrhoë had been held was immediately transferred to its successor, whose water continued to be used for religious and ritual purposes.

The sacred springs soon became architectural fountains all over Greece. Some were celebrated as medicinal springs, others were oracular, and each spring had its own genius, so that the invalid, or the person who wished to penetrate the future, might go on pilgrimage from fountain to fountain as in later ages men would visit the tombs of saints. With their infallible good taste, the Greeks designed shrines for the sacred water, temples were built near or above them, and many achieved celebrity all over the Mediterranean world. Pausanias, who travelled through Greece about the year A.D. 150, declared that in his opinion no place deserved the name of "city" that did not possess a decorated fountain dedicated to a god or a hero; and he saw in their prime some of the great fountains of Greece, such as that of Theagenes, at Megara, which was even then an antiquity; the famous Pirene at Corinth; the fountain in the grove of Aesculapius at Epidaurus; the oracular spring of Demeter at Patrae; the dragon-guarded spring

Fountain scenes on two Greek vases of the sixth century B.C. The left-hand vase apparently shows the famous Callirrhoë fountain at Athens, but may be only a stylized representation of a general type of fountain house

of Ares at Thebes, mentioned by so many ancient writers; the springs of Forgetfulness and Memory at Lebadia; the rain-making spring on Mount Lycaeus; and two strange salt-water springs, one on the Acropolis at Athens, the other in the temple of Poseidon at Mantinea.

Wherever the traveller turned in the Greek world, he would encounter a fountain that healed, blessed, or, though rarely, cursed. So we see in imagination the healing waters welling up in temple forecourts and issuing from majestic fountains, each one the focus of a complicated mythology of gods, goddesses and attendant nymphs, which the practical Roman mind reorganized in later ages as thermal spas. There were waters which the patient drank before he submitted to the dream cures for which the temples of Aesculapius were famous. The chief shrine of the god at Epidaurus has revealed a great number of votive tablets on which patients have described how, after having drunk water from the sacred fountain, they fell into the temple-sleep (which some believe was hypnotic treatment) and were cured, testimonials which have their modern parallel in the records of those who have been healed by the waters of Lourdes. There were also fountains in the oracular shrines, and in the most famous, the Oracle at Delphi, a spring, which still exists, was channelled to flow into the temple of Apollo, the shrine of the Oracle. There the Pythia – a middle-aged trance medium dressed as a young girl – would drink the water before uttering prophecies which the priests translated into ambiguous hexameters.

There was a fountain at Nauplia which had the reputation of restoring lost virginity, but it should be said that the favour was reserved for the goddess Hera when she bathed there once a year; though mortal women who did so were rewarded with the gift of unusual beauty. Vitruvius mentions the curious fact that certain fountains in Greece bore notices warning the traveller to avoid them. In Arcadia the visitor who appreciated "the joys of wine" was warned to give a wide berth to the "vine-hating" fountain of Clitor whose waters would not only destroy his palate but remove his taste for wine, and this Arcadian water was also celebrated as a cure for drunkards. There was a fountain on the island of Chios whose waters, though pleasant to the taste, were reputed to fossilize the brain, and in Asia Minor a fountain was credited with the power to make all who drank its waters see what they wished to see. Many magical springs were celebrated for divination. Their waters acted as the crystal of the fortune-teller, and sometimes, as at Cyaneae, in Lycia, as described by Pausanias, a mirror was gently let down into the spring until it almost touched the water, when prognostications were read from its surface. Similar beliefs and superstitions were common in all countries, and the well-dressing ceremonies in England, the wishing-wells, and the village superstitions connected with them, are part of the primitive reverence for the spirits of water; that every ancient well in England has been firmly dedicated to a Christian saint proclaims their rescue from paganism.

It is possible to visit what has been spared of some of the greatest fountains of the Hellenic world, but, remembering their fame and contrasting it with their present condition, the pilgrimage may be a sombre one. The Fountain of Arethusa still exists as a large, sunk pool, planted with papyrus and surrounded with a balustrade, on the island of Ortygia, off Syracuse, facing the great harbour where the fleets of Athens, Carthage and Rome cast anchor in their time. The story of this fountain is that of Arethusa, a water nymph who in a remote age was bathing in the river Alpheus, near Olympia, in the Peloponnesus, when the river god fell passionately in love with her. She fled from him across the Ionian Sea and came to Syracuse, in Sicily – a distance of about four hundred miles – where the goddess Artemis concealed her in the earth and transformed her into a spring; but to no effect, for the ardent Alpheus, pursuing her across the sea, found her and mingled his water with that of the spring. The story illustrates the ancient belief that the river Alpheus was connected with the fountain Arethusa in Sicily by a subterranean passage or fissure beneath the sea, four hundred miles in length. It was said that a cup cast into the Alpheus would later be recovered from the Arethusa, and it was also said that every fourth year, when the Olympic Games were held, the offal from the sacrifices which were cast into the river at Olympia, and the dung when racehorses bathed in it, fouled the fountain four hundred miles away. The story was believed as late as A.D. 397, when it was said that the news that Stilicho had defeated the Goths on the Alpheus was known at Syracuse when the Arethusa was seen to be stained with blood. Claudian, who relates this, does not explain how the Syracusans knew that it was Gothic blood! Milton mentioned the legend in *Arcades*:

> Divine Alphaeus, who by secret sluice
> Stole under seas to meet his Arethuse.

The name of Arethusa is heard nowadays only in coin auction rooms where numismatists are the last converts to her cult. She inspired the most beautiful coins that have ever been minted, the big silver decadrachms of 400 B.C., signed by the artist Kimon. The portrait shows the nymph as a fashionable young woman of the time, her hair elaborately curled and dressed and caught up in a net, and a string of pearls round her throat. Dolphins play round the edge of the coin, those friendly creatures who adopted fresh-water fountains centuries ago and frisked as charmingly in ancient Syracuse as they do today in Trafalgar Square.

Corinth also possessed its water nymph, Pirene, who, according to legend, shed so many tears upon the death of her son that she became a fountain; and such a famous one that the Delphic Oracle sometimes referred to Corinth as "the city of Pirene". Although the architectural fountain has vanished, the old spring still gushes out in ice-clear water from the ruins of Corinth. Possibly the only remaining evidence of this fountain is to be found in the coinage of Corinth, which shows a seated figure of Pirene which may have been copied from a statue that once formed part of the decoration. It is odd to think that during the Turkish occupation of Greece the Bey of Corinth had his seraglio here, in a garden watered by Pirene. Corinth was once a city of splendid fountains, and many of their sites were revealed recently by the American School of Classical Studies,

Lion's-head spout surviving in the ruins of the Sacred Spring, a fountain in the agora at Corinth

though the statues and architectural adornments have all disappeared. Among the fountains was a statuesque group which represented Bellerophon with his winged steed Pegasus, for it was while Pegasus was drinking at Pirene that he was caught and tamed by Bellerophon. As the steed sprang upward, water gushed from one of his hoofs. A second fountain was a colonnaded terrace where the townsfolk would walk and sit in the evening, charmed and cooled by the sight and sound of water; a third depicted Poseidon with a dolphin at his feet.

Perhaps the most celebrated of all the Greek fountains was the Castalian Spring at Delphi in whose water those who had arrived to consult the Oracle would wash their hair or take a ritual bath. It still flows vigorously in its rocky gorge in the shadow of Mount Parnassus and at the foot of the Sacred Way. The water is cool, clear and sweet to the taste, and the modern tourist has discovered that the famous spring is a pleasant place for a picnic luncheon near the ruins. Another Delphic spring which still flows, higher up the mountain, is the Cassotis, whose waters were brought underground to the oracular chasm and the Temple of Apollo.

One cannot leave the fountains of Greece without remembering their guardian spirits, the water nymphs, those spectral maidens who were in attendance on all fountains and were not unlike the fairies of English superstition. Generally amiable to mankind, they were, however, sometimes mischievous and were greatly feared for their sudden rages. They were physically attractive and, though not immortal, were credited with exceptionally long life. That they still haunt the Greek countryside will be well known to anyone who is familiar with the remote villages and the islands.

I remember hearing an old peasant in Arcadia confide to a Greek friend of mine a convincing description of a naiad who was often seen flittering through an olive grove, wearing trailing white garments; and much the same story is known to all who have written about Greek folklore. J. C. Lawson found that in country districts it was customary to propitiate the water spirits with adulatory names, as their ancestors placated the Furies by calling them the Kindly Ones, or Our Good Queens. "Their presence is suspected everywhere," he wrote, "grim forest depth and laughing valley, babbling stream and wind-swept ridge, tree and cave and pool, each may be their chosen haunt, the charmed scene of their dance and song and god-like revelry." J. C. Lawson collected stories of the love affairs between men and water nymphs – frequent, it appears, but invariably unsatisfactory – and of the malice felt by the nymphs for mortal women. A shepherd of Scopelos told him that one of his goats fell under the spell of a naiad and pined away from unrequited love, a story which surely might have been told to Theocritus or Pausanias. Lord Rennell of Rodd wrote that "mineral springs and healing waters are especially under the protection of the Nereids, and those who drink of them do so in silence and with a certain awe". More recent travellers have also found that such beliefs are as strongly held today as ever. Patrick Leigh Fermor describes the water spirits as being dressed in white and gold and of unearthly beauty. "Strangely enough they are not immortal," he writes, "they live a thousand years. But they are of a different and rarer essence from ordinary mortals and, in some way, half divine. Their beauty never fades, nor do the charm and seduction of their voices."

Such were the spirits of the Greek fountains, and I think that some of us, walking after sunset in an old garden and finding among dark cypresses "a stone fountain weeping out the years" will admit that we have glanced into the gathering shadows, half expecting to see the glimmer of a naiad's garments and to hear in the silence, above the drip of water, the mocking laughter of the pagan world.

The Greece that tutored Rome was not the Greece of antiquity but the inventive, Hellenistic Greece which arose in the steps of Alexander the Great, an age that in its scientific approach to life bears some resemblance to our own. Probably no cities more beautiful have ever been designed on more uncompromising sites than Pergamum and Priene on the west coast of Asia Minor, cities so steeply terraced upon mountainsides that one wonders how those who were no longer young and active managed to get about. The succession of brilliant cities from Assus in the north, by way of Ephesus to Halicarnassus and Aspendus, have revealed rectangular streets, splendid market-places, theatres, temples, docks: the cities of an age that looked upon steam power and compressed air as a delightful joke and, as it seems, failed only by the merest chance to invent a steam engine.

One can only imagine what the fountains were like in Ptolemaic Alexandria or in Seleucid Antioch, but they must have been worthy of the cities of that age. The pressurized water supply of Pergamum and the aqueducts of Priene, Magnesia and Ephesus no doubt fed superb fountains, though we know nothing about them. We do know, however, that the Hellenistic world contributed the *nymphaeum* to the art of fountain-making. This was an architectural city fountain unconnected with the temple, and religious only in a formal way as a place dedicated to the spirits of water. Even caravan cities such as Palmyra, in Syria, and Amman, in Jordan, had their *nymphaea*; and those elaborate constructions, which were often circular in shape, and always richly decorated with statues, mosaics and paintings, were in time adopted by Rome. The *nymphaeum* became so popular that many a palace and private house possessed one; a room full of plants and flowers where a fountain played or a grotto with running water had been arranged.

The mechanical fountain fitted with automata, the fountain that spouted wine, the water organ, the fountain decorated with birds that whistled and sang by means of compressed air, belong to the Hellenistic Age, and such works as the *Pneumatica* of Hero of Alexandria show how ingenious and varied these were. The author explained in that fascinating "how-to-do-it" book that temple doors might be made to open without human agency by the help of steam generated in boilers under the temple; and he illustrated with diagrams how compressed air could move figures, blow trumpets, and cause birds of bronze or brass to sing. Many of these delightful fountain tricks were revived by architects during the Renaissance. When Montaigne went to Tivoli in 1580 he found Hero's device of the owl and the singing birds in working order. This was a fountain worked

An elaborately decorated domestic fountain from Pompeii, first century A.D.

by pulleys, siphons and compressed air, on the rim of which perched a number of bronze birds all whistling merrily until an owl perched upon a nearby post suddenly turned and faced them. The design is perfectly simple, and anyone with a little mechanical knowledge, and a soldering iron, could make such a fountain from Hero's instructions. His hydraulic organ is rather more complex, but it presented no problems to the Romans and to the fountain-makers of the Renaissance.

It is from such circumstantial evidence, rather than from architectural remains, that we are justified in believing that the cities, parks and gardens of the Hellenistic world were full of impressive and interesting fountains. Their design, repeated in the fountains of ancient Rome, was revived during the Renaissance and later periods, and is reflected in the finer fountains of today.

The owl fountain from Hero of Alexandria's *Pneumatica*

II

THE AQUEDUCTS OF
ANCIENT ROME

THE ROMANS had no other water but that of springs, wells and the Tiber for the first four and a half centuries of their existence. The springs were numerous and some of them still flow under modern Rome as may be seen, and heard, in the Mithraic temple beneath the church of S. Clemente, which lies in the path of a subterranean stream. The most famous of the springs was the Fountain of the Camenae, which rose in a sacred grove just outside the old Porta Capena. The Camenae were a mysterious group of water spirits or nymphs who decided to befriend the young community and to guide it with their divine knowledge.

In the legendary prelude to Roman history, the warlike Romulus was succeeded by the peaceful and pious Numa Pompilius, who fell in love with a Camena named Egeria. Thirty-nine years of happy and constructive peace under a king wedded to a fountain goddess were explained by the story that Numa was divinely guided. It was said that he visited the sacred grove by night, when his Egeria would give him the advice which he later passed on to his people as law. Thus from the first of the fountains of Rome emerged the beginnings of Roman religion and law, though I wonder what a lawyer would say to a student who ventured to suggest that the mighty structure of Roman Law originated in water. However, the story of Numa and Egeria gives point and charm to the phrase, "the Fountain of the Law".

For centuries the fountain of the Camenae was the scene of a daily ceremony when the Vestal Virgins, who were forbidden to use water that had passed through pipes, came to the grove to fill their archaic water pots. These were shaped so that they could not be rested without spilling the water, a precaution taken to prevent contamination with the earth. It is not known for how long this ancient custom was observed, but Juvenal, writing about A.D. 100, said that in his time the grove was no longer venerated and was haunted by the poorest class of Jews with their baskets and bales of straw. It has been supposed that in later times the Vestals drew their water from the more convenient spring of

27

Juturna, whose remains are to be seen only a few paces from the House of the Vestal Virgins in the Forum Romanum.

Cities expand in proportion to their water supply, and as Rome developed and increased in population the springs and wells were no longer adequate. How curious it is that the words "writ in water" should be used sometimes to suggest something fleeting and ephemeral – as the dying Keats, for example, said that his name was "writ in water" – whereas water is necessary to permanence; indeed, all history might be said to be written in water since, lacking it, no life is possible.

Rome's problem of finding additional water was faced for the first time during the Censorship of Appius Claudius Caecus and Gaius Plautius in 312 B.C. It was the procedure in ancient Rome for public works approved by the Senate to be entrusted to the two Censors during their eighteen months of office. They had the task of employing the contractors and of supervising the construction; as a reward, they were often allowed the prized privilege of giving their names to the works they had directed. Plautius, entrusted with the task of finding the new water supply, discovered some springs about ten miles to the east of Rome; Appius Claudius, who was already supervising the Appian Way, was responsible for the aqueduct. However, the work was not completed when the time came for the Censors to resign. Plautius retired as he was required to do by law, but Appius Claudius was so determined to give his name to the aqueduct that he refused to resign and continued to remain in office, arguing that the *Lex Aemilia*, which limited the power of the Censors, did not apply to him. The moment the aqueduct was built and he had made certain that it would be called the Aqua Appia, he resigned. For most of its ten miles the Aqua Appia was buried underground in a channel of cut stone. Only when it had entered Rome was it lifted upon arches.

By A.D. 226, when the last of Rome's aqueducts was built, eleven aqueducts poured the water of springs, a river and a lake into the city. Nothing like this abundance of water had ever been seen, and it has never since been exceeded. It was, of course, out of all proportion to the actual needs of the population because many of the aqueducts were built purely to minister to the astonishing Cult of the Bath.

The aqueducts built after the Aqua Appia, in chronological order, were:

Aqua Anio Vetus, built in 272–269 B.C. This aqueduct was forty miles long and brought water from the Anio river (now the Aniene), near Vicovaro, east of Rome. Like its predecessor, it was an underground channel of cut stone.

Aqua Marcia, built in 144–140 B.C., by Quintus Marcius Rex, of whom nothing is known except that his *imperium* as Praetor was extended for a year that he might finish and give his name to the work. The length of the aqueduct was slightly more than fifty-six miles, and its source was a group of springs near Subiaco, east of Rome. For fifty miles the water flowed in an underground channel, then, as it approached Rome, it was mounted upon six miles of arches. Its terminus was the Capitoline Hill, and it was later piped to the Caelian, the Aventine, and the Quirinal hills.

Aqua Tepula, built in 125 B.C. This was eleven miles long and brought spring water from the Alban Hills. For five miles the aqueduct was underground and then for six miles it rode into Rome on top of the Aqua Marcia, both aqueducts using the same arches.

Aqua Julia, built in 33 B.C. This was the first of two aqueducts constructed by Marcus Agrippa, the friend and son-in-law of Augustus (Gaius Julius Octavianus), and named "Julia" in his honour. It was fourteen miles long, half underground and half carried into Rome on top of the Marcia and the Tepula. Thus three aqueducts entered the city one on top of the other. The water of the Julia came from springs east of Rome, not far from the source of the Tepula.

Aqua Virgo, the second aqueduct built by Marcus Agrippa, in 19 B.C. It was called "Virgo" because a young girl is said to have led the military engineers to a group of springs near the Via Collatina, to the east of Rome. It was fourteen miles long and about half of it was underground and half on arches which crossed Rome and terminated at Agrippa's Baths in the Campus Martius. The name survives in the modern Acqua Vergine, which ends at the Fontana di Trevi and is still one of the principal aqueducts.

Aqua Alsietina, built in 2 B.C. by Augustus. It was twenty miles long and brought water from Lake Alsietina, now Lake Martignano, to the east of Lake Bracciano, north-west of Rome. It was one of two aqueducts that came from the north-west: the other was the Aqua Trajana. The water of the Alsietina was of poor quality and was brought to Rome by Augustus to flood his theatre on the Janiculum, where mock naval battles were staged.

Aqua Claudia, built in A.D. 52, and named after the Emperor Claudius, who completed it. It was forty-three miles long and only a little more than nine miles were on arches when it approached Rome. The water came from springs near Subiaco, east of Rome, and terminated on the Caelian Hill. It was later carried to the Palatine Hill and was piped to the imperial palaces from the middle of the first century. The Porta Maggiore, which still stands and is one of the most

Above Ruins of an aqueduct near Rome, half its arches buried in the earth

Below A reconstruction of ancient aqueducts outside Rome at the point known as Campus Barbaricus, not far from the modern Cinecittà. The straight road leading to Rome is the Via Latina. The aqueduct which is twice crossed by the curve of the right-hand aqueduct carries the Aqua Claudia and the Aqua Anio Novus; the right-hand aqueduct carries the Marcia, Tepula, and Julia. The section on the extreme right shows how the aqueducts flowed one above another

impressive relics of the ancient aqueducts, was built to carry the Aqua Claudia into Rome.

Aqua Anio Novus, the companion aqueduct to the Aqua Claudia, and also completed by Claudius in A.D. 52. It was fifty-four miles long, and, as the water came from the Anio river, east of Rome, the aqueduct was called "the new Anio" to distinguish it from the ancient Anio Vetus of 269 B.C. It travelled upon arches for only eight of its fifty-four miles, entering Rome on the Porta Maggiore, on top of the channel of the Claudia. These two channels can still be seen above the three arches of the Porta Maggiore.

Aqua Trajana, built by the Emperor Trajan in A.D. 109. It was thirty-five miles long and mostly underground. Like the Alsietina, it came from the north-west and brought to Rome the water of a number of springs grouped to the north of Lake Bracciano. Like the Alsietina, it terminated on the Janiculum.

Aqua Alexandrina, built by the Emperor Alexander Severus in A.D. 226. It was about fourteen miles long and its sources were springs to the east of Rome in the marshland near the Via Prenestina. The Emperor built this aqueduct to supply his Baths, the Thermae Alexandrianae, which were on the Campus Martius, near the Pantheon.

At the time of the first Gothic sack of Rome in A.D. 410 the eleven aqueducts were feeding 1,212 public fountains, 11 great imperial *thermae*, and 926 public baths. Never before had a city known such a display of water. The Elder Pliny, who saw the system in operation, wrote: "But if anyone will note the abundance of water skilfully brought into the city, for public uses, for baths, for public basins, for houses, runnels, suburban gardens, and villas; if he will note the high aqueducts required for maintaining the proper elevation; the mountains which had to be pierced for the same reason; and the valleys it was necessary to fill up; he will consider that the whole terrestrial orb offers nothing more marvellous." Strabo echoed this tribute with: "And water is brought into the city in such quantity that veritable rivers flow through the city and the sewers; and almost every house has cisterns, and service pipes and copious fountains." Galen, the Greek doctor who saw Rome about the year A.D. 164, wrote: "The beauty and number of Rome's fountains is wonderful. None emits water that is foul, mineralized, turbid, hard or cold."

All trace of this triumph of hydraulic engineering vanished during the barbarian invasions, save for the ruins of some of the baths and fountains and of the aqueducts as they strode towards Rome across the Campagna: the methods employed by the Romans to control and circulate the immense volume of water that flowed in day and night became a mystery for a thousand years. Then, in 1429, the scholar and humanist, Poggio Bracciolini, who had found many lost Latin classics, made a great discovery. He found in the library of the Benedictine monastery of Monte Cassino a copy of a work written about A.D. 97 describing the aqueducts and their administration, and also the system of distributing water to public and private consumers in ancient Rome. The title of the book was *De aquis urbis Romae*, and the author was Sextus Julius Frontinus, who was the chief commissioner for water in the reigns of Nerva and Trajan.

The resurrection of an unknown work by a distinguished writer who was also an historical character mentioned by Tacitus, Pliny, and Martial, was an event of more than scholarly interest: the Roman commissioner had returned to life at the precise moment when, after a retirement of some thirteen centuries, he was able to reassert his influence on the restored water system of Renaissance Rome. I do not know if there is another instance of a technical adviser to the Caesars who was able to act after many centuries in the same capacity to the Popes. It has been said that his book, *De aquis*, "will always remain the starting point for any investigation pertaining to the water supply of ancient Rome".

Certainly no account of the fountains of Rome would seem adequate without some description of Frontinus, his career and his book; and what is known of him is of unusual interest. Most scholars agree that he was born about A.D. 35, in the reign of Tiberius, and some think that he may have been educated in Alexandria, the New York of the first century. That he was a Roman aristocrat is suggested by his rapid advance along the *cursus honorum*, and his appointment to positions of dignity and authority in the State. In the reign of Vespasian, when he was thirty-nine, he was sent to Britain as Governor, where his task during his four years of office was the subjugation of the Silures of South Wales. It was not his policy to exterminate the tribes but, having conquered them, to build new towns for them, and to romanize them. This was a contrast to the methods employed by his successor, Agricola, who massacred the northern Welsh without a touch of compassion. The steps of Frontinus in South Wales are marked by Roman forts and hill camps, notably Brecon Gaer, three miles west of Brecon, where the *praetorium*, which may well have been his headquarters, was uncovered in 1924–5. Other relics of his campaigns are the Coelbren and Neath forts in Glamorganshire, both recently excavated; and a road in the same country, the Via Julia, which was named after him.

Even without *De aquis*, the magnanimity displayed by Frontinus in Wales would have commended his character to us, but he reveals himself in his book as

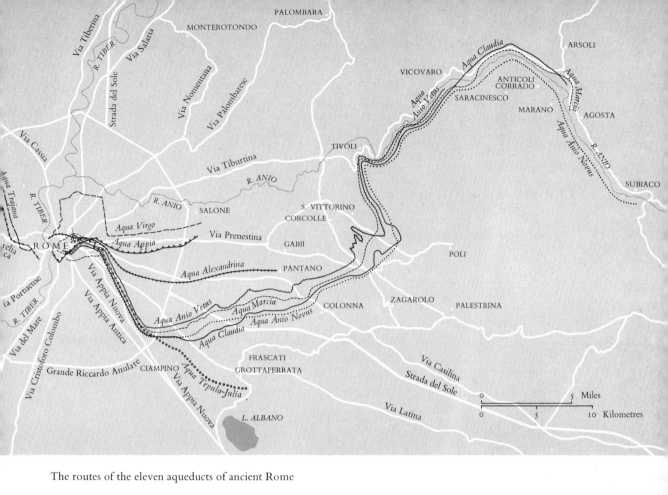

The routes of the eleven aqueducts of ancient Rome

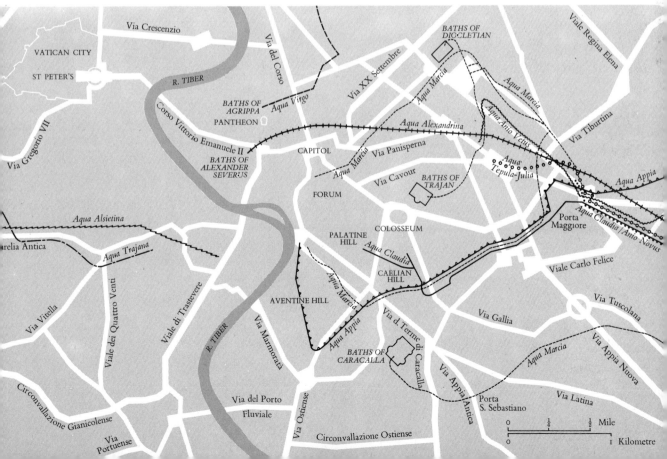

a man of inflexible integrity and full of the old Roman moral qualities; of *virtus*. The position of Chief Commissioner for Water (one, as he charmingly comments, that was bestowed only upon the most eminent men in the State), was conferred on him in A.D. 97, when he was in his early sixties. He described it as "an office which concerns not merely the convenience but also the health and even the safety of the City . . . therefore I deem it of the first and greatest importance to familiarize myself with the business I have undertaken, a policy which I have always made a principle in other affairs".

There was also another reason for his enquiry. The water department had fallen into bad ways and was riddled with dishonesty. Frontinus was resolved to put things right but, as a newcomer ignorant of the department, he wisely decided, first, to learn all he could and write down the facts to clarify the situation in his mind. In doing so, he has given us an unusual experience: he has taken us behind the scenes of an important government department of ancient Rome, and has shown how things worked and how they were prevented from working. His treatise is a rare glimpse into an obscure field of ancient life and custom.

When he wrote in A.D. 97, only nine of the eleven aqueducts had been built. The head office of the water department was called the Statio Aquarum and was staffed by clerks, who were probably freedmen. Frontinus was the Curator Aquarum and he had two officials to assist him, both of senatorial rank, the Procurator Aquarum and the Tribunus Aquarum. There was a staff of scribes, technical advisers and architects, and when Frontinus left Rome on tours of inspection he was entitled to be preceded by lictors, though he says that he dispensed with them as unnecessary, trusting to the dignity of his office to clear the way for him.

The head office controlled a group of some seven hundred workers known as the *familia*, a grand old Roman term which has survived only in its original sense in the Vatican, where the Pope's household is known as the *familia*. Among the members of the *familia aquarum* were water inspectors, plumbers, plasterers, stone-masons, bricklayers, and various other artisans as well as two groups of slaves, *aquarii*, or watermen, several hundred strong, who patrolled the aqueducts under their foremen. They also stopped leakages, uprooted trees from the "reserved strip" of fifteen feet on either side of the aqueduct, carried out general repairs and, in Rome, maintained the settling and distributing tanks and saw that an uninterrupted supply of water reached the fountains, the Baths and the public and private buildings. The *aquarii* also laid the lead and terracotta water pipes and patrolled the water mains. Tons of lead piping have been found in the ruins of Rome, much of it from Britain, which extended in a labyrinth beneath the streets, branching from the mains as in a modern city. An improvement on modern practice was the size of some of the mains which were large enough for men to enter and make their repairs without tearing up the pavement.

The popular conception of a Roman aqueduct is that of a water channel carried upon lofty arches, but Frontinus tells us that the channels were underground for most of the way and upon arches as rarely as possible, and only as they approached Rome. They were, in fact, modelled on the sewers. The total length of the aqueducts administered by Frontinus was approximately 270 miles, and of these only about 40 were above ground. The channels were lined with a special hydraulic cement whose composition is given by Vitruvius. Each aqueduct had frequent inspection points, since it was not only essential to be able to reach underground storm damage quickly but, as everyone knows who has had a bath in Rome, the water is hard and the deposits of carbonate of lime had to be cleaned out at frequent intervals. The brilliant idea occurred to the archaeologist Lanciani in the last century that the removal of mineral incrustation over centuries must have created dumps of lime at regular places along the lost routes of the aqueducts, and, setting himself to discover these dumps, he found, as he had expected, the underground aqueducts nearby.

Another popular belief is that the aqueducts were an efficient triumph of Roman engineering genius, whereas it is clear from Frontinus that they all leaked like sieves. Among literary references to the leakages are references by Juvenal and Martial to the moist drops that descended from the Aqua Marcia as it passed above the Porta Capena, but they were nothing compared with the serious leakages along the length of the aqueducts, some due to accident, some to deliberate punctures which the watermen had been bribed to make by landowners. "The public watercourses are actually brought to a standstill", wrote Frontinus, "by private citizens just to water their gardens." How one can sense and sympathize with the indignation of the new Curator Aquarum, yet how one's heart goes out to those ancient Romans who were trying to keep their gardens alive during the heat of summer!

Repairs were constant, and they often involved a regional water shortage in Rome. The same thing happens today, as anyone who has stayed any length of time there is aware, the reason being, of course, that the modern system is a copy of the old one. The underground portions of the aqueducts gave less trouble than the archways. The arches were not only vulnerable to storm damage and the weather, but also, one learns with some surprise, since those wonderful constructions impress us with their massive strength, were sometimes made of shoddy materials and were the work of dishonest contractors. The perpetual leakage needed constant attention and the Romans had devised a method of repairing an overhead channel without interrupting the flow of water. This was to clamp a bypass of thick lead at both sides of a fault and so to short-circuit the water, leaving the damaged section dry.

Frontinus mentions one or two curious facts about the water laws. Theoretically all water was the gift of the emperor, who granted it to public bodies and to private individuals who, of course, paid a water rate in return. Land carried with it no water rights, and grants of water expired with the owner of the property, whose successors had to apply for a new grant within thirty days, otherwise the water was cut off. Even leakage water was subject to the imperial permission. One recalls Martial's application to Domitian for a grant of water, in the course of which he explained that water was not laid on to the house on the Quirinal Hill where he lived, and that he was tantalized by the sound of Aqua Marcia bubbling up in a nearby fountain. Of course, such applications were never seen by the emperor: they went automatically to the Statio Aquarum and, reading Frontinus, one has the impression that probably the poet might have achieved his wish more rapidly had he disregarded the usual channels and bribed the local *aquarius* instead.

The water flowed through the aqueducts by gravity, but, had the Romans been able to manufacture cast-iron pipes, they probably knew enough about hydrostatics to have delivered water under pressure. They were familiar with the law that water finds its own level, and they understood the inverted siphon. They soon lifted water on lofty arches to the highest points in Rome. The first of the Seven Hills to receive water from an aqueduct was the Capitoline, which in 140 B.C. received the cool spring water of the Aqua Marcia; branches were eventually extended to the other hills.

Each aqueduct delivered its water to a terminal *castellum*, a word borrowed from the legionary engineers, which in its aqueous connection is often translated misleadingly as "reservoir", but that is exactly what the *castellum* was not: "settling tank" or "distribution point" would be a better rendering of this word as it relates to Rome's water. An aqueduct had numerous *castella* and the chief was invariably an impressive fountain with an inscription, while behind the scenes a maze of pipes carried the water to the fountains, the Baths, the public buildings, and the ground floors of private houses. Still moving, the water flowed on to flush the sewers and eventually to discharge itself into the Tiber.

A passage from the Monte Cassino manuscript of *De aquis urbis Romae* by Frontinus

When Frontinus took over the Statio Aquarum the first thing he wished to know was the amount of water that was lost in transit. Accordingly, he measured the water at the sources as it entered the aqueducts, and again as it was delivered in Rome. Though a modern hydraulic engineer might question his method of measuring water, and possibly his mathematics, Frontinus satisfied himself that an enormous discrepancy existed, and he set himself to find the reason why. In doing so he uncovered an old-established system of fraud, which he divided into fraud committed outside Rome and fraud committed in Rome. The chief culprits were the *aquarii*, who were mostly slaves who were probably saving up to buy their freedom. In the country it was not difficult to bribe the *aquarius* to forget to repair a leak, and even, maybe, to enlarge it; but in Rome a more complex system of fraud was literally uncovered, for it lay beneath the pavements and was hidden in the *castella*.

Frontinus discovered that the outflow pipes in the delivery tanks had been tampered with so successfully that many consumers were not receiving their correct allowance of water, a proportion having been drawn off by the insertion of illegal pipes and sold to unauthorized persons by the watermen. He also found that when a water right had lapsed and had been renewed to a new consumer, the watermen had sometimes put in a new supply pipe without removing the old one, which water again was sold. They had also found that by altering the position of the outlet pipes, or their angle in the delivery tanks, they could increase or decrease the volume of water that flowed out, of course to their own profit. The sad story was repeated under the pavements. "There are extensive areas in various places where secret pipes run under the pavements all over the City", wrote Frontinus. "I discovered that these pipes were furnishing water by special branches to all those engaged in business in those localities through which the pipes ran, being bored for that purpose here and there by the so-called 'puncturers'; whence it came to pass that only a small quantity of water reached the places of public supply. How large an amount of water has been stolen in this manner, I estimate by means of the fact that a considerable quantity of lead has been brought in by the removal of that kind of branch pipe."

Having opened the pavements and torn out the offending pipes, Frontinus then ordered that every water pipe must be stamped with the amount of water it was entitled to deliver and the name of the grantee, and that all pipes must be set at the same level in the distribution tanks. He also tightened up the administration of the public fountains, which it seems may have been tapped by night, and in other ways made it more difficult for members of the *familia aquarum* to earn the odd denarius. At last he was able to declare that he had almost doubled Rome's water supply. "Not even the waste water is lost," he wrote, "the appearance of the City is clean and altered; the air is purer; and the causes of the unwholesome atmosphere which gave the air of the City so bad a name with the ancients, are now removed."

A last glimpse of Frontinus was given in an epigram which Martial addressed to him. The old administrator, then in his seventies, had retired to the sea-coast near Baiae, where he spent his time in the delicious climate cultivating the Muses, as the poet put it. Poor Martial had to have his usual grumble. "Here

Marcus Agrippa, who built five hundred fountains in a ye

am I, tossed about in the vortex of the City," he wrote, contrasting his own depressing fate with that of his friend, "my life wasted in laborious nothingness. . . . By all the gods, I swear I love thee." And one can well believe that the tough old man was lovable: a man who had subdued South Wales (which no one has been able to do since), and also the watermen of Rome.

Oddly enough, *De aquis* has been cold-shouldered by scholars, presumably because of its technicalities, and it appears likely that there might have been no translations into modern European languages but for the fascination the work has had for practical men. The first translation was made in 1820 by the French architect Rondelet, and the next was the German version of 1841 by the builder Dederich. The English reader had to wait another half-century until, in 1897, an American civil engineer named Clemens Herschel became so interested in Frontinus and his reforms that he made what he called "a pious pilgrimage" from New York to Monte Cassino to see the original manuscript. His power of persuasion must have rivalled that of Poggio four and a half centuries earlier, for the Benedictines allowed him to take the manuscript to Rome and photograph it. Herschel published a facsimile of the manuscript in 1899, accompanied by a translation by Professor Charles E. Bennett of Cornell University, which, in a revised form, is that of the English version in the Loeb Classical Library.

The department which Frontinus managed so admirably had been founded a hundred and thirty years earlier by Marcus Agrippa, who was probably the greatest fountaineer in history; certainly no one else has ever built five hundred fountains in one year. Agrippa, and his lifelong friend and schoolfellow, Octavian (afterwards Augustus), were both in their early thirties when they defeated the murderers of Caesar, and brought the civil wars to an end. They found Rome in a deplorable condition, full of despairing mobs, of dispossessed landowners, ruined farmers and peasants, a city of shabby temples and horrible slums. This was the Rome of brick which Augustus was later in life to say he had transformed into marble.

Describing the city at that time, Dio Cassius said that no one would believe that Rome had a water supply. The sewers were clogged, and the aqueducts were leaking. Of the four existing aqueducts, one, the most recent, the Tepula, was nearly a hundred years old, and the oldest, the Appia, had been in existence for nearly three hundred. Though Agrippa had been consul, he willingly stepped down in rank to aedile to help his friend Octavian to clear up the chaos. His first act was to dismiss the contractors who had managed, or mismanaged, Rome's

Plate 1. The Neptune group in the Piazza del Popol
Overleaf Plate 2. The Trevi fountai

water supply for centuries and to form his own government department, which was the Statio Aquarum, and though the human element required attention in future years, Frontinus found that he had no need to alter Agrippa's organization. Having cleaned the sewers and repaired the aqueducts, Agrippa built a new aqueduct, Aqua Julia, and he erected five hundred fountains and seven hundred basins and pools for public use; and all this in one year of office. Having done so, he left Rome to take command of the fleet and to defeat Antony and Cleopatra at Actium in 31 B.C.

In the course of his aedileship, Agrippa had noticed that during the agony of the civil wars various speculators had opened bath houses all over Rome in which the poorest people could forget their worries in hot water for less than a farthing. He counted a hundred and seventy of these establishments. Such was the beginning of the Cult of the Bath which reached such fantastic proportions before the end of the Empire. The craze implied one of those reversals in thought and habit which many of those who live to be over sixty notice in contemporary life. The austere Romans of the Republic were reluctant bathers. Seneca noted that though arms and legs might be washed daily, complete immersion took place only once a week in a small room near the kitchen, and standards of modesty forbade Cato the Censor to take a bath in the presence of his sons, an attitude which still existed in Cicero's time. All this had changed by 23 B.C., when crowds filled the hot baths, which were often simple establishments run by a freedman with the help of a few slaves. It was probably during his year as aedile that the idea occurred to Agrippa to give the populace the most luxurious public bath that had ever been seen, but he was unable to do so until 13 B.C., when the Thermae of Agrippa were opened in the Campus Martius at the back of the Pantheon. A large garden was laid out with an artificial lake, where amid avenues of trees, statues and fountains, stood a palatial bath, which was also a club, a library, and a restaurant, in which hot, cold, steam, shower and plunge baths might be enjoyed. In general effect, Agrippa's Thermae were probably like a more sumptuous Athenian gymnasium, or grove of Academus, though more splendid, costly and extensive. In order that nothing should be missing, Agrippa built a special aqueduct to supply the Baths, the famous Aqua Virgo, which for many years was considered to be the finest water in Rome.

To anyone interested in the aqueducts and the fountains of Rome, the name "M. Agrippa" which has survived above the portico of the Pantheon must always be the most dramatic announcement in the city. He was the greatest of the *aquarii*.

III

THE FOUNTAINS OF
ANCIENT ROME

T HE FOUNTAINS of ancient Rome in their glory must have been one of the wonders of the world. They were adorned with statues by some of the greatest sculptors of Greece and they lifted their jets or showered their cascades against the imperial background of marble temple and palace. Augustus had been quick to adopt the Hellenistic colonnade – the "Street called Straight" – which he used with such good effect in Rome, and no doubt his architects were inspired by the Hellenistic fountains: thus the new Augustan Rome bore evidence of the travels of those who had pledged themselves to destroy the murderers of Caesar.

There were, it is recorded, 1,212 fountains in Rome at the time of Constantine the Great, but identifiable remains may be counted on the fingers of one hand. It is not difficult to imagine why. Of all works of architecture, the urban fountain is the most vulnerable once its function comes to an end. The very factor that made for its success and popularity, accessibility in a public place, then led to its downfall; and once the aqueducts ceased to flow in the Dark Ages, the fountains were swept away as useless obstructions and so destroyed. Stray references in Latin literature are practically our only information about them. We know that each of the eleven aqueducts terminated in a *castellum*, a display fountain of massive monumental proportions, which bore an inscription naming the emperor or the public benefactor who had brought the water to Rome, just as the modern fountains mention the popes. Some idea of the architectural and artistic character of the fountains is contained in the bare statement that during his aedileship in 33 B.C. Agrippa decorated the fountains with three hundred statues of marble and bronze and with four hundred columns.

Many of the fountains were named after the statues which decorated them, and we read of the Fountain of Prometheus, the Fountain of the Shepherds, of Orpheus, of Ganymede, of the Four Fishes, of the Three Masks, and of the Ox of Myron, which stood in the old cattle market of Rome, the Forum Boarium, on the banks of the Tiber near the modern Ponte Palatino. The Ox was one of the most famous and popular fountain statues in Rome, and inspired a great number of epigrams, some of which have survived in the *Greek Anthology*.

Myron lived about 430 B.C. and seems to have been the first great animal sculptor, and his works were eagerly sought by the Romans and shipped back to Rome to adorn the capital. The Ox, which was made of bronze, is said to have come from Aegina, and Procopius saw it standing uninjured above its fountain in the sixth century. The Ox was not the only statue by Myron in Rome, neither was it his only ox: four others were placed at the four corners of the altar of the temple of Apollo which Augustus, who built the temple and dedicated it in 28 B.C., considered to be one of the glories of his reign. Even its position on the Palatine Hill has now been lost, but, so fantastic are the chances of survival, a few breathless lines have survived which the poet Propertius wrote after hurrying away from the dedication ceremony and noting that the four oxen of Myron "seemed to live".

Of the 1,212 ancient fountains only the following can be identified now:

> The bronze Pine Cone (La Pigna) in the Vatican
> Marforio, the river god in the courtyard of the Capitoline Museum
> The two river gods, Nile and Tiber, nearby in the Piazza del
> > Campidoglio
> The site of the Meta Sudans, near the Arch of Constantine
> The fountain of Juturna in the Forum Romanum
> The ruins of the Julia fountain in the Piazza Vittorio Emanuele

I mention La Pigna, Marforio, and the Nile and Tiber later, among the fountains of the Vatican and the Capitol, but the other three, I think, should be described here.

The Meta Sudans was a curious, tall, cone-shaped fountain of original design near the Colosseum, which received its name, the "Sweating Goalpost", from its resemblance to one of the goals (*metae*) of the Circus which, as water descended or dripped from holes in the cone, appeared to be sweating (*sudor*); and it has been said that gladiators who had survived were in the habit of drinking there, though one has always fancied that they preferred stronger fountains. Seneca, who lived within earshot of the Colosseum, complained of a showman who would station himself near the Meta Sudans and make a great noise blowing a trumpet.

All that is left of the fountain today is a circle in the road between the Colosseum and the Arch of Constantine, marking the place from which it was removed in 1936 as an obstruction to traffic. Photographs of the Colosseum before that year,

Above The ruins of the Meta Sudans, by the Arch of Constantine; from a nineteenth century drawing

Below The ruins of the fountain of Juturna, in the Forum

and engravings of an earlier time, show the Meta Sudans as a tall brick cone which had been patched and shored up from time to time. Though it was beyond restoration and was not beautiful to look at, it seems a pity that one of the few ancient fountains, and one so closely associated with the Colosseum, should have been destroyed in favour of the motor traffic of Rome.

Like Egeria, Juturna was a water nymph to whom the Romans had dedicated a temple, and whose fountain in the Forum was fed by spring water. As every schoolboy once knew, this was the place where the great Twin Brethren watered their steeds and washed off the sweat and blood of conflict when they brought news of the victory at Lake Regillus. "White as snow their armour was; Their steeds were white as snow." Though Ovid clearly indicated the position of the fountain, it remained unknown until 1900, when it was discovered during Giacomo Boni's excavations in the Forum.

Few visitors give the fascinating relic a glance as they pass on to the house of the Vestal Virgins, and, admittedly, there is little to see but an opening about sixteen feet square and six feet deep, which was once lined with white marble. In the early part of the year the springs in which Castor and Pollux watered their horses are seen to fill the basin, but in late September they often dry up. The centre of the basin is occupied by a square brick pedestal which may once have held a statue above water level. A most striking feature of the fountain is a beautiful altar of white marble nearby. It is carved on all four sides: a graceful Jupiter is seen leaning on a long staff and holding in his left hand a small cone-shaped object which is one of his thunderbolts; on the second side is a beautiful figure of Leda; the third side shows her sons, Castor and Pollux, wearing their high cone-shaped caps, which are really half swan's eggs, a reference to their paternity; and the fourth side bears a female figure, probably Helen, the sister of the Dioscuri and, by sailors of old, held responsible with her brothers for the mysterious lights known as St Elmo's Fire that appear at mastheads in storms at sea.

During the excavations of 1900 a statue of Constantine and various dedications and inscriptions were found which suggested that the offices of the Statio Aquarum were in a neighbouring building. Should this have been so, it is interesting to think that in the very heart of the Forum Agrippa planned the Julia and the Virgo aqueducts, and hundreds of fountains, and that Frontinus in his day also worked there, side by side with the spring Juturna, the guardian of waters.

In the small garden in the Piazza Vittorio Emanuele, near Rome's Central

The Julia fountain and the Trophies of Marius. *Above* A sixteenth century drawing showing the Trophies in position; they were removed by Pope Sixtus V to the balustrade of the Capitol, where they may still be seen. *Below* An eighteenth century drawing by Piranesi. *Right* The Julia fountain today

Railway Station, is to be seen a tall, gaunt mass of ancient brickwork which, to an English eye, resembles a much desiccated Norman keep. It is all that remains of a great Roman fountain of imperial times, and the only relic of a terminal *castellum aquarum* to have survived. It is called the Julia fountain, or I Trofei di Mario, the name it bore during the Renaissance. The "Trophies of Marius" were two enormous stands of arms carved in white marble which once decorated the fountain and in 1590 were moved by Pope Sixtus V to the balustrade of the Capitol, where they may still be seen on either side of Castor and Pollux.

In 1575 Du Pérac published a print of the *castellum* in his *Vestigi dell'antichità di Roma*, which shows the Trophies in position fifteen years before Sixtus V removed them. The fountain was the terminus of Agrippa's Aqua Julia, which was built in 33 B.C. and, like all the aqueducts and fountains, had been repaired and reconstructed in the following centuries. The existing ruin is all that is left of an immense fountain, or *nymphaeum*, which Alexander Severus erected (A.D. 222-35) to replace an older one that had probably fallen into disrepair. In ancient Rome, as today, statues were migratory, and monuments had a habit of disappearing for a time and reappearing in another part of the city. It was evidently so with the Trophies, which the Emperor apparently took from some other fountain or monument since there is a quarry-mark underneath the marble which states that the stone was sent from Athens to Rome by the freedman Chresimus in the reign of Domitian (A.D. 81-96). The Trophies are therefore more than a century older than the *castellum* which they adorned.

It is difficult to make much of the battered ruin of the fountain today, but fortunately the architects of the Renaissance had a little more to guide them. It was a gigantic triumphal arch of water: a tall main archway flanked on each side by lower arches in which the Trophies were placed. All the other statues and columns have vanished without trace. The water poured in a series of jets and cascades into marble basins and, having been aerated, passed on to subsidiary *castella* and to various destinations.

The importance of this unique survival is in the influence it has had on the designs of the great terminal fountains of the sixteenth and seventeenth centuries. It showed the men of the Renaissance, and the architects of Sixtus V and Paul V, what a Roman terminal fountain was like, and enabled the classical *castellum* to be reborn in the Rome of the popes. Its influence is to be seen in the Fountain of Moses, the terminal fountain of the Acqua Felice, and in the Acqua Paola on the Janiculum, and also in the Fontana di Trevi, where the archway idea has been successfully adapted to Baroque conventions.

Plate 5. A detail of the Pantheon foun

IV

THE WATERLESS
MIDDLE AGES

WHEN THE Goths under Vitiges cut the aqueducts in A.D. 537, they camped in an area close to, if it does not, actually include, what is now the Cinecittà. In ancient literature the spot is called the *campus barbaricus*, and every modern Roman still knows it as the *campo dei barbari*. The juxtaposition of two such sites, one the scene of so many imaginary reconstructions of Roman history, and the other the place where history really happened, suggests a few reflections.

It is almost certain that should a film director stage the cutting of the aqueducts by Vitiges, he would in every possible way antedate the event by some four and a half centuries: he would build a set recreating the Forum as it was in the time of Nero, and people it with characters of the golden age. We should see some fine shots of hairy Goths hacking away at the aqueducts, then the camera would move to the Forum, where well-toga'd crowds would watch with consternation the drying up of the fountains while less fashionable Romans would demonstrate outside the closed *thermae*. The general effect would be that of disaster suddenly striking a thriving and brilliant metropolis.

In reality, the Rome of A.D. 537 was a miserable and depressed city that for two hundred years had been merely a sentimental memory, and the cutting of the aqueducts probably only reduced still further a water supply that, owing to administrative neglect, had been failing for as long as anyone could remember. Since Constantine the Great had moved the capital of the Roman Empire to Constantinople two centuries before, taking with him a crowd of patricians with their households and dependants, art corporations and their trained artisans as well as professional men and merchants, the history of Rome had been that of successive waves of refugees. The city had been sacked by Goths and Vandals, the surrounding countryside was covered by deserted estates, and thousands of Romans of all classes had fled to other cities in Italy, and to North Africa and Asia Minor; yet still the macabre make-believe of Rome continued within walls

te 6. Il Facchino

that were manned by a few troops from Constantinople. Perhaps the most serious deprivation caused by the cutting of the aqueducts (it seems that the high-level aqueducts were those chiefly damaged), was to drive the inhabitants of the hills down to the Tiber, and so form the shape of mediaeval Rome.

How many of the fountains which were playing when Constantine departed for Byzantium were still working in A.D. 537, we cannot know, but it would be surprising if there were a hundred. The archaeologist Lanciani examined the Aqua Marcia at Monte Arcese and found it to be choked with fourteen inches of chemical deposits, which reduced the channel from six and a half feet to a little over four feet. One of the first tasks of the gangs which patrolled the aqueducts in imperial times was to prevent this incrustation from forming, and the fact that fourteen inches of hard, glass-like deposit – "thin layers of alabastrine purity and transparency", as Lanciani called them – should have accumulated conveys a picture of neglect stretching over centuries. Who can believe that many of the fountains of Rome were still playing when the Goths severed the aqueducts?

The cutting of the aqueducts provided one or two of the best-known stories of the decline of Rome, thanks to the historian Procopius, who was present as secretary to Belisarius. He said that one night a sentry who was on duty near the ventilation shaft of an aqueduct happened to glance down into the then dry depths and was startled by what he thought was the gleam of a wolf's eyes. The story went the round of the garrison and eventually reached Belisarius, who did not treat it lightly but immediately sent a patrol into the aqueduct to make a report. They returned to say that they had come upon lamp and torch droppings, which proved that the Goths were investigating the possibility of entering Rome by way of the dry channels. Belisarius then ordered the openings into the aqueducts to be blocked with masonry.

In earlier times the enormous quantity of corn that was used each day to provide the bread dole was ground in mills worked by animals, but later they were worked by water from the aqueducts. When Vitiges cut off the water he put the corn mills out of action: but Belisarius mounted mills upon rafts and moored them in the Tiber in such a way that the current turned them. The siege went on for a year, then one day the Goths packed up and marched away. Fortunately for Rome, Vitiges was one of the most irresolute and incapable of her enemies.

Rome had a breathing space of nine years before she was again attacked, this time by the Goth Totila, a very different adversary. He captured Rome and decided to pull down the walls, an act, however, which he never carried out.

Instead, he ordered the evacuation of the city, and it is said, though difficult to believe, that Rome was without a single inhabitant for forty days. Nevertheless the most critical of historians have accepted the account of Procopius: J. M. Bury and, recently, Professor A. H. M. Jones, both use the word "deserted" to describe Rome after Totila's departure. The imagination plays round that extraordinary event, the lowest ebb of Rome's fortunes, for in the long history of the city there is no stranger moment than that when the only silent witnesses of her downfall were her statues.

Gradually a few inhabitants crept back to the shelter of the walls, but so few and so helpless, that no carpenter could be found capable of making city gates to replace those destroyed by the Goths. Some time later we learn that Rome, captured and garrisoned again, was able to exist on corn grown on the vacant land within the walls.

The story of the sieges and disasters is too well known to be repeated, but this brief mention is necessary to indicate how the fountains dried up during the Dark Ages. There was unhappily no Frontinus to leave an expert's account of what happened; and it is only by reading the tragic history of the time that one can guess how a great public service, created and extended in days of law, order and prosperity, collapsed under the impossible pressures of anarchy and invasion. Water, which so many townspeople never think about, having an obedient spring in the kitchen, is really among the most fragile of life's necessities. One's mind reverts to the nineteen-forties and the air raids of the last war, when in London, and in all cities where water mains had been hit, it was usual to see long queues of men and women waiting with buckets, pans, even jugs and cups, at some unaffected source. They were repeating in the modern world a scene that must have been only too familiar in Rome as fountains dried up and the aqueducts ceased to flow.

In the eighth century a new Rome had emerged bravely from the struggles of four hundred years. The Pope had replaced the Emperor, and the Papacy guarded all that was left of the traditions of civilization. In this city of churches water became holy water. The Christian passed through water in his initiation; he washed before he entered the church to pray or to receive the Sacrament. Water was a symbol of the new life; more than that, it was the "Water of Life" itself. The Lamb of God, glittering in apsidal mosaics, was to be seen standing in green grass with symbolic rivers springing from His feet. The fountains of Early Christian Rome had vanished from the streets, but were to be found in the courtyards of the churches. As the worshipper entered, he was faced by a *can-*

ROMA

A view of Rome in the sixteenth century

tharus of running water in the centre of the *atrium*, in which he was expected to perform an act of symbolic purification by washing his hands. If he wished food or a bath he would go to a *diaconia*, or church hall, where the imperial obligation to provide bread, baths and circuses for the populace had become Christian charity administered by the pontiffs through the deacons. During the pontificate of Hadrian I (A.D. 772-95), a wash house was opened near St Peter's where the poor could bathe when they went there to collect the dole.

If the history of imperial Rome and all its splendour may be said to have been "writ in water", the lack of water ruled the life of Early Christian Rome. The few who were still able to live amid the wreck of the palaces upon the hills did so because they possessed a well or a spring; the others migrated to the low land of the Campus Martius near the Tiber, and thus the map of Rome was settled for centuries; until, indeed, the hills again became habitable with the return of water during the Renaissance.

V

THE RETURN OF
THE WATERS

LACKING CHIVALRY, the Romans also lacked the faith, the beauty, the poetry and the compassion of the mediaeval world. They lived in slums and ruins, haunted by the past, the people of a nightmare. The Savelli had fortified the theatre of Marcellus and lived there with their men-at-arms; the Colonna possessed the tomb of Augustus; the Frangipani had established themselves on the Palatine, with a branch fortress in the Colosseum; the Crescenzi occupied the Baths of Alexander Severus; the Orsini were in Pompey's theatre. Like the earliest settlers of seven centuries before Christ, they drank the water of the Tiber and the water of springs and wells.

An Englishman, Adam of Usk, a contemporary of Henry V of England and of Charles VI of France, watched dogs and wolves fighting near St Peter's, and wrote, "O God, how lamentable is the state of Rome! Once it was filled by great lords and palaces; now it is full of huts, thieves, wolves and vermin, and the Romans tear themselves to pieces."

Anarchy had driven the Papacy from Rome (1304) and French influence had guided it to Avignon, where it spent more than seventy years. When the Popes returned (1377), they were hunted in and out of Rome like criminals for half a century. Martin V (1417–31), elected in Switzerland, was prevented by anarchy from entering Rome. Early in 1419 he settled in Florence, living with the Dominicans of S. Maria Novella until he left for Rome in the autumn of the following year.

Much has been written of Rome's debt to Florentine artists, but little about the three popes who lived in Florence during the bright morning of the Renaissance as they waited for the disorders of Rome to subside. The Florence which Martin V saw was that of Giovanni di Bicci, the father of Cosimo de' Medici. What a fascinating thought this is. How often the Pope must have contrasted the intellectual splendour of Florence with the mental squalor of Rome. He met the geniuses of the Renaissance in their twenties and thirties. Cosimo de' Medici was

59

Rome at the close of the Middle Ages: the Piazza Colonna before the construction of the fountain and before the statue of St Paul had been placed on the column of Marcus Aurelius.

thirty. His son, Piero (to be the father of Lorenzo the Magnificent), was three. Donatello was thirty-three and Fra Angelico thirty-two; Ghiberti was thirty-eight; Luca della Robbia was only nineteen; Brunelleschi – quite an old man! – was forty-two. And Michelangelo was not to be born for another fifty-six years. The time of the Pope's arrival coincided with the competition for the dome of the cathedral; it was the year that Brunelleschi began to build the Foundling Hospital; Donatello's saints had been newly erected in the niches of Or San Michele; and Ghiberti was at work on the doors of the Baptistry.

The Pope left that splendid scene in 1420 for the perils of Rome, a year as important as any in the city's history, for it marked the end of mediaeval Rome and the beginning of the Roman Renaissance. The ruin that met the Pope was indescribable. The Lateran, the ancient home of the Papacy, was falling to pieces; the Vatican was not habitable and Martin had to live in a private palace on the east bank of the Tiber. He was unable to originate anything: all he could do was to mend roofs and shore up walls. One great event of his reign cannot be over-emphasized in its bearing on the waters of Rome. In 1429, as I have already mentioned, the humanist, Poggio Bracciolini, one of the Papal secretaries, found the lost manuscript of *De aquis* by Frontinus in the library of the monastery of Monte Cassino. So at the earliest beginning of the revival of Rome, and years before it could be used, the men of the Renaissance were provided with a hand-book to the aqueducts, the fountains and the waters of Rome.

The next pope, Eugenius IV (1431-47), was driven from Rome three years after his election. Disguised as a monk, the head of the Church was carried pick-a-back by a pirate to a boat in the Tiber while the Romans flung stones and shot arrows after him. He sailed to Pisa and went to Florence where, once again, Dominicans sheltered a pontiff.

Fourteen years had passed, and the Pope saw the Florence of Cosimo de' Medici; in fact, he welcomed Cosimo from exile, and a friendship began between them which lasted throughout life. Brunelleschi's dome was now finished and the Pope was asked to consecrate the cathedral. A raised walk was built all the way from S. Maria Novella to the Duomo, decorated with tapestry and flowers, along which Eugenius passed to perform the ceremony on 25 March 1436, accompanied by his cardinals, thirty-seven bishops, the Signoria, and the representatives of foreign nations and the Italian States.

Though Eugenius was neither a scholar nor a humanist but a rigid and pious monk, the vitality of the new world inspired him. Back in Rome again, almost overwhelmed by the confusion of his times, he remembered the beautiful things

Above left Pope Martin V (1417-31)

Above right Pope Nicholas V (1447-55)

Below A scene from the bronze doors of St Peter's by Filarete, showing Pope Eugenius IV (1431-47) welcoming delegates from the Eastern Church to the Council of Florence

he had seen in Florence. Among these were the bronze doors which Ghiberti was still making for the Baptistry during the Pope's stay in Florence. Wishing to emulate them, the Pope commissioned Filarete to make similar doors for St Peter's ("a testimony of the Pope's good intentions rather than of his artistic feelings", said Bishop Creighton): and these are still the great central entrance to the basilica. Towards the end of his life Eugenius invited Fra Angelico to Rome to paint a chapel in the Vatican, and so began the association of Rome with the great artists of Florence, inaugurated by a pope who had lived in Florence and had seen her artists at work.

The link was strengthened still further by the next pope, Nicholas V (1447–55), who was a Florentine, if not by birth, at least by training and experience. He was the most learned scholar of his day and a great bibliophile. He had helped Cosimo de' Medici to form the library of S. Marco, and it was said of him by Aeneas Silvius (a saying wrongly supposed to have originated in Oxford) that "what he knew not, was not knowledge". He has been called the first great restorer of Rome; he was certainly the first pontiff who was able to see beyond the huddle of huts and tenements and battlements to a new and splendid Rome worthy of its place in history and of the dignity of the Holy See.

Nicholas reigned for only eight years, and it almost seems as if he knew that his time was short. He was always in a hurry. He filled Rome with stone-masons and carpenters. He gathered round him famous Florentine architects: Bernardo Gamberelli (Rosellino), Antonio di Fransecco and Leon Battista Alberti. He was the pope who decided to rebuild old St Peter's, a task which was to occupy fourteen architects through the reigns of twenty popes. He began to plan new streets and squares. He founded the Vatican Library. And in 1453 he restored the old Aqua Virgo, which then became the Acqua Vergine. His architect was the great Alberti, whose churches at Rimini and Mantua are admired by every visitor to the north of Italy, and he gave the water a new outlet at the Trevi, not the site of the present fountain, but nearby.

The Acqua Vergine continued to be repaired by successive popes, and it remained the only aqueduct in Rome for 133 years, while the Trevi was the chief source of pure water. In the following century a second aqueduct was built by Sixtus V (1585–90), and a third was built by Paul V (1605–21), but Rome had to wait another two and a half centuries for the fourth papal aqueduct, built by Pius IX in 1870. All these four aqueducts are still working.

With the return of the waters after so many centuries of neglect and disaster, the city rose from her ruins, and once more fountains sparkled in her streets.

VI

THE WATERS OF ROME

ODERN ROME is served by six aqueducts, all, save two, the gift of the
popes. As in ancient times, each aqueduct terminates in a different part of
Rome, whence its water is distributed. The six waters of Rome are:

    Acqua Vergine Antica (1453), which carries the name of the
       Aqua Virgo into modern times
    Acqua Felice (1586)
    Acqua Paola (1611)
    Acqua Pia Antica Marcia (1870)
    Acqua Vergine Nuova (1937)
    Acqua Peschiera (1949)

The first three are reconstructions of ancient Roman aqueducts. Two new aqueducts, which it is hoped will be completed by 1972, will be the Acqua Peschiera
II, bringing water from the Centrale di Salisano to the Monte Sacro district, and
another conveying water from Lake Bracciano to Monte Mario.

Four of the six aqueducts (Acqua Vergine Antica, Acqua Vergine Nuova,
Acqua Felice and Acqua Pia Marcia) have their sources to the east of Rome; one
(Acqua Paola) to the west; and one (Acqua Peschiera) to the north-east. The water
is rain and snow water from the central Apennines which, having filtered through
the volcanic earth, rises in groups of springs at various distances from the capital.
The source of the Acqua Vergine is nine miles away and that of the Acqua Felice,
seventeen miles away. The source of the Acqua Pia Marcia is forty miles away
and the source of the Acqua Peschiera, fifty-three miles. The only aqueduct from
the north-west, the thirty-mile-long Acqua Paola, brings water from ancient
springs round Lake Bracciano, and also water from the lake itself.

The most popular waters in Rome are those of the Acqua Peschiera and the
Acqua Pia Marcia, with the Acqua Felice and the Acqua Vergine Nuova in second
place. The Acqua Paola is not drinkable water and sometimes tastes strongly of
Lake Bracciano. It is used for industrial purposes, for fountains (the Vatican

fountains spout Acqua Paola), and for gardens. (Some kitchens have a special tap of Acqua Paola, which is used for washing up.) The contamination of the old Acqua Vergine with surface seepage is a recent affair, due to the growth of Rome during the last thirty years. Until then it had been prized since ancient times as the purest and softest of waters. It was the custom until the last century for every house to keep a supply of Acqua Vergine, called "Trevi water", in large jars. Five of these were found in Michelangelo's cellar in Rome after his death and appear in the inventory of his possessions. English visitors of the nineteenth century always made their tea in "Trevi water", which was ready at hand in the centre of the Piazza di Spagna. Still, though now chlorinated, the old Acqua Vergine manages to hold its head up in some of the most beautiful fountains in Rome.

The aqueducts are administered by the Municipality of Rome through a department known as ACEA, which stands for Azienda Comunale Elettricità ed Acque. The department occupies a new building of glass and concrete outside the Gate of St Paul, with a superb view over Rome: the pyramid of Cestius is to be seen below and also the cypresses of the Protestant Cemetery. The Azienda is the descendant of Agrippa's Statio Aquarum, for though that administration collapsed during the barbarian invasions of the sixth century, the revival of gravitational aqueducts by the popes of the sixteenth and seventeenth centuries produced identical conditions to those of antiquity; and a similar organization was devised to handle them.

In spite of a pressurized supply and modern methods, the hydraulic engineers are controlling, as their predecessors did, continuous streams of water that flow in and out of Rome without previous storage in reservoirs, and, again as in ancient times, the water is not mixed, owing to the different characteristics and qualities carried by the various aqueducts. No other great city is served in a similar way; and it is only now, with the enormous growth of Rome's population, that the Azienda is contemplating a break with ancient practice by the building of storage reservoirs.

The supply is measured, as in imperial Rome, by the amount of water that can flow in a given time through a pipe of a given length and diameter. The unit of measurement is the *oncia*, the classical twelfth part of a whole, of which there are two values: the *oncia vergine*, which equals forty cubic metres a day, and the *oncia semplice*, which is half that amount. The *oncia* is related to the *quinaria*, a word that appears hundreds of times in *De aquis*; indeed, the chief preoccupation of Frontinus was the *quinariae* he was losing through inefficiency and fraud. It is

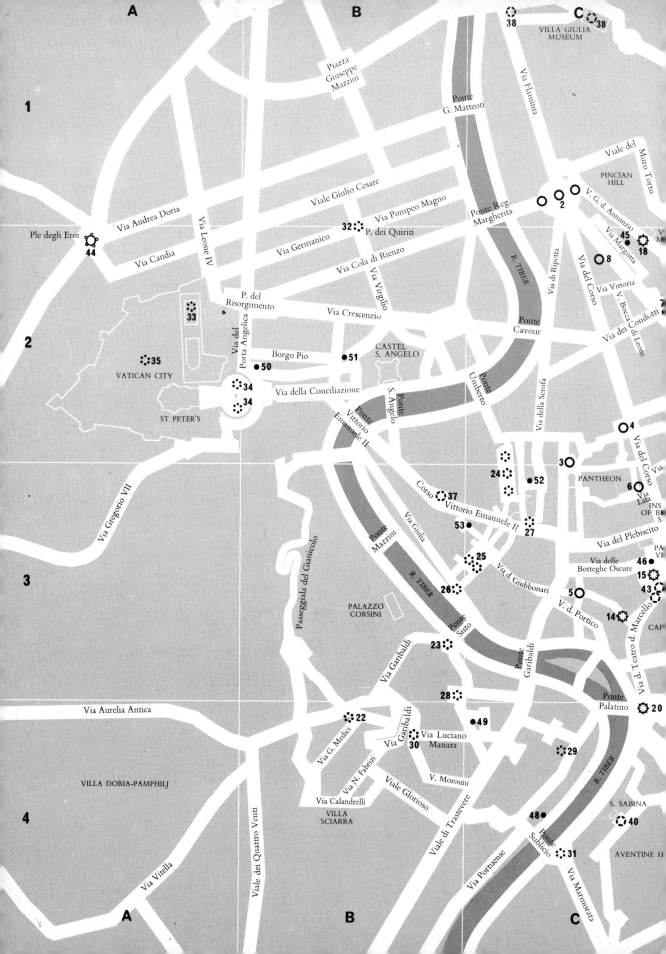

D   **E**   **F**

PINCIAN
GARDENS

ESE GARDENS

⚙ 42

Via Pinciana

Corso d'Italia

○ *Acqua Vergine*	
1 Fontana di Trevi	C 2
2 Fontænerne på Piazza del Popolo	C 1
3 Pantheon fontænen	C 2
4 Fontænen på Piazza Colonna	C 2
5 Fontana delle Tartarughe	C 3
6 Il Facchino	C 3
7 La Barcaccia	C 2
8 »Bavianen«	C 2

⚙ *Acqua Felice*	
9 Mosesfontænen	D 2
10 Monte Cavallo fontænen	D 2-3
11 I Quattro Fontane	D 2
12 Quirinal paladsets Have	D 2
13 Fontænerne på Capitol	C 3
14 Fontænen på Piazza Campitelli	C 3
15 Fontænen på Piazza d'Ara Coeli	C 3
16 La Navicella	D 4
17 Fontænen på Piazza Madonna dei Monti	D 3
18 Fontænen ved Viale della Trinità de' Monti	C 2
19 Triton fontænen	D 2
20 Fontænen på Piazza Bocca della Verità	C 4
21 Fontænen på Piazza di S. Maria Maggiore	E 3

⠿ *Acqua Paola*	
22 Paul V's fontæne	B 4
23 Fontænen ved Ponte Sisto	B 3
24 Fontænerne på Piazza Navona	C 2-3
25 Fontænerne på Piazza Farnese	C 3
26 Il Mascherone	B 3
27 Fontænen på Piazza S. Andrea della Valle	C 3
28 Fontænen foran S. Maria in Trastevere	B 3
29 S. Cecelia fontænen i Trastevere	C 4
30 Fontana del Prigione	B 4
31 Amfora fontænen	C 4
32 Fontænen på Piazza dei Quiriti	B 1-2

⠿ *Fontænerne på Peterspladsen og i Vatikanhaven*	
33 La Pigna	A 2
34 Fontænerne på Peterspladsen	A-B 2
35 Fontænerne i Vatikanhaven	A 2

⚙ *Acqua Pia Antica Marcia*	
36 Fontana delle Naiadi	D 2
37 La Terrina	B 3
38 Villa Giulia	C 1
39 Fontana delle Api	D 2
40 Parco degli Aranci	C 4
41 Fontana S. Giovanni in Laterano	E 4
42 Borghese-parken	D 1
43 Løverne ved La Cordonata	C 3

⚙ *Acqua Peschiera*	
44 Piazzale degli Eroi	A 2

● *Fontænerne i I Rioni*	
45 Il Rione Campo Marzo	C 2
46 Il Rione Pigna	C 3
47 Il Rione Monti	E 3
48 Il Rione Ripa	C 4
49 Il Rione di Trastevere	C 4
50 Fontana dei Quattro Tiare	B 2
51 Fontana delle Palle	B 2
52 Il Rione di S. Eustazio	C 3
53 Il Rione Parione	B-C 1

◇ *Levn af gamle fontæner*	
54 Juturna-fontænen	D 3
55 I Trofei di Mario	E 3

0   ½ Km

Via Vittorio V.
Via L. Bissolati

ITÀ
ONTI

39 ⚙   Via Barberini   ⚙ 9

19 ⚙

Via d.
Quattro

Via del Quirinale

Via XX Settembre

⚙ 36

Via Torino

11 ⚙

12 ⚙

Fontane

XXIV
Maggio

Via d. Serpenti

Via Nazionale

Via A. Depretis

Via d. S. Maria
Maggiore

⚙ 21

Via Panisperna

● 47

Via Giovanni Lanza

17 ⚙

Via Cavour

Via dei Fori Imperiali

Via d. Annibaldi

Viale del Monte Oppio

Via Merulana

Via Emanuele Filiberto

Piazza
Vittorio
Emanuele

V. Conte Verde

◇ 55

Viale Manzoni

CENTRAL
RAILWAY STATION

Via Giovanni

Via Tiburtina

3

Porta
Maggiore

Via Prenestina

RUM

◇ 54

PALATINE HILL

COLOSSEUM

Via di S. Gregorio

Via Claudia

Via Labicana

Via di S. Giovanni in Laterano

Viale Manzoni

Porta
Maggiore

CAELIAN HILL

Via della Navicella

16 ⚙

VILLA
CELIMONTANA

41 ⚙

S. GIOVANNI
IN LATERANO

Via dell'Anba Aradam

Via Magna Grecia

Via Appia Nuova

4

imo

Aventino

Via delle Terme di Caracalla

Via Druso

Via Gallia

*BATHS OF
CARACALLA*

D   **E**   **F**

astonishing to hear a hydraulic engineer, while seated in the most modern of
offices above the walls of Rome, pick up his telephone and discuss with a colleague
the measurement of water in terms that would be comprehensible to an engineer
of the XXth Legion.

Another aqueous link with the past is the *castello*. Most visitors to Rome are
too occupied in preserving their lives at street corners and crossings to have
noticed this word above iron doors in walls and buildings in various parts of the
city. It is the Italian for the Latin *castellum*, which was the name given by the
legionary engineers, who were trained in hydraulics and hydrodynamics, to the
distribution points of a water system. It was used all over ancient Rome, as in the
modern city, and was also applied by the ancient Romans to the great terminal
fountains and the *nymphaea*. The *castelli* of modern Rome are still the distribution
points of the aqueducts, and at certain times men wearing gumboots and overalls,
and carrying tool-kits and electric torches, unlock the doors and vanish into the
darkness beyond. They are the modern *aquarii*, and they ascend, or descend, to
chambers loud with the rush of an intake from an aqueduct, occupied by large
tanks from which pipes of various sizes protrude, some half an inch, some an
inch, some the size of a fist and even larger. (It is all described in *De aquis*.) So
unchanged are the duties of the watermen, that one feels could some *aquarius* of
the time of Trajan revisit Rome, he would see little to wonder at; he might even,
after a brief lecture on electricity, take his place in one of the Azienda's patrols.

The fountains of Rome, the spectacular expression of this unique and venerable
system, were originally erected by the popes, as the emperors had done before
them, to distribute aerated water to the population and, at the same time, to
gladden their hearts. No greater compliment has been paid by rulers to their
people than the gift of these beautiful poems in stone and water; and it is interesting to contrast them with the modest fountains which the popes made for themselves in the Vatican Gardens. The fountains have whispered their enchantment
to many generations, and in each age men have fallen in love with them. Charles
de Brosses wrote in the eighteenth century, "to my taste, the most interesting
thing in Rome are its fountains . . . the number of these fountains, which one
finds at every step, and the rivers that issue from them, are, I think, more surprising and pleasant than the buildings themselves". And Shelley, in the following
century, wrote, "The fountains of Rome are in themselves magnificent combi-
nations of art, such as alone, it were worth coming to see." Such travellers, of
course, saw the fountains at work, surrounded all day by Romans with buckets
and jugs; we see them now in their retirement.

As each aqueduct was built, it sprouted its own family of fountains: first, the Acqua Vergine, with the Trevi and its satellites, all on the low-lying land of Renaissance Rome; then the Acqua Felice on the Quirinal and the hills round about; thirdly, the Acqua Paola on the Janiculum, taking water to Trastevere and the Vatican. With the Acqua Pia Marcia we come to modern times and a piped supply to houses. Though the fountains are today purely decorative, they still continue to slake the thirst of the passer-by, and Romans are great drinkers at fountains. No one can spend a day there without observing this again and again. The result has been a slight redistribution of the waters. In order to provide the casual drinker with the purest supply, some of the old fountains have been separated from their parent aqueducts and connected with newer ones; thus a dolphin made in the sixteenth century may dispense water that was not introduced to Rome until 1870, or later. It even happens occasionally that a fountain may belong to two aqueducts. The old water still shoots from the central jet, but the lower, accessible, jets are fed by a different aqueduct. Many street fountains that have not been converted carry notices, "non potabile", though the warning

The routes of the six aqueducts of modern Rome

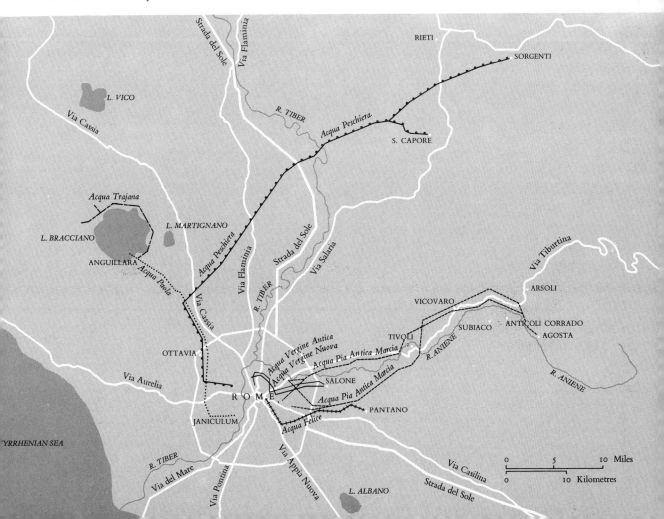

is constantly disregarded, in particular by homeward-bound schoolboys who leap up and eagerly, with enjoyment, drink from the tainted sources.

Even in these sophisticated days the sight – to me, a delightful one – may sometimes be seen of an old woman or a girl drawing water from a street fountain and departing through the crowded streets. It may mean, of course, that the water has been cut off in her flat, but it is also possible that some fussy member of the family prefers the water of the fountain (perhaps Acqua Pia Marcia) to that laid on in the building (perhaps Acqua Felice). I once asked an old man who was filling a bucket with Acqua Vergine Nuova from the wall fountain at Porta Castello, behind the Castel S. Angelo, why he was doing so. His reply struck me as entirely classical, almost like a quotation from Vitruvius. "There is nothing better than Acqua Vergine", he said, "for boiling vegetables."

The Azienda classifies the public fountains in its charge as *Fontane Monumentali*, which includes all the major fountains, *Fontanelle Artistiche*, a more numerous group of decorative fountains, and *Fontane Minori, Sarcofaghi e Abbeveratoi*, a large collection of beautiful and interesting fountains, which includes the wall fountains of the *rioni*, or wards, of the city. It also includes the wonderful collection of classical and early Christian sarcophagi which are to be seen all over Rome. Happily, any reflections on the base uses to which these have been put is made difficult by the time which separates us from the original occupants, and also because of the great beauty which these ancient marbles have achieved as they stand in a narrow street or square receiving the ice-clear water.

As I have said in the foregoing pages, it was the custom in ancient times for each of the aqueducts to conclude its journey to the capital at a splendid fountain, a *castellum* or a *nymphaeum*, which carried an inscription giving the name of the emperor who had built the aqueduct. The popes perpetuated this custom, and their names and insignia may be seen beneath the mitre and the crossed keys on all four of the great papal terminal fountains. The *castellum* of a modern aqueduct is known as a *mostra*, or show-piece, and the six *mostre* of the aqueducts are:

    The Trevi fountain (Acqua Vergine Antica)
    The Fountain of Moses (Acqua Felice)
    The Fountain of Paul V (Acqua Paola)
    The Fountain of the Naiads (Acqua Pia Marcia)
    The Fountain of the Pincian Hill (Acqua Vergine Nuova)
    The Fountain of the Piazzale degli Eroi (Acqua Peschiera)

It is time now to approach the aqueducts and their fountains in historical sequence, beginning with the Acqua Vergine.

Plate 7. Marforio, in the courtyard of the Capitoline Muse
Plate 8. The fountain in the Viale della Trinità de' Mc

VII

THE ACQUA VERGINE
AND ITS FOUNTAINS

THE SOURCE of the Acqua Vergine is to be found in a small village called Salone, about nine miles east of Rome, on the way to Tivoli. One leaves the Via Tiburtina by a side road and comes to a fenced tract of uneasy-looking country of tough marsh grass intersected by windbreaks of poplars. The fields are dotted with insignificant little constructions of brick and stone spaced at irregular intervals all over the area, reminding one of the sheds in an explosives factory. These are the buildings which seal the springs that feed the Vergine. A modern pumping station, humming with the sound of dynamos, bears above its gates the words *S.P.Q.R. Centrale di Sollevamento Acqua Vergine*, providing a contemporary touch in a landscape which otherwise must look as it did when Nicholas V sent this spring water on its way to Rome in 1453.

Crossing the fields, I was taken into some of the buildings. The water is sealed off by plate-glass at ground level; however, by kneeling and pointing an electric torch into the darkness, I could see a rush of water far below, passing through a stone culvert. This was the Vergine Antica and I was told that it takes a day to reach the Fontana di Trevi. Extraordinary to relate, the Vergine Antica flows by gravity, as its ancestor, the Aqua Virgo, used to do before the time of Christ, and for part of the way it flows through the stone channels made by the engineers of Agrippa. The Vergine Nuova, on the other hand, flows through cast-iron pipes and is pumped electrically, and though both aqueducts pump the same spring water, they lead separate existences even at the source.

The springs are formed by rain-water from the Alban Hills which, after passing through miles of volcanic tufa, wells up in this spot. I thought it impressive, watching the subterranean turmoil, to reflect that I was looking at to-morrow's cascades, and the subject of innumerable as yet untaken photographs. The dark flood would not see the light again until it gushed out in twenty-four hours' time over the rocks of the Trevi fountain or bubbled charmingly in the Piazza Colonna.

73

The old Vergine travels underground and passes into Rome on the north-east, under the Fosso Pietralata and, crossing the Via Nomentana, flows westward, making straight for the park of the Villa Ada, which it crosses. It then turns south, flows beneath the suburb of Parioli, crosses the western limits of the Borghese Gardens, and, deep underground, traverses the gardens of the Villa Medici. It then descends to the Piazza di Spagna and runs straight under the crowded streets to its terminal at the Trevi.

The new high-level Vergine takes a more southerly course. Entering Rome also from the north-east, under the Via Tiburtina, it flows beneath the main roads to the Porta Pinciana where it branches, one arm passing south-west to link up, but not mingle, with the Vergine Antica just behind the Piazza di Spagna; the other arm passing north-west under the Galoppatoio – Rome's Rotten Row – and curving through the Borghese Gardens, making a sharp southerly turn and lying beneath the Viale Giorgio Washington to the Piazzale Flaminio, where it cascades from the *mostra* on the hill above the Piazza del Popolo.

These two aqueducts feed some of the oldest and best-loved fountains in Rome. They include:

The Trevi fountain
The fountains in the Piazza del Popolo
The Pantheon fountain
The fountain in the Piazza Colonna
The Fountain of the Tortoises (Tartarughe), in the Piazza Mattei
Il Facchino (the Porter), in the Via Lata
La Barcaccia (the Old Boat), in the Piazza di Spagna
The "Baboon" in the Via del Babuino

The Trevi fountain

Critics of the last century who disliked the Baroque had decided that the Trevi (plate 2) exhibited "all the elements of decadence", though less learned people have always loved it as the most cheerful street spectacle in Rome. It is strange to remember that in the nineteen-twenties the Trevi was often deserted by day and sometimes at night. It was accepted calmly as one of the great fountains, and a visitor could go there on his last evening in Rome and toss in a coin with the fair certainty that no one would see him, and that he would be able to meditate in solitude on the marble orchestra stalls of this wonderful stage set.

That, however, was merely a lull in the fountain's history. The tumultuous waterfall was never intended to be a backwater, and today the Trevi, now a film star, is again the focus of noisy crowds, which, no matter how much the superior traveller may deplore the shouting and the electronic flashes of the street photographers, is a more natural background to this fountain than silence. The film, *Three Coins in the Fountain*, has had the effect upon a larger and more exuberant public that Mme de Staël's *Corinne* and Nathaniel Hawthorne's *Marble Faun* had upon the staid visitor of a century ago; and, as Roman fiction, the film is a not unworthy relative of those novels. Describing the Trevi as it was in his time, Hawthorne wrote:

> In the day-time there is hardly a livelier scene in Rome than the neighbourhood of the fountain of Trevi; for the piazza is then filled with stalls of vegetable and fruit dealers, chestnut-roasters, cigar-vendors, and other people whose petty and wandering traffic is transacted in the open air. It is likewise thronged with idlers, lounging over the iron railing, and with *forestieri*, who come hither to see the famous fountain. Here also are men with buckets, urchins with cans, and maidens (a picture as old as the patriarchal times) bearing their pitchers upon their heads.

In general effect the scene was not unlike that to be observed today at the height of the tourist season, but Hawthorne goes on to say that "at midnight the piazza is a solitude; and it is a delight to behold this untameable water sporting by itself in the moonshine". Today's crowds are still there at midnight, and the photographers are still flashing.

It is possible that if Horace or Pliny could see the Trevi they might recognize it as the fountain which, more than any other, recalled the great *nymphaea* with which they were familiar. It is an imperial gesture, flamboyant and triumphant, the kind of fountain that any emperor would have erected who desired to impress upon the populace the virtues of a new water and his own virtue in having introduced it.

In its present form the fountain of Trevi dates only from the middle of the eighteenth century, though its history goes back to 1453 when Nicholas V, reconstructing the old Aqua Virgo, brought the terminal of the aqueduct into the Piazza dei Crociferi, to the left of the present fountain. The first Trevi was a plain and dignified wall fountain designed by the great Leon Battista Alberti. The water fell from three openings into an oblong stone basin the size of a swimming bath. If the early prints do not exaggerate, the mouths of the fountain were large enough for three or four kneeling men to have entered abreast. The inscription was the first of a kind to become familiar in future centuries: beneath the papal tiara and crossed keys, and two shields bearings the letters S.P.Q.R.,

The horses of the Trevi fountain

large letters in the finest classical style stated that Nicholas V, Pontifex Maximus, had restored the aqueduct.

Some have derived the name of Trevi – "three-ways" – from the three mouths of the fountain; others think it may have been a reference to three roads – *tre vie* – which met there. For more than a century the Trevi offered the only pure supply of water in Rome, and for nearly two centuries it continued to be the modest wall fountain of Nicholas V. But Rome was becoming more splendid, and the time came when the Trevi was thought to compare unfavourably with the new head fountains of the Acqua Felice and the Acqua Paola. Nothing, however, was done until 1640, when Urban VIII asked Bernini to build a new Fontana di Trevi.

The architect began by pulling down the old fountain and moving the outlet of the aqueduct from the Piazza dei Crociferi to its present position, and for a peculiar reason. In the summer the popes were in the habit of leaving the *mal aria* of the Vatican for the more salubrious heights of the Quirinal Hill, and Bernini discovered that by moving the Trevi and pulling down some old houses in the line of view, the Pope, from the windows of the Quirinal Palace, would be able to look down on the fountain.

The first hint of the delays and difficulties which were to bedevil the building of the Trevi occurred when the Pope gave permission for Bernini to pull down the tomb of Cecilia Metella on the Appian Way to provide the stone. Although such demolition had been in progress for centuries and was a commonplace in the rebuilding of Rome, the public were so genuinely outraged that Urban was forced to bow to the outcry and cancel the order. The delays, which continued, defeated even Bernini, who turned his enormous energy to other things, building, among fountains, the Triton (1643), the Bee fountain (1644), and the Four Rivers in the Piazza Navona (1648–51). In the meantime, as a print of the period shows, the Trevi continued to stand in a more or less neglected condition, in appearance a large semicircular basin without any decoration, from which the people drew water, quenched their thirst and that of their horses and cattle, and washed their clothes. The fountain had some narrow escapes during this time, notably from Clement XI (1700–1724), who proposed to design it himself. His idea was to move the Column of Marcus Aurelius from the Piazza Colonna, mount it on rocks and train water to play over them. Happily this scheme did not leave the sketchbook, but it is interesting, proving, as it does, that Bernini's Four Rivers, and the rocky grotto, were in men's minds, and that rocks would probably be a feature of the new Trevi.

With Clement's successor, the Florentine Clement XII (1730-40), the Trevi project entered a decisive, though protracted, phase. Bernini had been dead for forty years and more, and the Pope decided to hold a competition, in the traditional Roman way, for a design for the fountain. Sixteen schemes were submitted, and were displayed to the public on the Piazza del Campidoglio. The winner was a Frenchman named Adam whose design featured seven figures all twelve feet high. Furious that a foreigner should have been successful, the Romans set up an outcry as loud as that which during Urban VIII's reign had preserved the tomb of Cecilia Metella, and the Pope cancelled the award. It seems that Adam, who was a *pensionnaire* of the French Academy, had also angered his principals and he was recalled to France as a punishment. The Pope then himself selected the design of a talented poet, philosopher and dilettante named Nicola Salvi who had recently delighted Rome by designing a "machine" or set-piece for a firework display in the Piazza di Spagna. The choice evoked the usual ironic Roman comment, but it was a good one.

Some of the most beautiful dream architecture of the seventeenth and eighteenth centuries went up in flames in the course of firework displays, and the greatest architects of the time were willing to design the ephemeral scenery of masques and public spectacles. It was probably the only way some could ever hope to see their more ambitious creations. Consequently the Trevi is probably that rare object, a reflection in stone of those fragile splendours. That Neptune should suddenly appear, escorted by Tritons and sea-horses and accompanied by a great waterfall, upon the placid façade of an Italian palace, a display of primitive energy as violent and unexpected as a burst water main in Piccadilly, is typical of the seventeenth century masque. Possibly that may be the reason why, as we descend the steps towards the fountain and seat ourselves in front of it, we have the impression that we have taken our places in a theatre.

Even under the direction of a stage-manager as capable as Salvi, the work dragged on; and Clement XII was succeeded by Benedict XIV (1740-58), who was not by nature a builder, neither was he the only pontiff who had inherited from an architecturally inclined predecessor an embarrassing number of half-finished monuments, and a crowd of sculptors, architects and contractors all respectfully holding out their overdue accounts. The moment he was elected, Benedict despatched two cardinals to inspect the Trevi, and, upon receiving their report decided to finish the work as quickly and as cheaply as possible. But that was not easy. When the work had been in progress for another eleven years, Salvi died, some said from a chill caught in the culverts of the aqueduct;

if the story is true, the Trevi is one of those works that have slain their creators. In the following year Giambattista Maini, the sculptor who had carved the figures, died; six years later the Pope himself died; and still the Fontana di Trevi was unfinished.

The next pope, Clement XIII (1758-69), awarded new contracts and, at last, after three years' work, the Fontana di Trevi, having occupied architects and sculptors for 122 years, and during the reigns of fourteen popes, was considered finished in May 1762; and Rome must have sighed with relief. The visitor cannot fail to read the names of Clement XII, Benedict XIV, and Clement XIII, on the inscriptions, but one misses that of Urban VIII, who set in motion the long process that eventually produced the lovely masque of water.

The fountain, as Salvi left it at his death, was a little different from the final version. To keep costs down, at the command of Benedict XIV, the figures of Neptune and his followers had been carved in chalk, but these were replaced by figures of marble. Also the left-hand niche was occupied in Salvi's time by a figure of Agrippa, which his successor removed and replaced with a figure of Abundance, perhaps to balance Health on the other side, possibly because Agrippa was already present, in the panel above, in the act of approving a plan of the Aqua Virgo. The "Virgo" herself is seen in the right-hand panel, not the child of the legend but a mature young woman, leading the engineers of Agrippa to the fountain-head.

Salvi, in his capacity as metaphysician and eighteenth century dabbler in physics, wrote a long and involved explanation of the symbolism of the Trevi, which most admirers, who think of the fountain as a simple water-tableau, will consider to have been an unnecessary effort. Nevertheless we have it on his authority that the Trevi is intended to be an essay on water. It is not easy to follow him all the way, but not difficult to understand that the left-hand Triton, who is having some trouble with his hippocampus, represents the ocean in an angry mood, while his companion, who leads a placid steed, is the ocean in tranquillity. Less obvious is the urn wreathed in ivy on the right, which Salvi intended to represent the virtue of stored water, while the tree and flowers, carved on the rock nearby, symbolize life nourished by water.

Of more general interest is the custom of throwing coins into the fountain, which makes the Trevi the world's leading receptacle for this form of propitiation. The antiquity of the custom is illustrated in a story told by Lanciani. He said that in 1852 the Jesuits who owned the warm springs at Bagni di Vicarello, on the northern shores of Lake Bracciano, decided to send a gang of workmen

Plate 10. The fountain in the Piazza Madonna dei Mo*

Overleaf Plate 11. Fidelity, one of the Quattro Fonta

from Rome to clean out the central spring, which had become choked up. In draining it, the workmen came upon a layer of bronze and silver coins of the fourth century A.D.; beneath this they found gold and silver of the imperial period, with votive cups of silver; lower still they found a stratum of Republican coins, and so on, layer after layer, until they came upon objects which represented offerings made before the time of minted coinage. These were rough scraps of copper. Even this was not the end. At the bottom of the spring was a deposit of stone arrow-heads and polished stone implements which had been cast into the water by prehistoric men to appease, or to enlist the sympathy of, the spirit of the spring.

As far as the Trevi goes, the custom is, of course, a revival, and a recent one. I have come across no reference to it earlier than the late nineteenth century. Hawthorne made his character Miriam go to the Trevi and sip the water in order to ensure her return to Rome, and that would be about 1860. But she did not throw a coin. The custom was, however, in full swing when Baedeker brought out the eighth edition of his guide to Rome in 1883. The ritual consisted of taking a drink of Trevi water (in the left hand, some purists insisted), and then of casting a coin into the water. Travellers in those days were, of course, drinking Acqua Vergine before it had become *non potabile*, but, should anyone wish to observe the rite in full, this can still be performed with perfect safety. In the right-hand corner of the fountain a kindly municipality has installed a supply of Acqua Vergine Nuova for the benefit of Roman lovers. This is known as the Fontanina dei Fidanzati, the little fountain of the sweethearts, and is sometimes visited by engaged couples if one of them must leave Rome. They should go there at night, taking with them a new glass, and, having filled it at the *fontanina*, they should each drink and then smash the glass on the rocks. This is said to make their reunion a certainty.

I rarely go to the Trevi without remembering that great collector of super-stitions, Sir James George Frazer of *The Golden Bough*. At the end of a learned dissertation on magic springs in his commentary on Pausanias, he confessed that during a visit to the Trevi he "did not scruple to comply with the custom". It was a great moment in the history of the superstition, and how astonished and amused the spirit of the fountain must have been! So few "scruples" are enter-tained by modern visitors that a weekly sum of about 70,000 lire is retrieved from the basin. Like all the great *mostre*, the Trevi is now electrically pumped, and once a week, on Tuesday morning, the old water is sent to join the Tiber, and, before the new supply arrives, men in sea-boots swarm all over the fountain

The four popes chiefly responsible for the building of the Trevi fountain: Pope Urban VIII (1623-44), Pope Clement XII (1730-40), Pope Benedict XIV (1740-58), and Pope Clement XIII (1758-69)

Nicola Salvi, designer of the Trevi fountain

with mops. They groom the hippocampi and scoop up a sample of the world's currencies in buckets. When this has been translated into lire, no mean task, a proportion is devoted to charity.

The atmosphere of fantasy created by the Trevi is so powerful that some visitors probably imagine that the palace in the background, from which Neptune and his outriders have so violently erupted, is part of the design and is not a real palace at all: but that is not so. It is the Palazzo Poli and was until the last century the Roman residence of one of the oldest and most distinguished families, the counts of Conti, afterwards dukes of Poli. The family produced four popes: Innocent III (1198-1216), Gregory IX (1227-41), Alexander IV (1254-61), and Innocent XIII (1721-4). When the dukes of Poli died out in the last century, the

Palazzo Poli housed the archives of the Italian Foreign Office. These were re-moved recently and the palace was, to the surprise of Rome, offered for sale, and it is believed that some offers were received. Once again, however, the public indignation, which the Trevi's affairs have been capable of provoking, erupted violently, and the Government stepped in and forbade the sale. The palace is now occupied by a learned society.

The fountains in the Piazza del Popolo (1572–1814)

Travellers who arrive along the Flaminian Way enter Rome by the Porta del Popolo and find themselves in the spectacular Piazza del Popolo, the most splendid, but perhaps the least Roman, of piazzas. The word "Popolo" has nothing to do with the populace or the people in the modern sense, but is de-rived from the old church in a corner of the piazza which, because it was built in 1227 with gifts from the Roman people, was known as S. Maria del Popolo – St Mary of the People.

Through the Middle Ages, and until the close of the eighteenth century, this square was a rural space surrounded by vineyards and monastery gardens. In 1814 it was decided to transform it into a splendid entrance to Rome, and the architect Luigi Valadier (Roman-born of French parents), who had been archi-tect to Pius VI and Pius VII, was chosen to re-design it. Ironically enough, at the moment when he was creating his vast arena, George Stephenson's first loco-motive was doing six miles an hour across the English countryside, frightening the horses, and before the century came to an end visitors were arriving in Rome by train, and the entrance was then no longer the Piazza del Popolo but the Central Station on the Viminal. Stranger still, in our own time the aeroplane has made the air-traveller's entrance to Rome (after a long drive) the most ugly and least hospitable of air terminals. If anyone were asked to imagine a departure point for the Siberian mines, or a convict settlement, he could do no better than recall that bleak and fearsome place.

In constructing the new piazza, Valadier removed an old fountain that had been spouting Acqua Vergine since 1572. No doubt a draught of this water was the first drink in Rome that thousands of travellers enjoyed when, having left behind them the dust of the Via Flaminia, they entered thankfully within the walls of Rome. This fountain had been standing in the centre of the piazza for seventeen years when, in 1589, Sixtus V provided a companion in the form of the great obelisk, which is still there; and these two were the first Roman monu-ments seen by every traveller who passed under the Porta del Popolo for 240

The Piazza del Popolo in the eighteenth century. The fountain shown in this engraving is now in the Piazza Nicosia

years. All the great travellers of the seventeenth century saw them, the noblemen, the scholars, the churchmen, the diplomats, just as they were seen by all who made the Grand Tour of the eighteenth century. What a number of interesting people have gazed upon them: Fynes Moryson, Inigo Jones, Tom Coryat, Velazquez, Milton, Evelyn, Horace Walpole, the President de Brosses, Joshua Reynolds, Gibbon, Goethe, Chateaubriand – just a few names chosen at random out of hundreds – but by the time Stendhal, Byron, Shelley, and their generation passed beneath the gate the old fountain was about to depart, or had already departed.

One of the charming characteristics of Rome is that some of her ancient monuments share with old soldiers the legendary ability to fade away yet not to die, and so to be discovered at some later time, by a surprised investigator, living quietly in retirement in another part of the city. This happily was the fate of the old fountain of the Piazza del Popolo. First, it crossed the Tiber and appeared on the Janiculum, in front of the church of S. Pietro in Montorio, where

The Piazza del Popolo today. *Above left* Valadier's splendid piazza is now used as a car park. *Above right* The Rome group. *Below* One of the lions of the central fountain

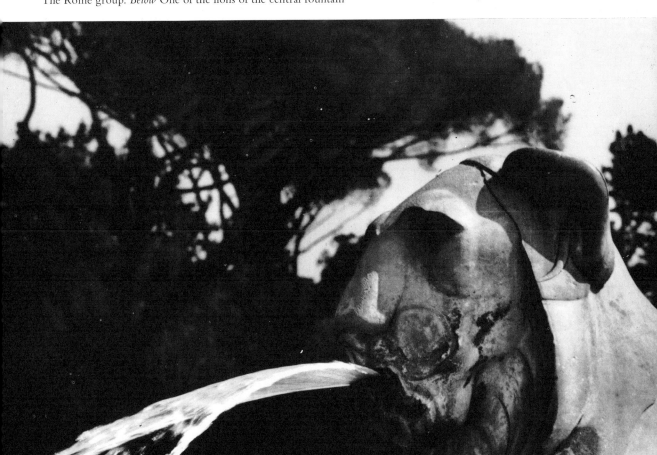

(an unfortunate come-down) it dispensed the Acqua Paola. It was not until 1950 that it recrossed the river and came, bringing its white beauty and its memories, to the Piazza Nicosia, where, like the end of a fairy story, it was reunited with the Acqua Vergine, with whom one hopes it will live happily ever after. Its new home is near the Tiber, midway between the Ponte Cavour and the Ponte Umberto I.

Those who love fountains will wish to salute it in the Piazza Nicosia, and, at the same time, to remember those travellers whose eager eyes alighted upon it in other days. It was the first fountain designed by Jacopo della Porta, and it is believed that it was carved from a huge block of marble from Aurelian's Temple of the Sun. It is approached by a flight of octagonal steps which provide a stately platform for the beautifully proportioned octagonal main basin. It is shallow, and the water is always whipped into miniature waves by four thin jets, which curve down from masks on the underside of a circular bowl above. The bowl is mounted upon a pedestal of carved dolphins, and, in its turn, carries a small marble mushroom, rather like those on the fountains in front of St Peter's, from the top of which bubbles a typical fat plume of the Acqua Vergine.

The plan of Rome made by Tempesta in 1593 shows the fountain side by side with the obelisk in the old Piazza del Popolo, a fascinating and peaceful scene. Vineyards climb the slopes of the Pincian Hill and every house has its garden, but it was not always as peaceful as it appears in the plan. In the last years of Gregory XIII, a *monsignore*, the brother of a cardinal, while driving across the piazza in daylight, was set upon by brigands and killed.

The Piazza del Popolo today provides a greater display of the Acqua Vergine than the Fontana di Trevi, though this is not obvious at a first glance because of the immense scale of the architectural scheme. It is also the only place in Rome where the waters of the two aqueducts are displayed together: the lions in the centre of the piazza are fed by the Vergine Nuova while the great *mostra* on the Pincian Hill and its fountains are fed by the Vergine Antica.

Valadier never saw the giant waterfall, which provides the perfect finishing touch to his great scheme, for a century was to pass before sufficient water could be spared for it. It comes gushing from a triumphal arch on the hilltop – Rome's finest cascade – and feeds two fountains at opposite sides of the piazza, both of them surmounted by statuary. One of these shows Rome, a muscular maiden, helmeted and spear in hand, who stands above the reclining figures of the Tiber and the Anio; the other (plate 1) displays a graceful Neptune escorted by tritons, one of whom has caught a fish whose size he will never need to exaggerate.

The cascade on the Pincian Hill above the Piazza del Pop

The four sphinx-like lions in the centre of the piazza are crouched with their backs to the obelisk. Each bronze mouth expels the thinnest conceivable fan, or wedge, of water, impelled by such power that it might be a sheet of glass. As each lion is mounted upon a pyramid of six steps, the water has space to disintegrate into a shower as it descends into the circular basins below. In various parts of Rome there are lions which spout water, and drip water, and even gush water, but I know of no others which practise so perfectly the rare trick of transforming water into glass or ice.

The Pantheon fountain (1517–1711)

The best time to see the fountain in the Piazza della Rotonda (plates 3 and 5) is at eight o'clock on Sunday morning. The piazza is then likely to be empty. The Pantheon is not yet open, and it is still too early for coaches, crowds, and the sellers of postcards, who lurk in odd corners whispering together, but have not yet set out their wares.

This fountain was the second member of the Trevi's family, the first being the fountain in the Piazza del Popolo, now in the Piazza Nicosia. It had been projected as early as 1570 by Pius V, but his death two years later left the scheme to be completed by Gregory XIII. As with the first fountain in the Piazza del Popolo, the designer was Jacopo della Porta, and he obviously wished to design something different. Instead of the octagonal basin of his first fountain, he made the main basin square, with a curved bow to each of its four sides, a pleasant and attractive design. From the centre of the basin rose the usual pedestal and cup, or chalice, from which water spilt over into the lower pool. Then he spoilt the simplicity of his design, in my opinion, by sinking in the water the grotesque masks which were originally carved for the Piazza Navona. So the fountain remained from 1575 until 1711, when, in the reign of Clement XI, the central cup was removed and replaced by the rocks and the obelisk, an obvious echo of Bernini's Four Rivers in the Piazza Navona. That is the fountain as we see it today. Despite the eighteenth century reconstruction, it remains a typical child of the Acqua Vergine, with its sprays and falls of water, but height and importance are given by the obelisk. To me, the chief beauty of this fountain lies in the steps and the splendid basin.

I cannot leave it without recalling the story of its predecessors in the piazza, which were a brace of Egyptian lions. During his attempt to clean up Rome, the harassed pontiff, Eugenius IV (1431–47), was able to make a decorative gesture towards the Pantheon by sending there two lions of grey porphyry and

The Pantheon in the sixteenth century; a drawing by Martin van Heemskerck showing the two lions and the sarcophagus placed in front of the Pantheon by Pope Eugenius IV

also a red porphyry sarcophagus. No water at that date was laid on to the piazza, and these objects were placed in the centre of the piazza, facing the Pantheon, in about 1440, and are to be seen in that position in prints of the following century. The sarcophagus was in the centre, with a lion on each side.

In 1586 the architect Fontana, who was building the Fountain of Moses as the *mostra* of the Acqua Felice, told Sixtus V that he would like four lions as decorations for this fountain. The Pope gave him two from the Lateran and authorized him to remove the two porphyry lions which had stood for a century and a half in front of the Pantheon. So those ancient beasts migrated to the Piazza S. Bernardo alle Terme and were mounted on the fountain, where for two and a half centuries they and their companions spouted Acqua Felice. When Gregory XVI (1831–46) was forming the Egyptian Museum, he removed the lions to the Vatican, where they can be seen today, and substituted copies on the Fountain of Moses. Thus these animals, created in ancient Egypt, brought to

Three details of the Pantheon fountain

Rome, to the Lateran, to the Piazza della Rotonda, to the Fountain of Moses, and finally to the Vatican, demonstrate the migratory possibilities of a Roman monument.

The fate of the red porphyry sarcophagus was stranger still. It remained in front of the Pantheon until 1740, the year in which Clement XII died. In that year it vanished, to reappear in St John Lateran as the Pope's tomb; and it may be seen there now in the Corsini Chapel, which is the first on the left as one enters the church.

Before one leaves the Piazza della Rotonda, one turns from the fountain to read that majestic inscription – the most impressive ancient inscription still *in situ* in Rome – above the portico of the Pantheon: M. AGRIPPA. L. F. COS. TERTIUM. FECIT. ("Marcus Agrippa, son of Lucius, Consul for the third time, built it.") This is probably the original inscription of 27 B.C. which Hadrian replaced when he rebuilt the Pantheon. One may contrast the joy of the local inhabitants of 1575, as they gathered with their pails and bottles to greet the arrival of water at the Pantheon, with the Roman crowds who splashed about in the Baths there when Agrippa had been consul for the third time.

The fountain in the Piazza Colonna

Whispering gently of other days, the fountain in the Piazza Colonna stands on the edge of a car park, but, alas, no one can now hear what it says. There was a time, pictured in ancient prints, when the bubbling of this plume of the Acqua Vergine was the only sound in a square in which the column of Marcus Aurelius rose in solitary state, the fountain at its base. Now the traffic of the Corso flows ceaselessly past, contributing to a scene of noise and movement remarkable even in Rome. If Rome may be said to have a centre, this is probably the place: Parliament is round the corner, the Stock Exchange is opposite; there are banks, some of the best bookshops in Rome, a confectioner whose chefs are artists in marzipan, and in the background may be seen an elegant building, formerly the General Post Office, whose portico of Ionic columns came from Etruscan Veii.

The fountain belongs to that small group erected in the time of Gregory XIII to take the water of the Vergine to some of the more populous squares of the city, its companions being the fountain of the Piazza del Popolo (now, as I have said, moved to the Piazza Nicosia), the fountain in front of the Pantheon, and the two marble basins of the north and south fountains of the Piazza Navona. The Colonna fountain was erected in 1575-7 from a design by Jacopo della Porta and

The Piazza Colonna in the eighteenth century

it bears a family resemblance to its contemporaries. The huge basin of Porta Santa marble is a graceful variation of a shape which della Porta developed from the simple octagonal basin of the Piazza Nicosia fountain to the more elaborate and flowing designs of those in the Piazza del Pantheon and the Piazza Navona. It is to me the finest of them all. Beneath the marble rim, and not difficult to overlook, are sixteen beautiful little lions' heads carved by Rocco Rossi in the sixteenth century.

It is not easy to examine a fountain when all around is bustle and noise, but the effort is worth while. The Colonna fountain, a typical low-pressure child of the Acqua Vergine, is fed by a fat bubbling jet of water that springs from a central decoration, in shape like a small marble pedestal table which rises in the centre of the main basin. The flow is adjusted so that the water streams over the edge of this "table" in a veil like a cloth of the finest and most transparent silk. This beautiful effect dates only from 1830, when the fountain was restored and the ancient and more ornate central jet removed. Two curious objects like cannonballs rising at water level bubble up and help to keep the water agitated, and to provide an effect of waves.

During the Middle Ages pilgrims would visit the Piazza Colonna and climb

The fountain in the Piazza Colonna. The lions' heads below the rim of the basin date from 1575-7, the dolphins and the central jet from 1830

the spiral staircase inside the column of Marcus Aurelius to admire the view from the top. Lanciani says there are two hundred and three steps and fifty-six loop-holes. Every year the column was put up for sale to the highest bidder, and it seems that the monks of S. Silvestro in Capite usually acquired it and derived an income from the gate money. It is still possible to climb the column with the permission of the Superintendent of Monuments, but I have never had the energy to do so myself.

The view of the column and the fountain at its foot, as they were in the time of Sixtus V, is one of the best in the series of lunettes in the Vatican Library. Women are seen washing clothes in the fountain; pigs, hens, geese and sheep wander about the piazza; a horse is being shod outside a forge, and groups of pilgrims and tourists admire the fountain and point to the statue of St Paul on top of the column, which Sixtus placed there in 1589. It is difficult to connect it with the scene today.

In later centuries the fountain was the meeting-place of farmers from the Campagna who would hire labourers there and sign agreements with hand-shakes which were said to be as binding as any notary's bond. The piazza also had the odd distinction of being the only place where coffee might be roasted in Rome. When first introduced to Europe, the smell of roasting coffee was considered unpleasant. During the seventeenth century, in London at least, one coffee-house owner, James Farr of Fleet Street, was charged with annoying his neighbours with evil smells, while in some countries it was necessary to obtain a licence to roast coffee. The fountain in the Piazza Colonna was in those days surrounded by portable stoves and kitchens where, on fires of coal or wood, the café proprietors would bring their sacks of berries to be roasted. Until 1900 the fountain was almost invisible beneath the blue and white striped tents of lemonade sellers who, as a guarantee of purity, would use the Acqua Vergine from the fountain to mix their brews.

The Fountain of the Tortoises (1581-4)

This most Florentine of all the fountains is to me the most beautiful in Rome. I envy those who, never having heard of it, wander by chance into the little Piazza Mattei and see it for the first time with a sense of discovery.

The piazza is small and distinctly grim. Shutting out the sunlight, ancient palaces stand round it, now divided into flats, the ground floors devoted to shops and storerooms. The pavement slopes downward towards the centre where the gayest public monument in the city stands, murmuring softly with the sound of falling water. Four life-sized bronze youths, naked and pagan, lean against the stem of the fountain and, with uplifted arms, push four bronze tortoises over the rim of the marble bowl above them. The effect is enchanting, no matter how many times you may see the fountain. Small wonder the legend is still repeated that Raphael designed it: the spirit is that of the early Renaissance carried into the sixteenth century, it seems, from the Florence of Verrocchio.

It was one of those fountains which, like that of the Pantheon, was suggested in 1570 by the water commissioners of Pius V, but not executed until the next pontificate, that of Gregory XIII. It was originally intended to carry the water main from the Trevi to the Piazza Giudea, but the Mattei family, whose palace was, and still is, in the Piazza Mattei, were able to influence the authorities to change the plans and take the water instead to their piazza.

The sculptor was the Florentine Taddeo di Leonardo Landini, who worked under the direction of Jacopo della Porta. The work began in 1581 and the fountain was completed in 1584. During the construction, the original scheme was altered; instead of the entire fountain, including the figures, being of marble, it was decided that the four youths should be in bronze. Though the cost of this alteration was higher than the original estimate, the extra money was obtained by a tax on meat!

The original design provided not for tortoises but probably for dolphins, which the youths were to push over the edge of the bowl, but, for some reason unknown, these were never added – so for more than seventy years the youths remained with their hands raised in mid-air. Who the genius was who added the tortoises is a mystery, though some believe that perhaps Bernini did so during a restoration in the year 1659. The little creatures, so anxious to escape into the water, their forelegs spread out eagerly on the marble rim as they struggle forward, their scaly hind-legs in the air, give the fountain a touch of humour and playfulness. Landini would surely have approved, and might have wondered why he had never thought of this himself.

Charming as these creatures are, and responsible to some extent for the affection this fountain inspires, they do not affect the superb harmony and the exquisite grace of the main figures. The youths – clearly related to fauns, though a searching investigation will fail to reveal tail or hoof – rest lightly against the stem of the fountain as though they had been running and had paused, one leg uplifted, a foot on the head of a dolphin, the other leg bent back to maintain balance, as, without the slightest sense of effort, each one gently pushes his eager little chelonian into the water overhead.

Plate 13. The Triton fount

Overleaf Plate 14. The Piazza Navo

There is nothing else like this in Rome: if we wish to compare it, we must look to Florence. The same grace, charm and humour are to be found in the lovely little Genietto, a cupid clasping an infant dolphin, which Verrocchio made for the Medici villa at Careggi in 1476, and now in the forecourt of the Palazzo Vecchio. Landini must often have admired it, and also those snub-nosed satyrs and the naked nymphs, only a few yards away, which Giambologna made for the Neptune fountain; indeed it might even be that the four youths of the Piazza Mattei are the sons of such a union, though fortunately they take after their mothers!

In 1965 it was discovered that one of the youths was ill. It was feared at first that he was suffering from the puzzling bronze disease which has attacked the horses of Lysippus in Venice, and some bronzes in Rome, and experts hurried to the patient. It was eventually discovered that he had existed for four hundred and eighty years with a bar of iron in one of his legs. The revelation suggested a crisis in the foundry similar to that described so vividly by Cellini in his *Life*, when, during the casting of the Perseus, finding that the metal was not running freely into the mould, the frantic sculptor cast every pewter plate and porringer he possessed into the bronze and got the metal flowing again. Fortunately, the chemical reaction set up after all these years in the bronze figure on the Tortoise fountain will, it is believed, respond to treatment.

A restaurant, which I considered one of the most pleasant and excellent in Rome, was to be found in the Piazza Mattei, only a few steps from the fountain, but the last time I was there it had vanished and its place was taken by a draper's store-room. Gone for ever now are those delicious meals at a table, with the fountain almost at my elbow, to which I looked forward with so much pleasure. Gone, too, for ever is that memorable moment in the spring when the scent of wood strawberries came to me as I entered the square; gone also are those meditations as I finished my wine, listening to the falling water and watching the four young figures in lamplight, or in moonlight, as if I half expected them to spring to life and resume their game.

I am one of those who find it pleasant to fix a work of art in time, and I often sat at my table reflecting that in the year 1584, when Landini had finished his fountain, Shakespeare was only twenty and had never been heard of in literary and theatrical London. On the other hand, Cervantes, a battered thirty-six, had written a number of plays but was still many years away from *Don Quixote*; and among the new books in England in that year were North's *Plutarch*, Hakluyt's *Voyages*, Sidney's *Arcadia*, and Spenser's *Shepherd's Calendar*. The year was also

Plate 15. The Fountain of the Four Rivers, in the Piazza Navona

Details of the Fountain of the Tortoises in the Piazza Mattei

an interesting one in the world of action. Raleigh had annexed Virgina; William the Silent was assassinated; the Duke of Alençon, who had had a long and absurd flirtation with Elizabeth Tudor, died of tuberculosis, the hereditary disease of the Valois, aged thirty, and so began the "War of the Four Henrys". In England, Elizabeth was facing the problem of Mary Stuart and the threat of Spain; in three years Mary was to die at Fotheringhay; in four, the Spanish Armada would set sail.

And in Rome the four youths in the Piazza Mattei continued to lean against their fountain as if there were no such thing as sorrow in the world.

Il Facchino (the Porter), in the Via Lata

Let into the wall of the Bank of Rome in the Via Lata, just off the Corso, is a wall fountain in the form of a man holding a little barrel (plate 6). He is called Il Facchino, the Porter, and is one of the best-loved fountains in Rome, though from the condition of his face, which has received blows which appear to have been anything but affectionate, one might never suspect this. Time has carried away his nose and otherwise obliterated his features, lending to the face in certain lights an expression of harrowing melancholy. Perhaps a supposed resemblance to Martin Luther may have been responsible for some rough treatment during intolerant centuries, though, as far as one can tell now, the resemblance must always have stopped short at the kind of cap, or bonnet, the figure is wearing.

Should you happen to find someone in the crowds of the Corso who was born in Rome (an unlikely event in these days) he would tell you that Il Facchino was the work of Michelangelo, though there is nothing to substantiate this. The story dates only from 1751, when Luigi Vanvitelli, in the course of a history of the Palazzo de Carolis – now the Bank of Rome – made the surprising claim, which has been accepted by the many and rejected by the few.

The fountain dates from the sixteenth century – some think from the reign of Gregory XIII – and was erected originally around the corner in the Corso. A woodcut printed in 1643 by Giovanni Domenico Fragini in his *Descrittone di Roma* shows the figure in good repair, but the water, which pours from the centre of the barrel, descends, not as it does today into a semicircular basin, but into a large, two-handled Greek urn, which may, of course, be artistic licence. The face is undamaged and is that of a middle-aged man with a beard. The fountain was removed from the Corso to its present position during alterations to the building in 1872.

There is a belief that the figure represents a well-known street character, a

porter named Abbondio Rizio, who was noted for his strength, his skill in carrying difficult loads, and his prowess in the local taverns. But was he a porter? Is
it not more likely that he was a more interesting character, an *acquarolo*, or
water-seller? Surely a porter would have been shown carrying a load upon his
back, not holding a barrel at waist level and dispensing water? Should he be an
acquarolo, he is a fascinating link with the waterless Rome of the fifteenth and early
sixteenth centuries when the only supply of good water was that of the Trevi,
and the water-seller was a figure as familiar in Rome as the milkman in a modern
city. The barrels, which were called *coppelle*, were made not far from the Piazza
Navona where a street, the Via delle Coppelle, a piazza, and a church, S. Salvatore
delle Coppelle, perpetuate the now obsolete word. The water, drawn from the
Trevi and the Tiber, was hawked from door to door by men like the "Facchino",
and also by women, for Rienzo's mother was an *acquarola* in her spare time. The
water was drawn from the Tiber some way upstream near the Porta Flaminia,
where it was believed to be less contaminated, and having been stored in tanks,
sometimes for six months to allow the sediment to settle, was drawn off into
barrels and sold.

One has always imagined that drinking the water of the Tiber must have been
one of the hazards of life in Rome centuries ago, yet many exalted persons,
including several popes, attributed their health to it. When Clement VII went to
Marseilles to marry Catherine de' Medici to the Dauphin, he took a supply with
him, and Paul III would never travel anywhere without barrels of it. Another
addict, Gregory XIII, who died at the age of eighty-four, drank Tiber water every
day on the advice of his doctor, Alessandro Petroni. These pontiffs must have built
up a magnificent resistence to typhoid.

An English enthusiast named Strother A. Smith published a book entitled
The Tiber and its Tributaries in 1877, and wrote as follows:

Being desirous to learn something about the quality of this water, and to form an
opinion as to the time within which it might be drunk, I filled a large flagon with it
at a time when it was greatly discoloured by a sudden flood. At the end of five hours
I found that it had deposited all its yellow mud, but still retained a slightly milky hue.
I had proposed to filter it, in order to render it perfectly transparent; but being otherwise engaged, and obliged to defer the operation, I was surprised to find on the fifth
day, inclusive, it had become as clear as crystal, and in no way distinguishable from
the water of the Acqua Vergine.

I drank a portion, used another portion for making tea, and found it excellent. A
trial of it with soap shewed it to be of a medium degree of hardness. In short, it was
very superior to the water with which Londoners are supplied from the Thames. A

bottle of it well corked was left at Rome during the summer, to see whether it would undergo fermentation owing to the presence of organic matter, and develop any unpleasant taste or smell. On my return, after an interval of four months, the water was found to be perfectly sweet to the taste, and free from any disagreeable odour.

The writer ended by admitting that to those who do not know how "clear and sweet" the water of the Tiber becomes after having been allowed to settle, the preference of many popes for it must seem incomprehensible.

To return to the "Facchino". His popularity in former times was increased by his status among the select company of Rome's "talking" statues. These were monuments to which critics of the papal government, and of everything else, attached sometimes witty, and generally acid, comments on current events, a custom which died out with a free press.

La Barcaccia (the Old Boat), in the Piazza di Spagna (1627)

The Piazza di Spagna, with its superb place of assignation, the Spanish Steps, imparts to the Roman scene a joyful sense of youth and gaiety. It is one of the happiest squares in the world. People have been meeting there, and resting there, for more than two centuries, and a few yards off, sunk in the roadway, one of the most admired fountains in Rome, La Barcaccia – the Old Boat (plate 4) – leaks Acqua Vergine at every joint.

One may fancy that the spirit of nineteenth century England still lingers in the piazza, which an Italian wit once described as the "English ghetto" (as the Via Vittorio Veneto is now the American "ghetto"); and one has only to look up at the old saffron-coloured house to the right of the fountain, as one faces the Spanish Steps, to imagine the face of the dying Keats at the window, gazing down towards the frail barque that was sinking like his own young life, a sight that must have been the poet's last memory of Rome. In the corresponding house to the left, Mrs Babington's successors uphold the traditions of the English tea-table and can no doubt be relied on to produce such Victoriana as crumpets and muffins. Between those houses, the old travertine boat bubbles and leaks away, having caught the eye of every traveller since the year 1627.

Charles I had occupied the throne of England for only two years when La Barcaccia arrived in the piazza, and seventeen years later a young Englishman, travelling in order to avoid involvement in civil war at home, took lodgings above on the Pincian Hill. It is strange that John Evelyn, who mentioned so many of the Roman fountains in his admirable description of Rome in 1644, did not spare a word for this one, though he must have seen it every day. It is also

La Barcaccia, in the Piazza di Spagna. *Above* A seventeenth century drawing showing the tree-lined path that led up to the church of Trinità de' Monti before the construction of the Spanish Steps. *Below* The Spanish Steps and La Barcaccia in the still uncrowded Rome of the nineteenth century

strange that even today you will often hear people explain that the jet of La Barcaccia was made low in order not to obstruct the view of the Spanish Steps, though one would imagine that everyone would know by this time that the fountain was there a hundred years before the Steps. Prints of the seventeenth century show the fountain with the same low-pressure Vergine jet, but instead of the Spanish Steps (which, incidentally, were the gift of a rich Frenchman and have nothing to do with Spain), a winding path led up through trees to the Trinità de' Monti.

It is said that the fountain commemorates an event which took place in 1598 when, during the worst Tiber flood ever recorded, eighteen feet of water filled the Pantheon, while a boat was cast up on the hillside which one day was to become the Spanish Steps. It has also been said that the fountain symbolizes the Ship of the Church sailing the sea under the insignia of Urban VIII, though it may occur to some that a happier symbol than a sinking ship might have been found. Nevertheless, the Pope himself did not think it inappropriate and composed a distich in which he said that the warship of the priest poured forth, not fire, but water to quell the flames of battle.

Some think that the fountain was designed by Pietro Bernini, but others believe it to have been the work of Lorenzo, his famous son. Bernini senior was a Florentine married to a Neapolitan wife, which may perhaps explain his son's cold, balanced mind and his passionate anger. The family arrived in Rome from Naples in 1604, when Lorenzo was a child of six, and, like many great artists, he gave proof of his genius at a precociously early age. He was probably capable of designing the Barcaccia when he was in his teens, and he was already an accomplished twenty-nine, with many works to his credit, when the fountain was started. It is a reasonable assumption that, if he did not conceive the fountain himself, he probably gave his father a hand with it.

No doubt father and son studied with care the only fountain in Rome which bears a resemblance to the Barcaccia. That is La Terrina – the Tureen – which Jacopo della Porta built about 1590 for the Campo dei Fiori. Facing the same technical problem which was later to face the Bernini – the low pressure of the Vergine – della Porta sank his fountain below pavement level, giving it the approach as if to a spring with steps leading down to it. This idea was adopted, but with greater dramatic effect, in the Piazza di Spagna.

The Old Boat is a memory of Rome which even the most fleeting of visitors takes away with him. Sometimes in the early morning the flower-sellers refresh their roses and carnations in the fountain, and throughout a summer's day

Plate 16. The figure of the Ganges, from the Fountain of the Four Ri

Romans drink the water, which for some years now has been Acqua Vergine Nuova. In those precious early hours before the traffic arrives, the scene is the same as that our forefathers knew so well, though one would dearly like to see again the artists' models who in past times gathered at the fountain and at the foot of the Steps as they waited to be engaged. They adopted the poses for which they were noted, piety, simplicity, senility or roguishness, which Dickens said were so familiar to anyone who had visited an art gallery. The best account of them was given by the American sculptor, W. W. Story, in *Roba di Roma.*

> Here in a rusty old coat and long white beard and hair (he wrote), is the *Padre Eterno*, so called from his constantly standing as model for the First Person in the Trinity in religious pictures. Here is the ferocious bandit, with his thick black beard and conical hat, now off duty, and sitting, with his legs wide apart, munching in alternate bites an onion, which he holds in one hand, and a lump of bread, which he holds in the other. Here is the *contadina*, who spends her studio life in praying at a shrine with upcast eyes, or lifting to the Virgin her little sick child – or carrying a perpetual copper vase to the fountain – or receiving imaginary bouquets at a Barmecide Carnival. Here is the invariable pilgrim with his scallop-shell, who has been journeying to St Peter's and reposing by the way near aqueducts or broken columns so long that the memory of man runneth not to the contrary, and who is now fast asleep on his back, with his hat pulled over his eyes . . . Sometimes a group of artists, passing by, will pause and steadily examine one of these models, turn him about, pose him, point out his defects and excellencies, give him a *baiocco*, and pass on. It is, in fact, a models' exchange.

One could see some strange things if one stood at La Barcaccia in 1887, less than a hundred years ago. "Today, as I am writing," wrote Story, "some hundreds of galley-slaves in their striped brown uniforms, are tugging at their winches and ropes to drag the column of the Immaculate Virgin to its pedestal on the Piazza di Spagna."

The "Baboon" in the Via del Babuino

The decayed figure of a reclining Silenus, known to irreverent Romans as the "Baboon", gave its name centuries ago to the Via del Babuino, which runs from the Piazza di Spagna to the Piazza del Popolo. Though he has lost both hands and is pitted and eroded everywhere, the figure has, generally speaking, stood up to the centuries much better than Pasquino, and his face is in a better condition than that of Il Facchino. In certain lights it wears the vestige of a crafty woodland smile and there is still something vigorous and indignant in the attitude of the statue, as if he would like to spring up and chastise the rude boys who cover the wall behind him with their graffiti.

Plate 17. The Neptune group from the northern fountain in the Piazza Navona

The ancient figure of Silenus in the Via del Babuino

Like other battered works of the kind, the Babuino was immensely popular in papal Rome and was numbered among the "speaking" statues to which satirical comments on current affairs were attached, to be answered by one of the other statues. The last thing Rome ever expected of this statue was that he should disappear, yet this happened in 1877. London could not have been more dismayed had Nelson been abducted from Trafalgar Square. The disappearance of the Babuino was due not, as Augustus Hare believed, to the malice of the new Italian government, but to street alterations. Unfortunately, like other monuments uprooted from ancient positions, the Baboon was lost, so that from 1877 until recent times many a visitor to Rome must have wondered why the straight and narrow street full of antique shops and expensive book shops should have been called "the Street of the Baboon".

In the nineteen-twenties the statue was discovered in the courtyard of the Cerasi palace from which he was rescued, soon to return in triumph to the street named after him, where he may be seen reclining above a marble fountain filled with Acqua Vergine.

VIII

THE ACQUA FELICE
AND ITS FOUNTAINS

Pope Sixtus V (1585-90), whose name was Felix Peretti, stands out among the benefactors of Rome like one of the better Caesars. His father was a poor jobbing gardener in the Adriatic coast town of Grottamare, in the March of Ancona. One night he dreamt that a son would be born to him who would lift the family fortunes to unimaginable heights, and that he was to call the child Felice - "happy" or "fortunate".

A manuscript of thirty pages, which was written after the death of Sixtus by one who knew him, and published by Ranke, gives some curious details of the Pope's birth and childhood. The writer states that Sixtus himself related that his father heard a voice calling him in the night, saying, "Rise, Peretti, and go seek thy wife, for a son is about to be born to thee and to whom thou shalt give the name of Felice since he one day will be the greatest among mortals!" At the time of this rather blasphemous dream, Peretti's wife, Mariana, a domestic servant, was living in the town, but Peretti, who was heavily in debt, did not dare to go to her in daylight in case he encountered his creditors. However, he managed to steal off at night under cover of a sea fog. Upon the birth of the child on 18 December 1521, Peretti formally assured his creditors that his debts would be settled, and advanced as a guarantee the future fame and greatness of the infant. "When he had the child in his arms, he would declare that he was carrying a pope, and would hold out the little feet for his neighbours to kiss."

In spite of these convictions, he made no provision for the child's education and young Peretti began life scaring birds from orchards and herding sheep. Like many great men, he knew the spur of poverty and also the stimulus of a stern mother. "When he discovered himself to have committed any fault, he trembled in every limb for fear of his mother." Perhaps she was attempting to counteract the dotage of her husband. Poverty prevented the future pontiff from attending school, but by borrowing the hornbooks of other children he managed to pick up the alphabet and to teach himself to read. A relative, recognizing the boy's capacity for learning, came to the rescue and paid for his education; and at an early age Felice entered the Franciscan Order.

He became a celebrated preacher before he was twenty, and had at his command a flow of words which in later life his enemies were to describe as worse than garrulity. While in his thirties he attracted the attention of two future popes, Pius IV and Pius V, and his reforming nature led to a friendship with Ignatius Loyola. He became Grand Inquisitor, then General of the Franciscan Order, and eventually Cardinal Montalto. In all his dealings he was feared and never apparently liked except, fortunately, by his architect, Fontana; and many detested him for his despotic methods and his domineering manner. It was clear to everyone what kind of a pope Cardinal Montalto would be.

He was, nevertheless, elected, and his election inspired the best-known conclave story of the sixteenth century. He was sixty-five at the time and it was said that, believing the Sacred College might prefer a stop-gap pope on the edge of the grave, he tottered into the Conclave with the aid of a stick, pausing to cough now and then, and looking desperately ill. The moment he was elected, however, he straightened up and flung away his stick to take it up again only to chastise those who opposed his will. The story may not be true, but it represents what men thought at the time. It is a fact that the quiet cardinal, who had been living in retirement editing the writings of St Ambrose, vanished, and in his place stood an autocrat.

In describing the life of Sixtus, Ranke said that "it would sometimes seem that even in confusion itself there exists some occult force, by which the man capable of steering through its mazes is formed and brought forward". Certainly it is not easy to explain how Sixtus was able to achieve so much in the five years of power granted to him. From the moment of his election he began to put down without mercy the bandits and murderers who for so long had infested the Papal States. On the day after his coronation he rejected the customary request for the pardon of prisoners with the words, "while I live every criminal must die". His mercy was reserved only for the poor and for debtors.

He demanded from his officials everywhere the heads of murderers, outlaws and bandits, and the grisly cargoes came trundling into Rome to be exhibited in public places. The Romans whispered, "Sixtus would not forgive Christ himself", and it was said that there were more heads on the Ponte S. Angelo one summer than melons in the fruit market. On one occasion the Duke of Urbino was ordered to expel a band of outlaws who had established themselves on a hill in his territory. Instead, he loaded a train of mules with food and wine and sent

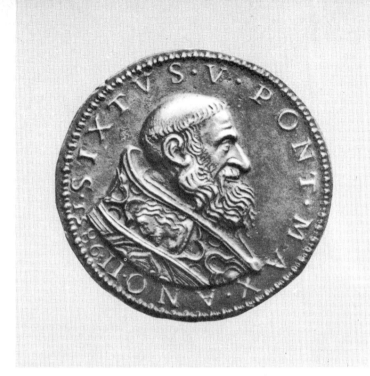

Two portraits of Pope Sixtus V (1585-90)

it past the hill where, as he had intended, the outlaws seized it. There were no survivors for the food was poisoned. And the Pope was delighted.

The result of such severity was that within a year the *banditi* had been executed or had fled the Papal States, and Sixtus had the satisfaction of hearing ambassadors assure him that on their way to Rome they had passed through a land blessed with peace and security. One of the best pasquinades of the time was inspired by the Pope's war on the bandits. It was a dialogue between the statues of St Peter and St Paul on the Ponte S. Angelo. "Why do you carry a burden on your back?" asked St Paul. "I am thinking of leaving Rome", replied St Peter, "for fear of being executed for having cut off the ear of Malchus."[1]

The achievements of Sixtus in five years were matched by the speed with which his plans were carried out, as if he knew that time was short. While he was putting down lawlessness, he was at the same time reforming the Curia and planning a new Rome with the aid of his friend, Domenico Fontana. Living frugally himself, and imposing economy upon his court, he managed to amass millions to pay for his schemes, and naturally he was hated for the taxes he imposed, the loans he raised, and the abrupt confiscation of the property of those who were rash enough to oppose him.

It is only since 1870 that Rome has ceased to be the Rome of Sixtus V, and even

[1] "Then Simon Peter having a sword drew it, and smote the high priest's servant, and cut off his right ear. And the servant's name was Malchus." *St John, 18, x.*

today every step we take reveals some evidence of his energy and vision. He completed the dome of St Peter's, a sight which Rome never thought to see. The architects asked for ten years. Sixtus brushed this aside and kept several hundred men at work day and night, with the result that the dome was completed in twenty-two months. He was the pope who married the obelisks to the fountains. He moved the Vatican obelisk to the front of St Peter's and erected the Lateran obelisk and the obelisk in the Piazza del Popolo; and upon the top of each he placed a cross to symbolize the triumph of Christianity over paganism. With the same intention he placed a statue of St Peter upon Trajan's column and one of St Paul upon the column of Marcus Aurelius. He rebuilt the Lateran Palace and swept away without a moment's regret all relics of that wonderful site; he rebuilt the Vatican Library whose gay painted walls and classical book cupboards every tourist sees today; he built the Via Sistina and the Via delle Quattro Fontane; he placed the "Trophies of Marius" on the Capitol and the "Horse-tamers" in front of the Quirinal Palace; he built the Sistine Chapel in S. Maria Maggiore, where he selected his tomb during his lifetime and where he is buried: and all this in addition to public works outside Rome which, as in Rome itself, he personally inspected, generally on foot. He restored and revived the Aqua Alexandrina, and was the first man to build a Roman aqueduct for thirteen centuries. In doing so, he made the abandoned hills habitable for the first time since the fall of Rome. Upon an arch of his aqueduct, two miles from Rome, at Porta Furba, may be read this imperially worded inscription, telling how he "had gathered the waters from afar, and brought them into Rome".

In the perspective of history the building of the Acqua Felice was the greatest of all his acts, though, strangely enough, the scheme was not his. It had slowly and painfully emerged in the course of preceding pontificates as the only way to relieve the pressure on the Acqua Vergine and to bring life to the desolate districts on the hills. The route of the aqueduct had been surveyed and everything was ready when the aged Pope, Gregory XIII, died in 1585. But without hesitating, Sixtus ordered the work to begin ten days after his election, and he followed up his command by a personal inspection of the source at Pantano de' Griffi, about twenty miles from Rome. Four thousand men were employed on the scheme under Matteo Bartolani of Città di Castello, who was so afraid of the Pope that he hurried on the work with such speed that the aqueduct reached Rome during the following year. Unhappily, in his desire to beat the papal deadline, Matteo had miscalculated his levels and, to the fury of Sixtus, when the water was turned on only the merest trickle emerged. Matteo was instantly

A contemporary print of Pope Sixtus V surrounded by some of his works, including the Mos
fountain and the obelisks of St Peter's, St John Lateran, and the Piazza del Popo

a Cappella di S.ᵃ M. Mag.

Spegere li tristi.

La libraria in Beluedere.

Labondantia.

Le Galere noue.

La fabricha di ponte Sixto.

La benedicione col palazzo di S. Giouani.

corpo di Pa Pio V.

La guglia di S.ᵗ Giouani.

La Colonna Troiana.

La Colonna Antonina.

guglia di S.ᵗ Pietro e Cup.ᵃ

La guglia di S.ᵗᵃ Maria Magiore.

SIXTVS · V · PONT · MAX · MINCON

Creatus ano Dñi 1585 die 24 Aprilis ætatis suæ anni LXVI.

Battista parmen for. Roma 1589

Ieronimo a ripetta.

La guglia del populo.

Scala Sant./Il palazzo di S. Giouani.

Le strade noue.

La fontana a Termine.

A plan of Rome in 1590

dismissed and one who could do no wrong in the eyes of the Pope was appointed in his place, Fontana. During the reconstruction of the aqueduct it was discovered that in places the water showed a tendency to flow away from Rome! Fontana, with his usual skill and efficiency, had put things right by 1587, when Sixtus was able to inaugurate the arrival of the Acqua Felice "near the gate of the vineyard dei Panzani, in Santa Susanna", or in what is now the Piazza di S. Bernardo with its speeding buses and motorcars. In the following year water reached the Capitol for the first time for thirteen centuries. That year, 1588 (in England, the year of the Spanish Armada), marked the second stage in the rebirth of Rome. The first was the revival under Nicholas V a hundred and forty years previously.

Panoramas like that which Antonio Dosio drew in 1561 show that half of Rome was then a hilly wilderness, yet what an attractive wilderness it was. The fascination which the Forum and the Palatine Hill hold for us today was then spread over lonely, haunted miles. Such are the last glimpses of that ghostly Rome which had inspired poets like Petrarch and political dreamers like Rienzo; a Rome that had been broken up, not by barbarians, but by Romans, yet was still able to whisper of greatness to those few who could hear. Winding country roads led over the hills, past belts of woodland to solitary little churches and monasteries which had managed to exist by virtue of an old well. Only the robber concealed himself in the caves and brambles, only the shepherd guided his flock at night into a marble pen; and one could wander all over the hillsides picking up scraps of porphyry or malachite, wondering maybe about the half-words on broken stones, words which had once spelt "Caesar" and "Senate". Brunelleschi one day sat there with his sketchbook, collecting cornices and capitals which would spring to life again in Florence; and, later, one might have met Raphael and his friends, perhaps taking a holiday from the walls and ladders of the Vatican, on their way to what they called "grottoes". Climbing down from an opening in the roof, they would descend into some imperial hall or bedroom, and see with delight how the "grotesque" cupids and sphinxes on walls and ceilings became alive in the light of their torches. Sometimes the word would go round that a man digging in his vineyard had found Venus or Apollo sleeping there.

That world, which had its own magic like that of any morning in spring, came to an end with the arrival of the Acqua Felice upon the Quirinal Hill. As the water neared Rome, it is said that two relatives of the Pope, thinking to please him, went out and hurried back with a cupful of it. Sixtus waved it away saying that it had no taste, a remark with which generations of Romans have been in agreement. Of all the great undertakings of the pontificate of Sixtus V, the making of the Felice aqueduct was the most costly. The account books of Fontana, which are preserved in the archives, say that it cost three times as much as the Sistine Chapel in S. Maria Maggiore.

Anyone interested in the reign of Sixtus V should study his splendid tomb in that church. It was begun by Fontana while the future pope was Cardinal Montalto, and its magnificence caused his predecessor, Gregory XIII, who disliked him, to cancel the Cardinal's allowance, saying that he obviously had no need of it. It is said that Fontana continued the work with his own money, but had the delicacy not to let his friend know, though if Rome then resembled the

Rome of today, the Cardinal probably heard all about it within the hour! Sixtus is seen kneeling in life-sized effigy, without the papal tiara: a square-set man with a square beard to match and an expression scarcely as stern as might have been expected. Above are his arms, a play on the name of Peretti: a lion rampant reaching for three pears. The story of his reign of five years is told in the bronze panels. We see the obelisk he moved to St Peter's, the arches of the Acqua Felice stretching into the distance, the dome of St Peter's and, less usual on a papal monument, men bearing the severed heads of bandits and robbers.

"If anything can still the spectator to silence, and awaken him to great recollections," wrote Gregorovius, "it is the monument of this astonishing man who, as a child, herded swine, and as an old man commanded people and kings, and who filled Rome with so many works that from every side his name, like an echo, rings in the traveller's ears."

It might also be said that had he not constructed so much, he might have been remembered as one of the great destroyers. He demolished the "Patriarchium" of the Lateran and the Oratory of the Holy Cross; he melted down the bronze doors of S. Agnes to make the statues of St Peter and St Paul for the column of Trajan and the column of Marcus Aurelius: he pulled down the Septizonium of Septimius Severus – the worst architectural vandalism of the century. He was equally busy in other directions. Among those whom he excommunicated were Elizabeth Tudor (for the execution of Mary Stuart), Henry of Navarre (for his Protestantism), Henry III of France (for the assassination of Cardinal Guise), and the half-witted Jacques Clement (for the assassination of Henry III of France). And still he had time to correct the *Vulgate*.

The source of the Acqua Felice is a group of springs about fifteen miles to the east of Rome at Pantano Borghese, just off the Via Casilina, along a rough country road. The word *pantano* means swamp or bog, and when I visited the source on a day when the October skies had opened with the first rains, I thought the name could not have been improved. The springs are fed by water from the Alban Hills which has filtered through the volcanic tufa like those of the Acqua Vergine; indeed both the Vergine and the Felice originate in similar country and owe their existence to the same geological formation. I was told that the water takes twelve hours to reach Rome.

The appearance of the springs was much the same as those of the Vergine, and finding little to interest me more than the thought of Sixtus V walking energetically over the swamp with his cardinals in 1585, I returned on the road to Rome to find the Acqua Felice as it emerges into the open air. This it does at a point about seven miles from the city, where the arcades of the old Claudian and Marcian aqueducts stride bleakly across the landscape, a sight that once delighted those visiting Rome for the first time as they drove in from the Ciampino airport. The aqueduct rises from the grass like a concrete drain, then, after travelling for some distance on the surface of the fields, mounts its ancient predecessors and enters Rome pick-a-back, sometimes on the Claudian aqueduct, sometimes on the Marcian, and always a hideous contrast to the grace and dignity of its ancestors.

Near the point of its emergence is an old farmhouse called Roma Vecchia, or Casale Torlonia. I never thought to see in these days a sight resembling so closely the Campagna as painted and described in the last two centuries. The old arches receded across the level landscape attended by clumps of stone pines, and, now that the rain had begun to fall again, the scene was one of the utmost melancholy. I turned for shelter to the farm. Like most ancient farms in Italy, its shape was that of a fortress. It was surrounded by a high wall pierced by an arched gateway that led into a courtyard from which an outside staircase of worn stone rose to the living-rooms. Beneath were the stables, the cow-sheds and the barns in picturesque disarray. One of the walls was studded from ground level to the top with the marble fragments of statues dug up in the fields and inset into the stone-work in the manner of Renaissance courtyards. It was a strange anatomical museum; arms, legs, fists, noses, rarely a complete object, even single fingers and toes, had been carefully preserved and added to the collection.

I was glad to shelter in a barn with turkeys, guinea-fowl, hens, and an odd-looking friendly animal which I took to be a goat that had been born with the wrong legs. (I was later to learn that it was a rare specimen of the Tibetan goat.) As I looked through the arch of the gate and saw the ancient Aqua Claudia and the Aqua Marcia gleaming in the descending rain with their escort of pines, the illusion was complete: that was the Campagna a century ago, and a depressing sight it was.

The farmer's wife, with a cloth over her head, said that her husband had gone off to rescue some waterlogged sheep, but if I cared to step up into the house I should be welcome. As I did so, a clatter behind indicated that the Tibetan goat was also coming; he leapt past me and, frisking on his short legs into the house, settled down like a dog. The woman told me that the farm belonged to Prince Torlonia and that it possessed water rights going back to the building of the aqueduct by Papa Sisto Quinto. When the rain stopped, we went down and saw the intake from the Felice, a direct puncture of the aqueduct exactly like those described by Frontinus in the first century, where a pipe of a certain length and diameter delivered the stipulated *quinariae* per hour.

Leaving the farm, I was almost immediately in modern Rome again, the Cinecittà on one side, the Campus Barbaricus on the other, and in between one of the incoherent suburbs which Rome extends in every direction. The place where Vitiges camped in A.D. 537, and cut the water supply of Rome, has itself been conquered; and there is already a Via Campo Barbarico. As the arches of the ruined aqueducts and the clumsy outline of the Acqua Felice, and the Rome-Naples railway, all proceeding on parallel lines, approach Rome, a stretch of the Aqua Claudia has been seized by squatters. They are known as *abusivi*, "the illegal", and are feared and detested by the authorities, who would like to evict them. They are poor, but not cringing, and are capable of making an official eat and swallow an eviction order as Barnabò Visconti once forced an abbot to eat a papal communication, wax seal and all. Hence a certain amount of sighing and tut-tutting about the *abusivi* in official circles.

Like some species of bird which forms its nest out of odds and ends, the squatters, raiding refuse dumps everywhere, have assembled battered sheets of corrugated iron, stray lengths of timber, discarded motorcar tyres, wooden boxes, old car bodies, and have managed to wall up the arches; and with true Italian spirit they have painted their lairs in attractive pastel shades of green, pink and yellow and have even made themselves, in the most endearing way, window-boxes. This heroic makeshift with its teeming population has the air of a Neapolitan slum. One of the more prosperous of the *abusivi*, having obtained a small secondhand car, has turned the next arch into a garage; another, with a sense of humour, has advertised his illegal den "for sale". It has probably not struck the indignant authorities in Rome that the *abusivi* are able to point to the most aristocratic of precedents: this camping in Roman ruins was started by the Colonna and the Orsini.

I had not been five seconds in the place before I was made to feel unwelcome. Hostile faces glared over walls and from windows. Little groups disintegrated and vanished, each person into his own covert. A gang of swaggering youths came swinging along, exchanging gallantries with any girl they could see, and I thought that, given cloaks and hoods, they would probably bear some resemblance to their distinguished predecessors in history. Above everything else, my attention was attracted by two girls, dark glossy hair falling to their shoulders, who, as they leaned from a window cut in a sheet of corrugated iron, addressed ironic comments and invitations to every passing male. Those unequivocal maidens, beautiful as they may have been, had still a rarer etymological beauty which dazzled me for the remainder of the day. The arch from which they were leaning was known to the Romans as a *fornix* and so notorious were the enticements of prostitutes in the arches of Roman circuses and amphitheatres that the word *fornicatio* suggested itself to ecclesiastical writers, from which spring the English and French derivatives.

From this point the course of the Acqua Felice became a little tedious. That bundle of water, that fat parasite clinging to ancient masonry for a hundred yards, then crawling for a time along a wall of its own, was entirely lacking in distinction, and I thought with admiration of the Roman engineers who brought their waters into Rome as if they were triumphant legions. Still, one must remember that they had all the spoils of Asia to spend.

The Felice goes underground again as it enters Rome and, missing the Porta Maggiore, that old water gate, by a matter of yards, runs underneath the Piazza Vittorio Emanuele and the Piazza della Repubblica, and then goes to its terminus at the Fountain of Moses in the Piazza S. Bernardo.

The new group of fountains called into being by the Acqua Felice were all upon the hills, first the Quirinal Hill, then the Capitoline, and among them are:

> The Fountain of Moses (*mostra*)
> The Monte Cavallo fountain
> The Quattro Fontane
> The fountains of the Quirinal Palace Gardens
> The fountains on the Capitol
> The fountain in the Piazza Campitelli
> The fountain in the Piazza d'Ara Coeli
> The Navicella
> The fountain in the Piazza Madonna dei Monti
> The fountain in the Viale della Trinità de' Monti
> The Triton fountain, in the Piazza Barberini
> The fountain in the Piazza Bocca della Verità
> The fountain in the Piazza of S. Maria Maggiore

The Fountain of Moses, in the Piazza S. Bernardo (1587)

The statue of Moses on the *mostra* of the Acqua Felice, squat, ungainly and ludicrously draped in a toga, has been a figure of fun for generations – "the most shameful parody of *Michelangiolismo* in Rome", as Venturi expressed it. Each coachload of tourists is told the story that the sculptor, Prospero Antichi of

Veduta del Castello dell'Acqua Felice
presso le Terme Diocleziano   Chiesa di S. Maria della Vittoria

Brescia, hearing the burst of laughter which greeted his work when it was first seen, fell into melancholy and committed suicide. The saddest part of the story is not always told: that the poor man begged to be allowed to correct the proportions which he had miscalculated, but the fierce old pope, Sixtus V, refused to allow him to touch the statue, saying that it must remain for ever as a monument to his incompetence. The story may not be true, but it is in character.

One wonders how the sculptor proposed to put the statue right. It would appear to defy correction. The strange and distraught figure holds what one can only assume to be advance copies of the Ten Commandments, since these were not given to Moses until after the incident of the water. It has been suggested recently that Prospero Antichi may not have been the sculptor, but merely his assistant, and that the real culprit may have been Leonardo Sormani, a Milanese sculptor whose work has earned a paragraph in Vasari. Should that be so, and if Prospero Antichi has been the scapegoat for nearly four centuries, then another Old Testament character has been added to the fountain!

Unfortunately, visitors are rarely asked to admire the proportions of this fountain, the lettering of the inscription, the beauty of the two angels who stand on the summit holding the pope's coat of arms, the rampaging lion and the pears, and the perfect travertine balustrade that surrounds it at ground level and on which four of the most docile and friendly lions in Rome are seated. These are the four modern lions which, as I have said, were placed there by Gregory XVI (1831–46), in place of the four Egyptian lions which he moved to the Vatican Museum. These charming beasts hold little pipes in their mouths through which they primly and expertly expel four fine arcs of water as if performing a trick.

In designing the fountain Fontana revived the Roman idea of an archway through which the water of the new aqueduct, like a victorious army, gushed from its *porta triumphalis* for all to see and admire. Not only was it the first terminal *castellum* of a new aqueduct to be seen in Rome since the time of the Caesars, but it was to influence the future designs of the Acqua Paola, on the Janiculum, and also of the Trevi. The rustic scene which it invaded has now become one of the most crowded crossways in Rome. In the year of its inauguration, 1586, the nearby church of S. Susanna, which Pius XI gave to Roman Catholics of the United States of America in 1922, was still a mediaeval church standing among fields and vineyards; the round church of S. Bernardo nearby was still the ruins of a terminal hall of Diocletian's Baths and had not yet shocked the Cistercians with frescoes which they whitewashed.

Among those who saw the Fountain of Moses when it was comparatively new

Plate 18. The Fountain of Paul V on the Janicu[l]

was John Evelyn, who described it in 1644, fifty-seven years after its erection, when, oddly enough, the fountain, which is now jet black, struck him by its whiteness. He wrote: "Opposite to this is the Fontana delle Terme, otherwise called Fons Felix; on it is a *bassorilievo* of white marble, representing Moses striking the rock, which is adorned with camels, men, women and children drinking, as large as life; a work for the design and vastness truly magnificent. The water is conveyed no less than twenty-two miles in an aqueduct by Sixtus V, *ex agro Columna*, by way of Praeneste, as the inscription testifies. It gushes into three ample lavers raised about with stone, before which are placed two lions of a strange black stone, very rare and antique."

The back of the Fountain of Moses, which is not open to public inspection, is entered by the watermen from a door around the corner, in the Via Venti Settembre. Once inside, it would appear that nothing has changed much since 1587. The sound of traffic is drowned by the rush of water entering from the aqueduct and flowing out from the fountain into the great basins; flights of old stone steps lead down into clammy caverns where some of the lead piping, the bronze stop-cocks and the valves are those used when the water was first turned on in the reign of Sixtus V. Most surprising of all to anyone who has seen the fountain only from the outside is that it still contains the quarters of the watermen of 1587, who had to live on the premises in days when the water supply of the Quirinal and Capitoline hills was controlled from the building.

I climbed a flight of steps which led to this flat and, opening a door, entered, unexpectedly, a neat dormitory where beds were arranged side by side. The impression was that of a hospital ward. Then I noticed an odd thing about it. The disposition of the bedclothes suggested that the sleepers had awakened at the same moment and had all instantly leapt from their beds, dressed, and fled the dormitory. And that, I imagine, is exactly what happens when the alarm goes off, for the rooms are occupied by waiters of the nearby Grand Hotel. It is the perfect bedroom for those who are lulled to sleep by the sound of water, among whom have been popes, emperors and caliphs. The rooms are palatial in proportion, and I wondered whether Fontana had designed them for his own use.

The Monte Cavallo fountain (c. 1588)

Probably nothing would have dismayed Gregory XIII more than the knowledge that his successor would be the cardinal he most disliked, Felix Peretti, who became Sixtus V. The antipathy was of long standing and was mutual, and so strong that when Gregory became pope, Cardinal Montalto, as Sixtus then was, thought it prudent to retire to his library. The irony which haunts the lives of popes, as of more ordinary mortals, was therefore present when, of all men, Sixtus V was called upon to carry to conclusion two of his predecessor's most cherished schemes: the construction of the new aqueduct and the establishment of the Quirinal Palace.

We must go back to the earlier years of the sixteenth century to see how that building developed, a palace that has sheltered popes and kings and is today the residence of the President of the Italian Republic. It stands upon a high spur of the Quirinal Hill, with a steep fall to the west, and a marvellous view, over the roofs of Renaissance Rome and the Tiber to St Peter's. About the middle of the sixteenth century, when the hill was still waterless and more or less deserted, a few cardinals bought land there and built themselves villas to escape from the notorious fevers and agues of the Vatican bred from the stagnant moat round the Castel S. Angelo and the standing water in gardens and vineyards.

The most admired retreat upon the Quirinal was the Villa d'Este. It had been a simple dwelling called the "Vineyard of Naples", the property of the Carafa family, when the talented and scholarly Cardinal Ippolito d'Este, the son of Lucrezia Borgia and Alfonso, Duke of Ferrara, transformed it into a delightful country house. Having been appointed Governor of Tivoli, where he created another Villa d'Este which still carries his name down the years, his property on the Quirinal was bought by Gregory XIII as a summer palace.

The Pope was then in his eighties. Perhaps his transactions with Time – he devised the Gregorian Calendar – gave the impression that he was indestructible, since at the age of eighty-two he could spring into his saddle without assistance and had buried thirty cardinals all younger than himself; he also attributed his health and vigour, in part, to daily draughts of Tiber water. Montaigne, who had a private audience in 1580, described him as "a very handsome old man, of middle height and upright, his face full of majesty; a long white beard", but he noted that his speech was halting and that he spoke Italian with a Bolognese twitter. Unlike his successor, Sixtus, who, as a good Franciscan, went everywhere on foot, Gregory was a fine horseman. Upon state occasions he rode a white mule, but was usually astride a Spanish horse. Montaigne saw him set off one day wearing riding-boots of leather with the hair inwards and a white leather cross on each boot. As he descended the steps of St Peter's, his groom was waiting, holding two or three pairs of gilt spurs for the Pope to choose from. On another occasion Montaigne saw him in a procession, twenty-five horses led before him richly caparisoned with housings of cloth-of-gold and ten or twelve mules with foot-cloths of crimson velvet.

Such cavalcades came to an end when Gregory, suddenly deserted by his celebrated health, died, aged eighty-three; and Cardinal Montalto emerged from his library leaning on a stick. Under Sixtus V the building operations took on a faster tempo. The Pope was said to "love hurry". The dismounted cardinals, led now by a tireless, inquisitorial figure, were required to explore building sites and road-making operations, while Sixtus, climbing over bricks and stones, or ascending ladders, would harangue the workmen and rebuke in the sternest manner any slackness or dereliction from duty. The Quirinal Palace delighted him so much that he decided to live there; he was also the first pope to die there.

When Sixtus glanced from the windows of the Quirinal he would see a sight that had fascinated visitors and pilgrims for centuries. The marble statues of two prancing horses attended by two marble men on foot had been in position on the Quirinal Hill since classical days, and they were among the few works of art which had never been buried or concealed from view since the fall of Rome. They appeared in most of the mediaeval guide books and maps and were among the objects which every pilgrim wished to see. They were known simply as "the Marble Horses" and are called today "the Horse-tamers" or "Castor and Pollux". They once stood at the entrance to, or inside the vestibule of, the *thermae* of Constantine, which occupied the western spur of the hill.

Though Sixtus had sent many a precious marble to the lime-pits, he looked with a kindly eye upon Castor and Pollux and decided to make them the decoration for a fountain. Unfortunately, the figures had their backs to the Quirinal Palace, but Fontana, turning them to the left, made them face the Strada Pia (now the Via del Quirinale), and placed a fountain, with two basins and a jet, between them. So one of the most famous fountain groups in Rome first took shape, but more than three hundred years were to elapse before it took the form which we admire today.

At first the scene was rustic. Old prints show that, attracted by the fresh shower of the Acqua Felice, carters often pulled up to water their horses at the Monte Cavallo fountain, and that wayfarers, having climbed the steep spur (still an ordeal now by way of a superb flight of steps), were glad to rest a moment there.

Sixtus had been dead for 195 years when an obelisk was dug out of the ground behind the church of S. Rocco. It was the companion to the obelisk which Sixtus had erected outside S. Maria Maggiore, and both had probably stood at the entrance to the tomb of Augustus. Pius VI (1725-99), who was then pope,

The Monte Cavallo fountain. *Above* An engraving by Piranesi showing the fountain that was demolished in 1782, shortly before the erection of the obelisk. *Below and right* The fountain today

The Forum in the time of Piranesi; cattle are drinking from the huge basin that is now on Monte Cavallo, in front of the Quirinal Palace

had the idea of linking the two detached statues of the Dioscuri by placing the obelisk between them; and that was done with great success. Some may like to remember, as they admire this famous monument, that Pius VI was the pope who began his reign as "Il Papa Bello", like a pope of the Renaissance, but ended it in France twenty-four years later, ill, humiliated, and eighty-one years old, as the prisoner of Napoleon.

Thirty-two years later, in the reign of Pius VII (1800–1823), a remarkable addition was made to the fountain, and one upon which few, unaware of its extraordinary history, bestow a glance. This is the giant granite basin at pavement level which was brought from the Forum in 1818, a Roman relic that, like the Dioscuri themselves, had survived in its original position all the storms and stresses of the centuries. It stood originally not far from the arch of Septimius Severus in the Forum, with the river god Marforio reclining above it and pouring into it the contents of his wine jug. When Marforio was removed to the Capitol in 1595 the huge granite basin was turned into a drinking trough for cattle and horses, and as such it is seen in sketches and engravings of the Forum made in the seventeenth and eighteenth centuries, notably by Piranesi. Thus the fountain of the Piazza del Quirinale is formed of three ancient monuments which have survived from the days of imperial Rome: an Egyptian obelisk, two marble groups, and a granite fountain, all of which were familiar to the Romans of centuries ago, and which now, by the apparently capricious chances which rule survival, have been granted a second life in another Rome.

And not in Rome alone. The Dioscuri have appeared, as their habit was, in many places: they are to be seen on the Berlin Museum; and the so-called Achilles statue in Hyde Park, the gift of English womanhood to the Duke of Wellington and his armies, is Westmacott's version of one of them. Arthur Hugh Clough apostrophized them in the following hexameters:

Ye too, marvellous Twain, that erect on the Monte Cavallo
Stand by your rearing steeds in the grace of your motionless movement,
Stand with upstretched arms and tranquil regardant faces,
Stand as instinct with life in the might of immutable manhood, –
O ye mighty and strange, ye ancient divine ones of Hellas.

This was Shelley's favourite fountain. After describing the Trevi and the fountains in the Piazza Navona, he wrote:

The fountain on the Quirinal, or rather the group formed by the statues, obelisk, and the fountain, is, however, the most admirable of all . . . On a pedestal of white marble rises an obelisk of red granite, piercing the blue sky. Before it is a vast basin of porphyry, in the midst of which rises a column of the purest water, which collects into itself all the overhanging colours of the sky, and breaks them into a thousand prismatic hues and graduated shadows – they fall together with its dashing water-drops into the outer basin. The elevated position of this fountain produces, I imagine, this effect of colour. On each side, on an elevated pedestal, stand the statues of Castor and Pollux, each in the act of taming his horse; which are said, but I believe wholly without authority, to be the work of Phidias and Praxiteles. These figures combine the irresistible energy with the sublime and perfect loveliness supposed to have belonged to their divine nature. The reins no longer exist, but the position of their hands and the sustained and calm command of their regard, seem to require no mechanical aid to enforce obedience.

The Quattro Fontane (c. 1588)

The year 1588 – a vintage year for the Acqua Felice – saw a series of new fountains spring up simultaneously upon the Quirinal and the Capitoline hills. As usual during the pontificate of Sixtus V, no time was lost, and the mains were immediately laid along what is now the Via Venti Settembre to Monte Cavallo and the Quirinal Palace, and on to the Capitol. Among the first fountains to spring to life were three of the four little wall fountains which gave their name to the Via delle Quattro Fontane.

The Pope, unlike his predecessor, was no horseman, but loved to take long walks, especially on Sundays after Mass, to see the new buildings that were growing up in Sixtine Rome. This habit, distressing to his elderly court, often took the Pope along the Via Felice (now the Via Sistina), and up the steep road (now the Via delle Quattro Fontane), where new streets were opening the way to the Pope's favourite church, S. Maria Maggiore.

It was not altogether easy to persuade people to build houses or consent to live on hills which had been depopulated for centuries, and Sixtus offered various inducements, such as tax exemption and building material, to those who would leave the crowded streets of Renaissance Rome and make their homes in the purer air of the hills; and to do so was a certain way to papal favour. The diarist Ameiden said that Mutio Mattei built the Villa Mattei (now the Palazzo del Drago), simply to please the Pope, and that in return Sixtus gave him a grant of stone from the Septizonium, some of which went into three of the "quattro fontane".

These are inset at the corners of the four buildings at the crossroads and are now blackened by age and by the exhalations of Roman traffic. I have never thought them beautiful, but they are a fascinating relic of Sixtine Rome, and one associates them with those Sunday walks of long ago when the Holy Father, accompanied by his footsore cardinals, came up the hill to admire the new roads and villas and to hear the cheerful sound of the Acqua Felice. It is easy to forget that in 1588 this was the most important "crossing" in the new town-planned Rome, and I have sometimes wondered whether Sixtus, as he surveyed his heated followers after their climb uphill, himself suggested four drinking fountains in this place.

They depict four figures, two male and two female, reclining in a classical pose while water drips from the urns they are holding, and in one instance from the mouth of a lion. They are unobtrusive fountains, and even at night one has to listen to catch the faint tinkle of the falling water. The two male figures are river gods, the Tiber and the Anio, though some say the Nile; the two females are Strength symbolized by the lion on which a matron is leaning, and Fidelity (plate 11) or Loyalty (who seems to be asleep), and a second glance reveals a dog at her side, a pleasant and unusual touch.

The Tiber, one of the Quattro Font

The Quirinal Palace Gardens

Among the attractions which the Quirinal Palace had for Sixtus V was the peace and quiet of the hill at night. He slept badly at the Vatican and was often irritated by bells, drums, the barking of dogs and the crowing of cocks, as proved by his order silencing bells and ordering the other sounds to be kept to a minimum. Like some bad sleepers, he sometimes failed to notice that others were nodding, and he often kept his court up late, and in summer led reluctant cardinals at night into gardens where mosquitoes dive-bombed their purple ankles. Incurably voluble, Sixtus loved to discuss the new Rome that was growing wherever his Acqua Felice spouted; sometimes he enjoyed a picnic in the gardens of the Villa Medici or a visit to the Franciscans of Ara Coeli when the pontiff, who handled and hoarded millions, would take with him not only his frugal luncheon but also a little firewood to heat it.

It is probable that Sixtus was living at the Quirinal and busy, among other things, with the Monte Cavallo fountain, when the news of the defeat of the Spanish Armada reached him (which did not surprise him), and it may have been at the Quirinal that he uttered his surprising praise for the queen he had excommunicated. "She is certainly a great queen", he said of Elizabeth Tudor, "and were she only a Catholic she would be our dearly beloved daughter. Just look how well she governs! She is only a woman, only mistress of half an island, yet she makes herself feared by Spain, by France, by the Empire, by all." Elizabeth returned the compliment with the remark that Sixtus was the only man worthy of her hand.

The palace, however, is more usually associated with later popes; the gentle Pius VI who, at Napoleon's orders, was arrested in his rooms there and taken to France where he died, ill and humiliated, at the age of eighty-one. Eleven years later French soldiers overpowered the Swiss Guard and arrested Pius VII, who was taken to France, but he returned to Rome and survived his captor. During the Revolution of 1848, Pius IX, disguised as a priest, escaped from the palace in a hackney coach: twenty-two years later he left the Quirinal for ever to become the "Prisoner of the Vatican", and a month later King Victor Emmanuel entered the palace and selected as his own the apartments of the popes.

During its four centuries as an Apostolic palace, the Quirinal was more accessible to visitors than during its seventy-seven years as a royal residence, and while most Romans and visitors to Rome have passed beneath the gardens, by way of the Quirinal Tunnel, few have ever walked through them. They are comparatively unchanged since the sixteenth century and are among those fortunate gardens in which gardeners have never ceased to clip, mow and plant for nearly five centuries. Their original shape was a number of geometrical squares divided by hedges of cypress, laurel, and myrtle; and so they remain today. The hedges are now stupendous. They were above the height of a man when Evelyn saw them in 1644: they are now more than three hundred years older and have reached the greatest height to which laurel and myrtle can attain.

An earlier visitor than Evelyn was Frederick, Duke of Württemberg, who in 1599, in the time of Clement VIII, admired the trees and the foreign plants, and "the very wonderful and peculiar water devices", and "a grand organ piece with four registers most cleverly made which, if you turn the water on with a tap, begins to play by itself just as if a good organist was playing it". This was the water organ of Clement VIII, which still exists. Forty-five years later, in the time of Innocent X, Evelyn admired the "exquisite fountains, close walks, grots, piscinas, or stews for fish, planted about with venerable cypresses, and refreshed with water-music aviaries, and other rarities".

The palm trees which now attract the eye had evidently not been planted in Evelyn's time or he would have mentioned them: they appear to be the same age as those in the Piazza di Spagna. Evelyn failed to note a feature of the garden which is one of its greatest attractions, the fine stone terrace with its miniature obelisks, which offers a splendid westward glimpse over Rome to St Peter's, a view similar to that from the gardens of the Villa Medici. The living architecture of the Italian garden has often disappointed the English eye, and the dark hedges, the contrived vistas, the deliberately posed statue at the end of a greenwood street, the fountains enclosed by walls of laurel, none of these seem to compensate for the lack of flowers. It is certainly so in the Quirinal Gardens, which fulfil the Renaissance ideal of "secret places such as are desired by poets and philosophers", and, indeed, as one progresses from one *giardino segreto* to the next, each walled in by giant hedges, the picture presents itself of rival philosophers or cardinals holding their separate courts, or such absurdities, for which Italian gardens seem designed, as Malvolio's declaration of love. On a warm and sunny day, and by summer moonlight, the Italian garden has its own grave magic, but in rain, when so many English gardens look beautiful and smell so sweetly, the streets of laurel and box, and a grassy forum where a mournful cypress sheds its tears, are places to avoid.

Most of the Quirinal fountains date from papal times and still display the Acqua Felice. I came with pleasure and surprise upon a fountain which I had read about called La Rustica, said to have been designed by Maderno. It is a mossy grotto overgrown with ferns and choked with water plants, and in front is a circular pavement with the arms of Gregory XV (1621-3), worked in mosaic. My companion, having deliberately placed me in the centre of the mosaic, made some unconvincing excuse and vanished into a shrubbery with such an air of conspiracy that I knew some trick was about to be performed. Sure enough, a circle of small holes round the edge of the mosaic sent up powerful jets of water which imprisoned me. It was a kindly version of those "trickes" which delighted travellers of the seventeenth century, who almost seem to have enjoyed getting drenched to the skin. Montaigne mentions a water-joke that "sends up stray jets to a man's height, and fills the petticoats and thighs of the ladies with its refreshing coolness", while Francis Mortoft, who visited Italy in 1659, would appear rarely to have been really dry. He says of one garden "as wee entered, the water flew up from the ground and wet us", and in another, "wee were saluted by spouts of water for a fare well, without perceiving from whence they came"; but these "pretty devices" roused only laughter among those well-tempered travellers. La Rustica is perhaps the only trick fountain still in working order into whose rather obvious precincts popes decoyed their cardinals.

The most impressive sight in the Quirinal Gardens is the water organ of Clement VIII (1592-1605), which, though badly in need of repair, is still, even in its silent and decayed condition, one of the unknown Baroque marvels of Rome. It occupies a special building, like the apse of a church, called the Ninfeo Aldobrandini, which is enclosed by wrought-iron rails and approached by a flight of marble steps. The organ stands in an immense and splendid archway every inch of which, with the neighbouring walls, is decorated with raised and moulded panels representing the Creation, the story of Moses, and the mythology of water. The paint is peeling off or has vanished altogether, yet even in decay the work is fine and deserves preservation.

Thirteen pipes of the organ are visible in an oval opening in a Baroque screen upon which two cupids, seated upon rocks, hold trumpets to their lips and, so ancient accounts say, blew them at appropriate moments as the organ played. The blazons of several popes may be made out in the peeling paint and plaster. Clement XI (1730-40) restored the instrument, and Gregory XVI (1831-46) added two tunes by Verdi to its repertoire. It is the urgent duty of one of the many departments and societies whose task it is to care for the works of art and antiquities of Rome to save this delightful example of an ancient and lost craft.

The water organ of Pope Clement VIII, in the Quirinal Palace Gard

Pope Clement VIII (1592–1605)

The whole scene is charming. It recalls the lighter moments of the papacy. One imagines the pontiffs of the seventeenth and eighteenth centuries, seated in the alcove with their cardinals, smilingly beating time as the hydraulic organ gurgled out its melodies.

Nearby is another hydraulic marvel, also badly in need of restoration. It is a dark cavern, representing the forge of Vulcan, where several almost life-sized figures of marble are grouped around a forge fire, and, presumably, when working, brought down their hammers upon an anvil. Other automata in the background moved at the same time, carrying pincers, pokers and other blacksmith's tools. The figures, in their motions, must have resembled those which strike the hours on ancient clocks, and the scene, when in movement in the gloomy cavern, must have been most realistic.

My companion told me that Queen Marie José used to be interested in both the organ and the forge and wished to see them restored, though nothing was ever done. He also told me that when he had entered the royal service twenty-four years previously, an aged gardener had been at work who remembered the Quirinal as a papal palace. He used to tell the other servants how he had seen Pius IX walking in the gardens with his cardinals while gilt coaches drawn by black horses drove round and round the Piazza del Quirinale, waiting for their eminences to emerge.

The Forge of Vulcan in the Quirinal Palace Gardens

The fountains on the Capitol (c. 1588)

During the Middle Ages, and for long afterwards, rubbish and dunghills accumulated in the streets of a city until a distinguished visitor was expected, when the magistrates would order the streets to be cleaned up. One of the most energetic spring-cleanings in history preceded the visit of the Emperor Charles V to Rome in April 1536. In the short time of fifteen weeks Paul III and his adviser, Latino Giovenale Mannetti, pulled down two hundred tenements and several churches and made a paved road three miles long, which they decorated with triumphal arches. They also cleared away the slums that clung to the Baths of Caracalla, the Septizonium, the Colosseum, and other famous monuments; and so exposed these ruins to view.

This clean-up was unusual because the improvements continued after the imperial back had been turned, and also because it is often said that modern Rome did not take shape until the time of Sixtus V – thirty-eight years and six pontificates after the death of Paul III. It was, however, the admirable and beloved Paul III, with his excellent Mannetti, the *maestro delle strade*, who first tackled the reconstruction of sixteenth century Rome, and also the Commune of Rome, which for the first time began to take an interest in town planning. During this period the Corso replaced the Via Giulia as the chief street of Rome, and the Capitol was reclaimed from its ancient squalor by the hands of Michelangelo. Though he did not live to see the Capitol completed, Michelangelo superintended the removal there from the Lateran of Marcus Aurelius, and he supervised the majestic steps to the Senator's Palace; but later hands were to modify his plans and to create the most perfect piazza in Rome. There was, of course, no water on the Capitol in 1538, and Michelangelo made no provision for fountains, though it is interesting that he should have placed two old Roman fountain figures, the river gods Tiber and Nile, beneath the staircase there, almost as though he foresaw a time when they would again preside over water.

Thirty-eight years after the death of Paul III, the Acqua Felice began to pour from the Fountain of Moses, and the engineers immediately carried the water main to the Quirinal, and on to the Capitol. The next year, 1588, the fountain on Monte Cavallo and the two river gods on the Capitol were in working order, proudly announcing that at last after a thousand thirsty years water had returned to the hills of Rome.

There are two fountains on the Capitol, but one is not immediately visible. They are the fountain under the senatorial staircase, and the celebrated Marforio (plate 7), who hides modestly in the courtyard of the Capitoline Museum, the

Plate 20. A detail of the fountain in front of S. Maria in Traste

building to the left as one enters the square. These figures have the unusual distinction of never having been lost or buried since the fall of Rome: they remained throughout the Middle Ages and the Renaissance more or less in their original positions until they were moved to the Capitol. Marforio survived all the perils of history in the Forum, not far from the Arch of Septimius Severus, and the Tiber and the Nile were originally on the Quirinal, near the Dioscuri. A great river was symbolized by the Romans as a bearded man in the full strength of maturity, naked to the waist, who reclined at ease, one arm resting upon some emblem of the river he represented, the other holding a flowing cornucopia, emblematic of the wealth and fertility created by fresh water. The air of grace and tranquillity, as well as the flowing lines of the drapery, make these statues clearly symbolic of the natural phenomena they represent. They are essentially a Roman convention and owe nothing to Greece, a country which is not noted for its rivers. They belong to an age when the Roman Empire contained within its frontiers the Nile, the Tigris, and the Euphrates, as well as the Rhine, the Seine, and the Thames. I think the two river gods on the Capitol among the most moving public statues in Rome, and I can never see them without feeling something of the delight I experienced when I saw them for the first time.

The Nile leans upon a sphinx and the Tiber upon Romulus, Remus, and the Wolf. Pirro Ligorio, the Renaissance genius who designed the gardens of the Villa d'Este at Tivoli, tells how the Tiber was originally the Tigris and was leaning upon the head of a tiger, but as the Romans of his day had no interest in the Tigris, the tiger was re-carved and, notes Ligorio, the fingers of one of the Twins were originally part of the tiger's fur. The two benevolent gods preside over a fountain which fits so perfectly into the architectural scheme that few perhaps could describe it, even after a second visit. It was selected as the winning design in a competition held hurriedly in 1588, as soon as the Acqua Felice had arrived on the Capitol. No one has ever criticized this lovely and dignified fountain, which adapts itself so perfectly to the stairway, and it may be that even Michelangelo would have approved of the use a later generation made of the two river gods. The only false note is the genuine but commonplace statue of Minerva in the central niche of the fountain, a figure out of scale with its surroundings.

Though not as handsome as the Nile and the Tiber, Marforio has a stronger personality, and one can understand not only his celebrated career as the partner of "Pasquino", but also his survival during the Dark Ages. He is obviously a powerful character and one would like to know how it was that, of all the

Above The Piazza del Campidoglio, with the statue of Marcus Aurelius and the two river gods. *Below* The two river gods, Nile (*left*) and Tiber

statues in the Forum, he alone remained *in situ*. It is recorded that Marcus Aurelius survived at the Lateran because it was believed he was Constantine the Great and no one had the nerve to melt down the first Christian emperor into coin or cannon. Perhaps some similar case of mistaken identity cast its protective shield around Marforio, and possibly an air about him of Teutonic chieftainship, due maybe to a drooping moustache and a luxuriant beard, may have stayed the destroyer's hand. In any event he continued to recline tranquilly at ease in the Forum through some of the most appalling events in the history of Rome. During the Middle Ages he became one of the sights to be visited and was mentioned in the early itineraries. He was seen reclining above the huge granite basin which is now on the Monte Cavallo.

Once Marforio had been moved from his ancient resting-place he became a rather embarrassing wanderer, since no one could decide what to do with him. During the great period of fountain-making which followed the arrival of the Acqua Felice, it was suggested that he should grace the fountains in the Piazza Navona, but nothing was done. Though there is no evidence, I suspect that Sixtus V would not tolerate such an obviously pagan deity as the decoration for any of the Felice fountains.

However that may be, four years after the death of Sixtus, Marforio was

moved to the piazza of the Capitol by Jacopo della Porta, where he joined the Nile and the Tiber, who had been there since the days of Michelangelo. Here the god was treated as an important person. In 1594, the year of his removal, only the Palazzo del Senatore and the Palazzo dei Conservatori had been built, and the left side of the square (as you face Marcus Aurelius) was not to be built upon for another sixty years. However, della Porta, who was a great admirer of Marforio, erected a high wall across this vacant side of the square with a central niche in which he placed the statue, a fountain once again after centuries of tragic drought. Here Marforio remained until the Capitoline Museum was erected, but it was not until 1679 that he was moved into the forecourt of the Museum, and only in 1734 that, as an inscription above him states, he received as companion a small bust of Clement XII.

Though the fate of many a Roman relic has been a fantastic one, no statue in Rome has had a stranger history than Marforio. Romans of the first century drank the water he dispenses so gently and courteously, as if filling the wine glass of a guest at a banquet, and it is possible that he was as well known to the first twelve Caesars as to the last. When disasters overtook Rome, he still reclined there as if nothing were happening, while the hordes of Alaric, Genseric, the Saracens, the Normans, and the ruffians of 1527, swept over the Forum and still further reduced the feeble heartbeats of the ancient capital. It is not surprising that he should have lost his right foot and ankle, his right arm to the elbow, and his left foot, but these were restored by Jacopo della Porta when Marforio was reinstated to his ancient dignity and function and the happily named Acqua Felice began to circulate once more between his urn and the basin of his fountain. It is one of the miracles of Rome that we can mount the stairs to the Capitol and see this statue as perhaps Virgil saw it, and to know that if Marcus Aurelius, who rides nearby, could revisit Rome, there would be much that he could not understand or recognize, but at least he would greet Marforio as an old friend.

The "speaking" statues of Rome were the product of an alert and intelligent society which had no Press or any other means of self-expression. Satire always was, and still is, the most popular form of Roman wit, and the statues were a perfect medium for the exchange of views on a number of current topics, of which papal government and the papal court were the most frequent. There were several of these loquacious statues: there was "Madame Lucrezia", a battered marble at the back of the Palazzo Venezia; the "Facchino" fountain in the Via Lata; the "Abbate Luigi" of the Piazza della Valle; the eroded "Babuino" in the Via del Babuino; and an almost forgotten oracle, the statue of S. Ann, by

Jacopo Sansovino, in the church of S. Agostino. But the most popular of all were Pasquino and Marforio.

Pasquino is still visible outside the Palazzo Braschi, near the Piazza Navona, a sadly mutilated torso of what must at one time have been a superb statue. He took his name from a tailor who had a shop nearby where the courtiers, prelates and *literati* were fond of gathering to repeat scandal and pass the time, and Pasquino was himself either a notable wit or one who was ready to have witticisms fathered upon him. The first "pasquinades" were directed against Alexander VI, the Borgia Pope, and they continued until the eighteenth century. Many of them were in Latin puns, most of which defy translation, and the majority, even in the original, seem rather silly; but then topical wit is a fragile blossom. Sometimes, however, the couplets were barbed and were capable of wounding sensitive and unworldly characters like Hadrian VI, who wished to cast Pasquino into the Tiber; but more sophisticated pontiffs dismissed the "pasquinades" as a modern politician laughs off a cartoon.

The method was for a question, usually a two-line verse, to be attached one morning to Pasquino – who was always the inquirer as Marforio was the one who answered – and for the reply to be discovered on Marforio on the following day. I think the wit and pungency of "pasquinades" may perhaps have been exaggerated, and having read at least a hundred of them, of various periods, I have come across only one really deadly one, and this was aimed at the Borgia Pope, Alexander VI, when his son, Don Juan, Duke of Gandia, was murdered and his body found in the Tiber. A translation of the Latin reads:

> Lest we should think you not a fisher of men, O Sixtus,
> Lo! you fish with nets for your own son.

This was abominably heartless. The Pope was overwhelmed with grief, and even Johann Burchard, his Master of Ceremonies, who had no love for him, wrote that Alexander "shut himself away in a room in grief and anguish of heart, weeping most bitterly"; which shows how cruel a lampoonist can be. But when Marforio was enclosed by the *cortile* of the Capitoline Museum, where we find him today, his utterances became fewer and eventually, like all oracles, he became dumb. He was once more his old, dignified, stoical self, and, thanks to Jacopo della Porta, one of the greatest of the fountains of Rome.

Everyone who has walked up the Cordonata to the Capitol will have noticed at its foot two Egyptian lions which aim spouts of water into travertine urns.

They no longer spout the Acqua Felice, as they used to do, but have been connected with the Acqua Pia Marcia; and their history will be found under the description of that aqueduct and its fountains.

The fountain in the Piazza Campitelli (1589)

This fountain (plate 9), to me one of the most elegant designed by Jacopo della Porta, was built in 1589 at the request of certain private individuals whose palaces stood in the neighbourhood. The fountain was originally erected in crowded streets some hundreds of yards away from its present site, but now the palaces have vanished and street reconstructions have placed it in retirement upon a picturesque cobbled square with the Theatre of Marcellus in the background.

A small marble pedestal basin casts upward a jet of water which drips into a main basin of unusual design. Della Porta's ingenuity in avoiding geometrical repetition in the design of his main basins was in the highest degree skilful. The Campitelli fountain is decorated with the weather-worn shields and coronets of the noble families who commissioned it in the sixteenth century.

The fountain in the Piazza d'Ara Coeli (1589)

The fountain in the Piazza d'Ara Coeli is one of those which were eagerly erected in 1589, the moment the precious Acqua Felice was piped to the Capitol. It is a fountain designed by Jacopo della Porta, with a central jet descending into a basin which drips water into a larger basin beneath, which, in its turn, overflows into a pool almost at ground level. The first basin is for display, the second for human beings, and the third is for animals.

The most interesting feature is a short column which rises from the upper basin, terminating in the three heraldic hills of Sixtus V. Immediately beneath are four smiling infants back to back around the column, each one holding a vase from whose spout springs a jet of water. These Roman figures were copied by della Porta from the most popular fountain of the fifteenth century, and they are the only surviving memory of it. This was the fountain erected in front of St Peter's in 1490, in the reign of Innocent VIII, nearly two centuries before the present piazza was designed. Though St Peter's and the Vatican were short of water at that time, the Pope gathered water from springs on the Vatican Hill and was able to maintain a flow which was admired by everyone and was considered, with the old Trevi fountain, to be the purest drinking water in Rome. This once famous fountain vanished when the present piazza was constructed in the seventeenth century.

The fountain in the Piazza d'Ara Coeli   The Navicella

Now the four happy children, whose ancestry is so unexpected, gaze down upon one of the grandest sights in Rome. To their left rises the long flight of steps to S. Maria in Ara Coeli, and next to them is the gentle gradient, La Cordonata, leading to the Capitol.

The Navicella

In the reign of the Medici pope, Leo X (1513–21), the models of some ancient Roman galleys were discovered beneath the gardens of the Villa Celimontana. They were *ex votos*, offerings from those who had safely returned from voyages. The Pope was interested in them and placed one outside the church of S. Maria in Dòmnica sul Celio on the Caelian Hill, where it stands today.

If the Navicella were a fountain when first erected it must have been fed by one of the local springs, since the Acqua Felice did not arrive until seventy years later. The ship is a massive hull of travertine some eight feet long whose vanished mainmast is replaced by a jet of the Acqua Felice. It still stands above the main basin of the fountain mounted upon the original pedestal carved four and a half centuries ago. Upon the weathered stone the Medici *palle* may be made out, ubiquitous in Florence but rare in Rome, commemorating the Pope, who was the son of Lorenzo the Magnificent.

The Navicella is among the most interesting and striking of the Felice fountains; it is also the third of the famous ship fountains in Rome. Its two companions are La Barcaccia in the Piazza di Spagna and the wonderful galley fountain in the gardens of the Vatican.

The fountain in the Piazza Madonna dei Monti

In 1588-9 Jacopo della Porta built a simple and effective fountain (plate 10) mounted upon an octagonal flight of four steps in front of the baroque church of S. Maria dei Monti. It bears some resemblance to the fountain of S. Maria in Trastevere, which may, to some extent, have influenced the design. Still it remains a typical della Porta fountain. A plume of Acqua Felice bubbles up from a small circular marble basin which, in overflowing, descends into a larger basin from which it pours through masks into the main basin in four graceful arcs.

The piazza is small and the fountain, though generally deserted save by the thirsty, bears all the signs of having been the main water supply of the neighbourhood for centuries. When one has admired it, a couple of steps take one into the Via Serpenti where can be seen ahead to the left a superb view of the Colosseum at the end of the Via degli Annibaldi.

The fountain of the Viale della Trinità de' Monti

One of the best-loved fountains in Rome whispers its enchantments beneath the ilex trees opposite the Villa Medici on the Viale della Trinità de' Monti (plate 8). The most modest of fountains, its charm is due to its simplicity and to its surroundings. A bowl of granite receives a plume of the Acqua Felice from a small sphere which rises from the surface of the water and might be described as an orb, though tradition has insisted since the seventeenth century that it is a cannonball. The water, filling the bowl to the brim, slides over and falls into an octagonal pool at pavement level.

The boundary wall of the Viale stands only a few steps away on the edge of the hill where the ground falls steeply to the Piazza di Spagna. The view from the fountain westward over the roofs and domes to St Peter's is among the finest in Rome. On warm summer nights before the invention of the motor-car, those who stood there must surely have heard the nightingale. Even now, when the traffic dies down late at night the Acqua Felice sings the sweetest of arias, and when the moon is full the granite bowl becomes a cauldron of molten gold.

Rome owes this lovely fountain to Ferdinand de' Medici, a cardinal at fourteen who, at the age of thirty-eight, was able to resign from the Sacred College, since he had not taken holy orders, and succeed his brother as Grand Duke of Tuscany. He built the fountain in 1587, the year he left Rome and decided to marry and found a family. He can be seen today in the Piazza della Santissima Annunziata in Florence, mounted upon a bronze horse; both the Grand Duke and the horse were cast by Giovanni da Bologna from the metal of captured Turkish guns.

The granite bowl of the fountain was purchased from the friars of S. Salvatore in Lauro, and probably its origin, like that of other fountains in Rome, should be sought in some ancient bath. The so-called cannon-ball from which the water rises is said by tradition to date from 1655 during a salute from the Castel S. Angelo in honour of the arrival in Rome of Queen Christina of Sweden. The illustrious convert had been brought up by her father as if she were a boy, and the story goes that, proud of her Amazonian achievements, she insisted on firing a shot herself. She was feminine, however, in her aim, and the cannon-ball described a dangerous arc over Rome and hit the Villa Medici. Whether the story is true or not, it is a fact that the round object displaced the Florentine lily which originally displayed the jet.

The Triton fountain, in the Piazza Barberini (1642–3)

Bernini's Triton (plate 13) has been one of the famous characters of Rome for three centuries. He might have sprung up, like a mushroom, overnight, the result of some long dormant fountain spawn germinating in the Roman earth. Larger than life, he is seated upon the open hinge of a scallop shell; his head is well back, with a conch shell to his lips from which a tall jet of Acqua Felice shoots into the air, to return upon itself and drench his muscular torso. In the course of three centuries the water has stained him and has blurred his outline without depriving him of his dignity or his power. The shell upon which he is seated is supported by four dolphins whose open mouths receive the water from a lower pool and so maintain the level. The beautifully carved Barberini bees date the fountain to the pontificate of Urban VIII, and the actual year of construction was between 1642 and 1643.

I once heard someone who has a right to be heard on such matters call Il Tritone the most pagan figure in Rome; and this may be so. His creator was, however, a devout Catholic who attended Mass every day and saw that his

A detail of the Triton fountain

labourers did so; who prayed every evening in the Gesù and who practised the *Spiritual Exercises* of Ignatius Loyola. Bernini lived to be eighty-two and Rome is filled with expressions of his piety: churches, saints innumerable, the canopy above the high altar of St Peter's, the fantastic Cathedra Petri at the end of the basilica, the colonnade which Bernini thought of as the open arms of Mother Church; and this strange pagan figure. Of all Bernini's fountain sculpture the Triton remains most clearly in the memory, and it is interesting to know that the sea-god did not spring unaided from Bernini's brain. The inspiration was a small triton in the Vatican Gardens, half worn away by water, in the confusing fountain known as the Eagle. It was carved thirty years before the Triton by Stefano Maderno. The pose is the same, and many who have seen it must have thought it a copy of Bernini's Triton instead of the other way round. It would

A detail of the Triton fountain

be interesting to know whether Urban VIII was attracted to Maderno's figure and asked Bernini to repeat it, or whether Bernini, while working in St Peter's, admired the pose and, as genius has always done, stored the idea away and eventually improved it.

When he designed the Triton, Bernini was forty-four years of age and the most celebrated sculptor and architect in Europe. Everywhere we look in Rome we see evidence of his genius and wonder how any man, even though he lived to be over eighty, managed to achieve so much. The explanation is that he employed and instructed nearly every capable sculptor in Rome. "Year by year," writes Rudolf Wittkower, "artists went to Rome, particularly from the north of Italy, hoping to get a share in the many commissions the centre of Christendom had to offer. Yet more often than not they were disappointed, and sculptors were lucky if they found a corner for themselves in Bernini's vast organization or in one of the studios more or less dependent on him. And when they returned home they spread the new gospel. Thus it was by direct transmission that the style was disseminated throughout Italy and beyond her frontiers."

There is a picture in the Museum of Rome, in the Palazzo Braschi, which shows that as recently as 1845 the Triton presided over a simple countrified scene. He stood in the centre of a narrow square hemmed in by rickety buildings whose balconies supported lines of washing; country carts filled the narrow side lanes; and it is difficult to reconcile that peaceful scene with the turmoil of the Piazza Barberini today.

I sometimes advise friends who are visiting Rome for the first time to rise not later than six o'clock in the morning and see the Triton before he is hemmed in by traffic. I also suggest to them that, having admired him, they should walk along the Via Sistina to the Villa Medici and look at the lovely fountain opposite the main gate; then, descending the Spanish Steps, visit La Barcaccia. Having come so far (though it is not yet seven o'clock), it seems a pity not to return to the Triton and walk to the Piazza del Quirinale and the Monte Cavallo fountain, and on down the steps, and along the Via della Dataria, to the Fontana di Trevi. To visit five of the great fountains before breakfast seems to me a good introduction to Rome.

Though John Evelyn was in Rome in 1644, just two years after the Triton was completed, and though he visited the Palazzo Barberini, he does not mention the fountain. Possibly he approached the palace from the upper road (now the Via Venti Settembre) and never penetrated the humble and crowded little square at the bottom of the hill, where he would have been rewarded by the sight of Bernini's great fountain shining, white and new.

The fountain in the Piazza Bocca della Verità (1717)

The Piazza Bocca della Verità – the Piazza of the Mouth of Truth – lies a few steps from the Tiber and the Ponte Palatino in one of the most romantic corners of Rome. It contains two temples built a century or more before the Christian era. One is the stately little temple of Fortuna Virilis, which is probably the shrine mentioned by Pliny which contained a statue of Fortune clothed in a woollen toga which lasted without decay for more than five centuries, and the other is the enchanting little round temple known as the Temple of Vesta.

Upon the opposite side of the square stand the Middle Ages, represented by the church of S. Maria in Cosmedin with its twelfth century campanile. The strange object which gives the piazza its name, the "Mouth of Truth", is to be seen in the church porch. It is a circular marble stone, some five feet in diameter, carved in the form of a bearded human face with a slit for a mouth. It is believed to have been a Roman drain cover, perhaps in a street or a bath. The rain or bath water escaped through the mouth. It is possible to insert the fingers into the opening, and the legend that anyone doing so and at the same time telling a lie would have his fingers bitten off, is a superstitition of great antiquity. Mediaeval wives suspected of infidelity, when asked to clear their characters, were sometimes required to submit to this ordeal; and to this day Roman schoolchildren, though their consciences may be clear, may often be seen thrusting their hands timidly into the opening with feelings of delicious apprehension. Augustus Hare mentioned an English traveller of the last century who, having scoffed at superstition in general, boldly thrust his fingers into the "Mouth of Truth" and was immediately bitten by a scorpion that happened to be lurking at the back!

The finishing touch to this beautiful square was provided in 1717 when Clement XI (1700-1721) commissioned the fountain. Signor Carrieri photographed it at that moment just after sunset when the stone pines are black against the western sky (plate 12). The architect was Carlo Bizzaccheri who was obviously inspired by Bernini. Upon a massive pedestal of rough rock two sad and emaciated tritons hold a vast shell above their heads from which a plume of the Acqua Felice rises into the air and falls over shell, tritons and rocks into the main basin of the fountain. This basin is unusual, indeed there is no other like it in Rome. Its shape, an eight-pointed star, was suggested by the arms of Clement XI.

The fountain in the Piazza of S. Maria Maggiore (1615)

The beautiful fountain which Carlo Maderno built for Paul V in 1615 stands upon the south-eastern side of the church of S. Maria Maggiore and in front of the tall column which Paul V brought from the Basilica of Maxentius.

Eight spouts of water descend in graceful arcs from a central marble pedestal into the main basin of the fountain. Upon the long sides of the oblong basin two small semicircular bowls resembling holy water stoups receive water from the main basin, and above them, now much eroded by time and the Acqua Felice, are sculptured the Borghese eagle. Old prints show that in former times two Borghese griffins spouted water on the short sides of the basin, but these have now vanished. That it is still a lovely fountain in spite of neglect that must be reckoned in centuries, is a tribute to the design and to the workmanship of Maderno and his collaborator, the architect, Gaspare de' Vecchi.

IX

THE ACQUA PAOLA
AND ITS FOUNTAINS

IFTEEN YEARS after the death of Sixtus V, when the planned Rome which he
had created so rapidly was still shining and new, and while the fountains of
the Acqua Felice were the envy of those who lived on the opposite bank of
the Tiber, a pope was elected who bore a certain resemblance to him. He was
Camillo Borghese, who took the name of Paul V. As with his predecessor, the
moment of his election was the signal for the transformation of a quiet, retiring
cardinal into a harsh and despotic pope. He reigned for sixteen years, from 1605
to 1621.

Among his ambitions was the desire to rival, or even excel, the architectural
and civic achievements of Sixtus. In the year of his election the Villa Borghese
was founded, and in the course of his pontificate he enlarged the Vatican and the
Quirinal; he built the Borghese Chapel in S. Maria Maggiore; he altered the
plans for the rebuilding of St Peter's by lengthening the nave and adding the
façade (and also putting his name above the portico); and he built a new aqueduct,
the Acqua Paola, whose waters still display themselves in the piazza of St Peter's.
When Paul came to power the right bank of the Tiber had little water and the
population still used the local springs and the river. Every time the inhabitants of
Trastevere crossed the Tiber they saw the fountains of the Vergine and the Felice
sparkling on the left bank, a display of good fortune which made their own
mediaeval conditions hard to bear. The Pope accordingly decided to bring an
aqueduct to the right bank whose waters would be distributed from the
Janiculum.

Just as Sixtus V had revived the ancient Aqua Alexandrina, so Paul V decided to
revive the ancient Aqua Trajana, which the Emperor Trajan had built in A.D. 109.
This aqueduct had played much the same role on the right bank during the Middle
Ages that the Aqua Virgo had played on the left: it was an intermittent source
of supply, patched up century after century, and frequently failed altogether. Its
waters came from a group of clear springs about thirty miles to the north-west

Two portraits of Pope Paul V (1605–21)

of Rome, close to Lake Bracciano, and it was this water which Paul V decided to bring back to the Janiculum.

In the year 1608 the Pope, having purchased from Virginio Orsini, Duke of Bracciano, the waters of the ancient springs and rivulets which had fed Trajan's aqueduct, engineers were immediately set to work to bring the water on its thirty-mile journey to Rome. The *mostra* on the Janiculum, which was its terminal, was designed by Giovanni Fontana, the brother of Domenico, in collaboration with the Pope's favourite architect, Flaminio Ponzio. Unfortunately, when the Acqua Paola began to flow four years later – in 1612 – it was discovered to be neither as copious nor as sweet to the taste as had been promised. Indeed the early records of this aqueduct are filled with bitter complaints. It appears that many property owners along the route failed to respect the reserved strip on each side and planted trees whose roots penetrated the underground masonry; others tapped the pipes in the impudent manner of landowners in the time of Frontinus. These offences were so numerous that in 1616 a fine of two hundred golden scudi was imposed on anyone found guilty of them, "and other penalties at the discretion of His Holiness the Pope". Despite this, the offences continued, and fifty years later the punishment was stepped up to "a fine of three hundred golden scudi, three strapados, the galleys and the whip".

Four pontificates later, during the reign of Alexander VII (1655–67), it was estimated that owing to the tapping of the aqueduct, mismanagement, illegal sales of water, and the gift of free water to friends and relatives, to cardinals, monasteries and convents, Rome was receiving only half the volume of water which entered the aqueduct; and here again one is reminded of the problem which faced Frontinus in the first century A.D. until he tightened up the regulations.

In 1659, knowing that the supply of water was inadequate, Ferdinand Orsini, then Duke of Bracciano, suggested to Alexander VII that it would be a simple matter to increase the flow by including in the aqueduct the water of Lake Bracciano. Although the Pope was anxious to see the new fountain in the piazza of St Peter's in action – there was then only one and it was often dry – he refused the offer, believing that the lake water would still further reduce the quality of the Acqua Paola. The next duke, Flavio Orsini, repeated the offer in 1672 to Clement X, when it was accepted; and from that time the Acqua Paola has been mixed with water from Bracciano. Later, in 1829, in the reign of Leo XII, the waters of the small lake of Martignano were also added to the sources of the aqueduct.

I motored out to Lake Bracciano in early October, on a day when there was scarcely a breath of wind and the water lay still and blue, reflecting hills and woods already stained with the first glows of autumn. The lake intake for the aqueduct is in a village called Anguillara, on the south-eastern shore, but the springs of Trajan are grouped along the northern shores. I went there first and was interested to see, dotted at intervals not far from the road, a number of stone structures which resembled Muslim tombs, each one a cone-shaped object about two feet in height, mounted upon a square base of masonry. These were the first *cippi* I had seen. They are mentioned by Frontinus as the usual Roman method of marking the line of an underground aqueduct, and are its milestones. The *cippi* I had seen marked the line of the old Aqua Trajana, still in use and bearing water to join the Acqua Paola at Anguillara. An engineer told me subsequently that much of Trajan's masonry is still in use.

A small stone building on the edge of the lake at Anguillara controls the intake of water, which has to pass through an eel-trap before it flows into the pipes of the aqueduct. Some distance away is another building named the Botte d'Unione, where the Trajan water meets that from the lake. Descending steps into a clammy vault loud with the rush of water, I saw the Trajan water pouring from a Roman tunnel to mingle with the lake water. From this point it takes the water eight hours to cover the thirty-odd miles to Rome. It is not always easy to assimilate the

Plate 22. The fountain in the Piazza dei Q

wealth of information imparted in such places by technicians, but no one can descend into these vaults and see the dark floods passing on their way without the reflection that he is sharing, in a minor degree, of course, a god-like sense of predestination. At the source of the Acqua Vergine I had seen tomorrow's Trevi water rushing to its photographic fate; and now, again, I saw water which in eight hours or so would be ascending from the mighty fountains in the piazza of St Peter's.

The course of the aqueduct, as it makes its way across country, is not spectacular save for a fine stretch of arches quite in the ancient manner as it crosses a valley a few miles east of the Botte d'Unione. As it reaches the outer suburbs of Rome, it becomes more interesting. There is a brick building in the centre of the road at the Piazza di Villa Carpegna where the supply of water for the Vatican City is tapped from the main aqueduct; and here is a second eel-trap. When the aqueduct reaches the Villa Doria-Pamphilj a few miles from its destination, it emerges and mounts the wall of the park where it might easily be mistaken for some ancient fortification; then, still above ground, it is carried forward along the Via Aurelia Antica to the Porta S. Pancrazio upon the half-buried arches of its ancient predecessor, the Aqua Trajana.

The Acqua Paola today is no longer drunk with safety or enjoyment. However, one daring connoisseur who has drunk it told me that it is a tepid fluid tasting of Lake Bracciano. He compared it to the water of Chicago which he said was equally unpleasant, though never having been there I am unable to say whether this is a fair comparison or not. The water is, however, used for gardens and for industrial purposes; it is also magnificent fountain water. The pressure is tremendous and many of the finest fountains in Rome are fed by it. These include:

The *mostra* – the Fountain of Paul V – on the Janiculum
The Fountain of the Ponte Sisto
The fountains in the Piazza Navona
The fountains in the Piazza Farnese
The Mascherone, in the Via Giulia
The fountain in the Piazza S. Andrea della Valle
The fountain in front of S. Maria in Trastevere
The fountain of S. Cecilia, in Trastevere
The Fountain of the Prisoner, in Trastevere
The Fountain of the Amphorae, in the Piazza dell'Emporio
The fountain in the Piazza dei Quiriti
The fountains of St Peter's and the Vatican (see chapter X)

23. The Fountain of the Amphorae in the Piazza dell'Emporio

The mostra of the Acqua Paola, on the Janiculum (1612)

I think it was Jean Jacques Ampère (whose father bestowed his name upon an electrical measurement) who said that you could get to know Rome superficially in ten years, but that twenty would be better. I think this is a little optimistic since I believe that several lifetimes would hardly be long enough to become omniscient, though it is possible to become familiar with some aspects of Rome in the short time allotted to man. In my own brief explorations I have noticed that certain famous monuments which did not at first impress me greatly became, upon close acquaintance, almost an obsession. It is, of course, the same with music and painting. The ignorant eye and ear requires training before it should expect to appreciate or understand many works of genius. I can scarcely believe that I did not care much for the Pantheon when I saw it for the first time, neither did I recognize the Fountain of Paul V (plate 18) as the outstanding monument that it is.

Mounted high upon the Janiculum, with the whole of Rome beneath it, this fountain stands magnificently situated amid the last surviving tranquillity of the nineteenth century. It is off the tourist run so that the thousands who linger around the Trevi are unaware of its existence, while many who follow the antiquarian route laid down in the eighteenth century generally lack the time to go there. I think it is one of the most rewarding sights in Rome. I have found that it often offers the unusual experience in these days of being alone with a famous monument. I have also found it stimulating, after contemplating the dead triumphal archways of Titus, Severus, and Constantine, to find an arch that is still alive: that announces with a flourish the triumphant arrival of an aqueduct's water in Rome.

The design is based upon that of the Fountain of Moses, and as that fountain was inspired by the ancient *mostra* whose ruins are in the Piazza Vittorio Emanuele, both these watergates have ancestors in imperial Rome. In size, the Fontana Paolina rivals those of Severus and Constantine. Beneath three arched openings, flanked by two of lesser height, gush five streams of water which, falling into marble basins, overflow and cascade into a large semicircular pool below. The façade is adorned by six tall columns of red granite which support an architrave bearing the inscription, "In the year of our Lord, 1612, and the seventh of Paul's pontificate." The entablature above carries the most beautiful copy of classical calligraphy in Rome, the work of one who had evidently studied the best inscriptions of the age of Trajan and Hadrian. Each letter is a model of grace and dignity, the spacing of each line a work of art. The inscription reads: "Paul V,

The *mostra* of the Acqua Paola before the large pool had been added by Carlo Fontana

Pontifex Maximus, collected this water, drawn from the purest of springs in the neighbourhood of Bracciano, and brought it for thirty-five miles from its source over the ancient channel of the Aqua Alsietina, which he restored, and over new ones, which he added." Above this inscription two delightful baroque angels support the Borghese coat of arms, a dragon and an eagle, surmounted by the papal tiara and keys.

Engravings of the fountain before 1690 show it in what, to modern eyes, appears to be a sadly unfinished condition. The water pours abruptly from the five arches into small bowls beneath: there is no pool. This was added by Carlo Fontana in a happy moment, an improvement which gives the austere structure life and movement and the gaiety of rippling water and, in certain lights, a reflection.

The *mostra* also resembles the Fountain of Moses in its internal arrangements, though it would probably never occur to anyone that these fountains were anything more than an architectural screen for the display of water. Like the Fountain of Moses, it was designed for a resident staff of watermen who controlled the pressure and arranged the outflow of water to the entire district. I have already mentioned that the living quarters behind the Fountain of Moses are rented by the Grand Hotel; those behind the Fountain of Paul V are used by the Accademia di S. Luca.

When the gate is unlocked to the private region behind, one steps into a charming scene, but one likely to distress a gardener. Here lies a sadly neglected little paved and walled garden of the seventeenth century that, with a season's digging, manuring and planting, might be made enchanting. Two neglected vines climb a trellis, there are lemon trees in tubs, and one orange tree covered with fruit, but weeds flourish in the pavement, the soil is starved, and the structure of the fountain at the back is as neglected as its front is cherished. This is not one of the Municipality's happiest efforts, and I thought how delightful it would be to live for a year or two in the rooms of the Acqua Paola and bring the garden back to life.

Like the Fountain of Moses, the *mostra* of the Acqua Paola is a museum of water, and it is surprising to see the force of water, like a river in flood, still controlled by valves and gigantic turn-cocks made in 1612. Fifty stone steps lead to the top of the building where, with an unusual view from the back of two Borghese eagles, it is possible to see over the balustrade the whole of Rome lying in the soft, silky air: the domes, the towers, the Tiber flowing beneath its bridges, the crowded streets of Renaissance Rome in the foreground, the Capitol upon its hill in the centre, and, behind it, the green belt of the Villa Borghese. Of all the famous views of Rome, this, I think, is the one I like best. Now that the noise, the traffic and the clutter of parked cars, which fill every piazza and street, make walking in Rome a doubtful pleasure, I advise anyone who would like a little tranquillity to cross the Tiber and enjoy the peace of this calm and noble fountain.

The Fountain of the Ponte Sisto (1613–1898)

The most distinguished of the migratory fountains of Rome is the Fountain of the Ponte Sisto in Trastevere, which once stood at the opposite end of the bridge. Its unusual history began with Paul V who, having brought the Acqua Paola to the Janiculum, wished to carry the water over the nearest bridge to the left bank of the Tiber, and to announce its arrival by a splendid fountain. Giovanni Fontana, who was charged with the task, found it difficult to select a site. In 1612 the Tiber was, of course, not yet embanked and the old Via Giulia, still a famous street, ended at the bridge-head in a dignified building which Giovanni's brother, Domenico, had built some twenty-seven years previously for Sixtus V. This was

a hospice which accommodated two thousand beggars, the *Ospizio dei Mendi-canti*.

Finding it impracticable to design a detached fountain, Fontana decided to incorporate it in the wall of his brother's building. He designed a striking and noble fountain which is unlike any other in Rome. It is, in a sense, a companion fountain to the magnificent Fontana Paolina, but in the form of a single classical archway, and instead of bringing the water in at the lower portion of the arch, Fontana introduced it at the top. It gushed out and, after breaking its fall in a projecting bowl, streamed down like a waterfall into the main basin. Fontana also introduced two Borghese dragons, or griffins, at each side of the fountain which spouted water sideways towards each other in two thin streams, recalling the lions of the Fountain of Moses.

This unusual display of Acqua Paola took its place among the most popular fountains of Rome and was admired until the last century, when the scheme for the Tiber embankment condemned it, with many other celebrated old buildings, to demolition. One of the shrillest and most passionate voices raised in protest was that of Ouida (Louise de la Ramée) who, in a letter to the London *Times* deplored the destruction of the fountain as "an outrage to art and history". Of all the novelists of the last century, Ouida's description of the fountains in her Roman novel *Ariadne* are the best and the most sensitive: she had a feeling for them and managed to convey the delight they gave to the eye and the ear in the eighteen-seventies. Her favourite seems to have been the Fountain of the Ponte Sisto with "its two streams crossing one another like sabres gleaming bright against the dark, damp, moss-grown stones".

In spite of the agitation which Ouida helped to sustain, nothing could keep the fountain in its original position, and in August 1879 it was pulled down and vanished from the Roman scene. Four years later, lovers of the fountains began to agitate for the re-erection of the Ponte Sisto fountain in another position, but nothing was done for fourteen years. As the agitation continued, the engineer Rodolfo Bonfiglietti was appointed in 1897 by the Municipality to rebuild the fountain on the right bank of the bridge in Trastevere. First he had to find out where all the stones had been stored. This was not easy. Some portions were found in the municipal warehouse of Testaccio; the epigraph with its beautiful lettering was discovered in the warehouse of Volturno; some fragments were buried in the ground and had to be dug out; others were lying in various yards; the papal coat of arms was unearthed on the Janiculum, and a lion's head, having been dredged from the Tiber, was in a museum. After a year's detective work most of

The Fountain of the Ponte Sisto in its original position in the wall of the Beggars' Hospital

the fountain had been recovered and the rebuilding began. Among the problems to be faced was that of the inscription, which stated that Paul V had taken the water to the other side of the Tiber for the use of that part of the city, which, of course, now that the fountain had crossed the river, was meaningless. A second inscription by Professor Giuseppe Cugnoni of Rome University, written in smaller lettering and explaining the removal, was therefore added beneath the bowl, in the interior of the arch. When the fountain is not playing, it is possible to read this explanation.

Naturally enough, since human nature detests the removal of landmarks, those who remembered the fountain in its old position disliked the reconstruction in Trastevere. But we, who have no such memories and can judge the matter only by studying old prints and photographs, must think the fountain a great improvement as it is today; its detached position, elevated upon a platform approached by a shallow flight of fifteen steps, and its background of trees, give it a dignity and an importance which it could never have commanded when crowded into the façade of a building.

The fountains in the Piazza Navona (1575–1651)

The Piazza Navona reproduces in size and shape the Roman stadium which stood upon the site in the first century. The houses that surround it are built upon the foundations of the tiers of seats: the long central oblong, with its three groups of fountains extending down the centre, represents the arena; and if, on a winter's night before the lamps are lit, you should approach the square by any of the several narrow entrances, so like gateways, you will have the impression that you have entered a vast, roofless auditorium. There is in Rome no more striking example in architecture of the present springing from the dead bones of the past. It is said that the Circo Agonale, which the Emperor Domitian built between A.D. 81 and 96, held 30,000 spectators, and perhaps something like the same number may now be crowded into the flats and tenements which surround the square. How strange it is to see human faces still looking down from windows and roof gardens, from cafés and restaurants, upon the central oval, as faces did centuries ago; one difference now is that the audience is permanently present: the ghostly stadium is never closed.

The ruins remained until the Renaissance. Throughout the Middle Ages crowds would perch upon them to witness tournaments and bull-fights; but at last the temptation to use the beautiful masonry became too strong. Bit by bit everything to ground level was carted away to be transformed into churches and into one supremely lovely building, the Villa of Pius IV in the Vatican Gardens (plates 27 and 28). And so the site was cleared, leaving the substructure of the arches as a solid foundation for the new houses. In many of the cellars, remains of the stadium may be seen, the most accessible being the crypt of the church of S. Agnes. Here is preserved perhaps the most unlikely Christian relic in Rome, or anywhere else. It is the remains of a Roman brothel which existed centuries ago in a *fornix*, or arch, of the stadium, into which the patron saint of chastity was flung for having repelled the advances of a rich and influential Roman. Her virtue was miraculously preserved, though she was subsequently beheaded; and so this strange surviving fragment of the vice of imperial Rome, now sanctified and smelling piously of incense, is today approached reverently upon bended knee.

In the most extraordinary way, the group of three fountains stretching down the centre of the piazza (plate 14) still further revives memories of the old stadium. If the faces at the windows recall the spectators, the marble figures wrestling with dolphins, or standing with poised trident, and the movement of the water, suggest the athletes who once struggled for victory on the sanded arena. The

Plate 24. La Pig

Overleaf Plate 25. The piazza of St Pete

best place to receive such an impression is from the upper windows of the Palazzo Braschi, at the south end of the piazza.

The two terminal fountains are the oldest in the piazza; Bernini's central group with its obelisk came seventy years later. At the end of the sixteenth century, when the Acqua Vergine was piped to the Piazza Navona, Jacopo della Porta built the fountains at each end (1575), but the central fountain remained a problem for years. At first it was a horse trough to which della Porta, perhaps wishing to provide a more worthy companion for his two fountains, desired to add the statue of Marforio; but this idea was happily abandoned. The Braschi Museum has several pictures which show the Piazza Navona while a tournament was in progress, and also as a market-place, with stalls, jugglers, mountebanks, coaches, and an escaped horse. There is also an oil painting of 1630 which shows the southern fountain complete with four seated tritons, but, of course, still without Bernini's central figure, known as Il Moro. But how deceptive is Rome! Should you, after seeing this picture, descend to the square and examine the four tritons, believing them to be those of the painting, you would be mistaken. They are nineteenth century replacements. It is, however, typical of Rome that the original tritons should not have been lost or destroyed, but should have migrated to the Borghese Gardens, where you will see them still blowing their wreathed horns over gravel and grass (plate 35). Should any fountaineer be sufficiently interested to track them down, he may agree with me that they are superior to the tritons at present in possession in the Piazza Navona, and he will wonder, as I do, what secret machinations or nepotism resulted in their dislodgement and exile.

The central figure of this fountain is one of the inanimate "characters" of Rome, like the Triton and Marforio. Bernini is said to have modelled it himself. It is a large, muscular, naked figure, probably Neptune, who is in difficulties with a huge fish which he grasps by the tail, while, at the same time, he turns his head slightly with rather an angry expression, as if asking someone to bring a gaff quickly. The fish, in its frantic efforts to regain the water, has twisted under Neptune's left leg, so that he stands astride it, and, as the monster hangs head-down with bulging eyes, it expels from its gaping mouth a mist-thin spray of water. The figure of Neptune is powerful and arresting and has been called, for no apparent reason, Il Moro, which is the usual Italian designation for any outlandish figure, probably a relic of the Crusades or the Barbary pirates. The "Moro" might be the brother of Bernini's Neptune in the Victoria and Albert Museum, London, and the latter's trident would have been of the greatest use

One of the tritons of the southern fountain in the Piazza Navona

Gian Lorenzo Bernini (1598–1680)

to his Roman relative; indeed it is perhaps the implement for which Il Moro is angrily calling.

The statuary of the fountain at the northern end of the piazza, known as the Neptune fountain (plate 17), is the work of the nineteenth century sculptors, Antonio della Bitta and Gregorio Zappalà, who, as so often in Rome, have courageously faced the dilemma of competition with the work of a greater artist. Neptune, again in difficulties, is this time in the act of spearing a gigantic octopus which has wreathed its tentacles round his thighs. The other figures include two infant tritons, one of whom has managed to bridle a sea-horse and has it under control while the other, having been unseated by his sea-horse, is in trouble. Two mermaids, absorbed in their own problems, have emerged charmingly from the water, each exposing a long fishy extremity and also the curly tail of a satyr, an anatomical curiosity which I do not remember having seen before.

It is, of course, the central Fountain of the Four Rivers (plate 15) which claims all the attention, and is generally agreed to be Bernini's greatest triumph in the art of fountain design. He was fifty years of age when he began it in 1648, and it took three years to complete. His patron, Urban VIII, in whose eyes he could do no wrong, had been dead for four years and had been succeeded by Innocent X,

a gentle septuagenarian who was dominated by his masterful sister-in-law, Donna Olimpia Maidalchini. Having been too successful, and having had his own way for more than twenty years, Bernini, once his patron was dead, became an easy target for the envy of less successful rivals, and, having a hasty temper and the gift of words (his mother being a Neapolitan), one thing led to another and he fell from favour. The story is, though how true it may be I cannot say, that the Pope was easily turned against Bernini who, however, managed to make friends with Donna Olimpia, the real wearer of the tiara. As Innocent X would not even consider Bernini's design for the Four Rivers, the story goes that Donna Olimpia asked the artist to make a model of it in silver which she placed in a conspicuous position in a room through which she knew the Pope would pass that evening. It is said that Innocent paused in front of it and was immediately captivated and would consider no other design.

However that may be, Bernini's organization took over the centre of the Piazza Navona in 1648 and three years later gave to Rome the most spectacular fountain of the century. It is interesting to glance at the genesis of this fountain. The Pope himself was anxious to erect it, possibly because his family palace, the Palazzo Pamphilj, was in the square, and he was determined that an obelisk should form part of the design. In order to further his aim, he had transported a broken obelisk from the Via Appia to the Piazza Navona. Thus the starting point of Bernini's design was a 54-foot shaft of granite. He did not think of this feature himself: it was an inescapable fact imposed upon him to which he had to adapt his ideas.

The effect he achieved is one of effortless rightness, and one would need to look far to discover so many tons of marble which give such an impression of weightlessness. There are rocks, four immense marble figures, a lion, a horse, an armadillo, and suchlike, and these extraordinary objects have been assembled as if by magic into a sophisticated composition of the utmost harmony. There is not a false note. The whole thing might have grown out of the earth like the Triton, but from a more complicated seed. One admires the art as much as the architectural good manners by means of which the fountain concentrates interest upon the formerly derelict centre of the piazza, without, at the same time, destroying the harmony of the scene or monopolizing the piazza. Whether Bernini was conscious of the various implications of his fountain we cannot say, but, as one looks at it, the Fountain of the Four Rivers completes, with the other fountains, the impression of a Roman *spina* dividing the course, while the obelisk recalls the cone-shaped goals.

The four figures are of marble and the rocks and the other sculpture of travertine. The figures represent the four continents: the Danube (Europe); the Ganges (Asia); the Nile (Africa); and the river Plate (America). The four giant river gods recline upon rocks from which water fans out in fine-blown sprays or gently drips into the huge circular pool beneath, in which the fantasy rises, or appears, in spite of its tonnage, to be floating. Europe is holding the shield of Innocent X, three lilies and a dove bearing a sprig of olive in its beak; the Ganges (plate 16) is tranquil (and entirely European in appearance); the Nile reclines with veiled head, a reference to its then unknown source; the Plate is looking up in astonishment, as well it might, at the obelisk. The rocks on which these deities are reclining form an open archway with a view through to a rocky cave or grotto, from which a horse comes galloping at one end while at the other a lion steals down to drink and a creature with a scaly body and the head of a crocodile, and intended to be an armadillo, emerges from the water nearby, all creatures symbolic of the four rivers. The horse represents the Danube, the lion is symbolic of the Nile, the armadillo represents the river Plate, while the beautifully carved palm tree and a serpent represent the Ganges.

It is a calculated part of the illusion that one is not aware, unless one analyses the fountain, of its most extraordinary feature: the weighty obelisk has been posed on the open arch as if its tons of granite were as weightless as plywood. The feat has given rise to one of those Roman stories which have now passed into folklore. It is that Bernini, hearing that his critics were complaining that the obelisk was not secure and might fall, appeared one day and, having attached thin strings to it and tying them to the buildings opposite, departed. There is so much to see that few, if any, ever look at the top of the obelisk. If they did, they would see not the usual cross but a bronze dove, the emblem of Innocent X.

When one is told that it took Bernini three years to build this fountain, one cannot conceive how any man could have performed such a task in the time; and, of course, the explanation is that, while Bernini designed every detail of the fountain and probably made models of some of the figures, the actual carving was executed by members of his school, or studio. The Danube was carved by Antonio Raggi; the Nile was the work of Giacomo Antonio Fancelli; the Ganges was carved by Claude Poussin and the river Plate by Francesco Baratta. There is evidence that the master himself carved the rock, the palm tree, the lion and the horse, also the coat of arms, and no doubt he touched up all the figures here and there. The armadillo was carved by G. M. Fracchi under the guidance of Bernini, though neither seems to have been too familiar with the animal.

The flooding of the Piazza Navona, an eighteenth century engraving by Giuseppe Vasi

Evelyn was fond of wandering about the Piazza Navona in the hope of picking up Roman coins, pictures and antiquities, and "to hear the mountebanks prate and distribute their medicines". But the custom of flooding the piazza had not begun in his time: it started the year after the Fountain of the Four Rivers was completed, in 1651, when presumably the greater volume of water made it possible. The custom lasted until the pavement level was raised in 1867.

During the heat of August the outlets that carried away the fountain water were stopped on Sunday evenings and the piazza was soon transformed into a shallow lake. The windows and the balconies of the palaces round about would be crowded with spectators as the coaches of the nobility, two abreast, one line moving to the right and the other to the left, splashed through the water. Residents in the piazza sent out invitations to their friends to witness the "Lago di Piazza Navona", and when, at the first note of the Ave Maria, the outlets were opened and the parade concluded, supper parties were held in the palaces.

The custom remained fashionable into the eighteenth century and a delightful picture by Pannini, now in the art gallery at Hanover, shows what the occasion looked like in 1756. It was a full-dress affair and was conducted with great

decorum except when, as Pannini records, a pair of horses, excited by the unusual experience, became unmanageable and, galloping into the centre of the
piazza, overturned their coach. Ecstatic dogs (again one relies upon Pannini),
sometimes swam valiantly beyond the lines of coaches towards the centre of the
piazza, enjoying the cool water and no doubt accumulating a supply which they
would later shake off on the beautiful satin dresses and breeches of their masters
and mistresses.

Among those who watched the spectacle on Sunday, 11 August 1720, from
the scarlet and gold bedecked balcony of Cardinal Acquaviva, were James
Stuart, the Old Chevalier, and his wife, Maria Clementina. Some years later,
in 1727, Prince Charles Edward ("Bonnie Prince Charlie"), then a child of
seven, was allowed to be present and enjoyed himself so much that he returned
the following year. Upon that occasion, profiting possibly from the absence of
his mother, he threw down small coins into the water in order to watch the
urchins fight for them; "hardly decent behaviour for a king's son", commented
the diarist, Valesio.

The American sculptor, William Wetmore Story, the friend of the Brownings,
who lived in Italy from 1850 until 1857, saw the "Lago di Piazza Navona" in its
last years, and left a spirited account of it. After describing the flooding of the
piazza, he wrote:

> From the surrounding streets crowds of *carrettieri*, *vetturini* and grooms now pour into
> the piazza, mounted on every kind of horse, mule and donkey; some riding double
> and even treble, and all laughing and shouting at the top of their voices. Then, with a
> clang of trumpets, come galloping in the horses of dragoons and artillery, accompanied
> by hundreds of little scamps with their trousers rolled up on the crotch, – and splash
> they all go into the water. The horses neigh, the donkeys bray, the people scream, the
> little boys are up to all sorts of mischief, pelting each other with rotten oranges,
> squeezed lemons and green melon rinds, till the Piazza echoes with the riot of voices
> and the splashing of water.
>
> The next evening the sport is better. The populace crowd the outer rim of the Piazza,
> where numbers of booths are erected. The windows of the houses are thronged with
> gay faces, brilliant floating draperies and waving handkerchiefs. Not only horses,
> mules, and donkeys are now driven into the artificial lake, but carriages welter nave-
> deep in the water, and spatter recklessly about; whips crack madly on all sides like the
> going off of a thousand India crackers; and horses plunge and snort with excitement,
> sometimes overturning their carriages and giving the passengers an improvised bath.

It is evident from Story's account that the stately and aristocratic amusement
pictured by Pannini had become one of the popular festivals of Rome.

The fountains in the Piazza Farnese (1626)

The stately twin fountains in the Piazza Farnese (plate 19) are Roman bath-tubs of grey granite which were found in the Baths of Caracalla. In shape, they have a recognizable descendant in the ordinary modern bath. Remove the beautiful central decoration and they are revealed as the same kind of baths which one has encountered, though not perhaps in such massive proportions, in old country houses, made sometimes of porcelain and even of marble. What their function was in the Baths of Caracalla is a little difficult to determine, but we can assume that if the *habitués* of the Baths were able to observe them now in a position of such honour and dignity, they would doubtless be amused.

The baths were discovered in 1466 by Paul II, the Venetian pope who began to build the Palazzo Venezia; and it was he who removed them to what was then called the Piazza S. Marco and is now the Piazza Venezia. They were not at first adapted as fountains: their function was purely decorative and they were valued simply as relics of the classical past. So they remained for sixty-eight years until Alexander Farnese, Paul III, another palace-builder, looking for a suitable ornament for the Piazza Farnese, moved one of the bath-tubs and placed it directly in front of the main gateway of his palace.

A print of 1545 shows bull-baiting in progress in the piazza. As two bulls career about the square, and one lies dead, several of the *toreros* have jumped into the bath-tub in front of the palace, where they are in an impregnable position, or it may be that they are privileged spectators. Perhaps the bath was placed there for this purpose. The sport was evidently as beastly then as it is now and the animals were teased and provoked by men with long spears and clubs. One man is rolling a barrel in front of him as protection against a charging bull, while another, perhaps the matador, advances with sword and shield.

The second bath was not moved to the Piazza Farnese until 1580. It was intended to adapt them as twin fountains, but, the supply and pressure of the available water from the Acqua Vergine being considered inadequate, the scheme was dropped for nearly fifty years. In the year 1627, however, when the Acqua Paola was available from the Ponte Sisto fountain (then on the left bank of the river), the idea was revived and the granite baths were mounted in decorative basins of marble and in each was placed an exquisite urn terminating in a Farnese lily. A jet of water bubbled over into the urn and dripped into the bath below. The centre pieces, possibly the work of Girolamo Rainaldi, are among the most elegant fountain decorations in Rome.

The shell-like delicacy does not blend too well with the uncompromising

outline of the baths. The artist was clearly conscious of the problem of harmonizing his curves with the rigid lines of the granite, and he attempted to soften the design with upward jets of water, two in each bath and four in each basin, but these are not always playing and one frequently sees the fountains only at half strength.

An old print, dated about 1652, which shows a man wading knee-deep in water near one of the Farnese fountains while a horseman prepares to ride into the flood, has suggested the theory that the custom of flooding a piazza during the heat of August may have originated in the Piazza Farnese and have spread to the Piazza Navona. On the other hand, the scene may depict one of the Tiber floods which so frequently placed this part of Rome under water.

It is always a delight, after having explored the picturesque street market in the Campo dei Fiori, to pass in a few yards into the Piazza Farnese and to see the two exalted bath-tubs in front of the mighty palace. One often reads that the Palazzo Farnese was built with stone from the Colosseum, though there appears to be no evidence of this: it is, on the other hand, a reassembly of other classical monuments, among them Aurelian's Temple of the Sun – that mighty stone quarry – and the *thermae* of Caracalla and Diocletian. Lanciani says that the columns of *verde antico* which adorn the palace came from Zenobia's bath house near Tivoli. The palace itself stands upon the site of the barracks and stables of the Red Faction of the Charioteers, and a mosaic floor depicting the "Reds" performing feats of horsemanship has been preserved in the cellars.

The twin fountains sound an appropriate note in this compound of Roman memories. They also belong to a select company of double fountains: the two fountains in front of St Peter's; the side fountains in the Piazza del Popolo; Vansantio's twin fountains in the Villa Borghese; and perhaps one might add the two spouting lions at the foot of the Cordonata on the Capitol.

The Mascherone, in the Via Giulia (c. 1626)

A combined wall fountain and horse trough has been celebrated in the Via Giulia for three hundred years. It takes the form of a colossal marble face of Roman date which has been made into a fountain by cutting away the mouth from which water descends in a steady stream (plate 21). This has had the effect, together with the staring eyes, of giving the face a surprised expression, and though it is an unusual fountain, it is not one of the most beautiful in Rome. It remains in the memory as one of three enormous enigmatic marble faces; the other two are the Bocca della Verità (Mouth of Truth), in the vestibule of

S. Maria Cosmedin, and the still larger face with a drooping moustache – another wall fountain – in the charming little square near S. Sabina on the Aventine.

The Mascherone – the big mask – is sometimes called Il Mascherone di Farnese because of a tradition that the fountain was erected by the Farnese family, whose palace is only a few paces away, and a stone lily surmounts the Mask, supporting the tradition. It is probable that the history of the Mascherone is similar to that of the two fountains in front of the Farnese Palace, which had to wait for water until, under Paul V, the Acqua Paola was piped across the Ponte Sisto to the left bank in 1613. The Mask still expels Acqua Paola.

The fountain in the Piazza S. Andrea della Valle (1614)

When the processional way to St Peter's was cut out of the heart of the Borgo in the nineteen-twenties to celebrate the signing of the Lateran Treaty, which reconciled Church and State, many ancient landmarks were demolished. Among them was the charming Piazza Scossa Cavalli, which is now merely a humble "via". Among its finest features was a noble fountain made by Maderno for Paul V in 1614. Those who deplored the State's well-meaning but clumsy architectural gesture of reconciliation, mourned the disappearance of this fountain, to be mollified in time when they discovered that it had migrated to another, and more populous, part of Rome. It may now be admired in the Piazza S. Andrea della Valle, off the Corso Vittorio Emanuele II.

The fountain, which is entirely of travertine, is designed on the heroic scale and recalls its contemporary, the senior of the two fountains in the piazza of St Peter's, which is the one nearest the Vatican. The stout stem that supports the smaller of two basins is decorated with the Borghese eagle and griffin, and the water drips into the large main basin from whose surface four jets rise and fall back upon themselves, an unusual and effective device.

The church of S. Andrea della Valle is associated with several fountain-makers. The building was completed by Maderno; the façade was added later by Carlo Rainaldi, who with his brother, Girolamo, adapted the Roman bath-tubs for the Piazza Farnese; the first chapel on the right was designed by Carlo Fontana, and that on the left contains a bronze John the Baptist by Bernini.

The fountain in front of S. Maria in Trastevere (restored 1658–94 and 1873)

A fountain which has a claim to be considered the oldest in Rome stands in front of the church of S. Maria in Trastevere. The church was founded either by S. Calixtus, who was pope from A.D. 217 to 222, or in the next century by Pope

Julius I, on the site of a hostel for old soldiers. According to Dio Cassius, a fountain of oil had sprung up there when Christ was born, a story which explains the name *Fons Olei* given to the Church in early times. Some scholars believe that the fountain of oil may be a reference to the fountain which had stood in front of the church for centuries and may even have been its precursor.

This beautiful and impressive fountain, so often restored though never radically changed, still wears a mediaeval air which relates it to the Fonte Gaia in Siena and the Fonte Maggiore of Perugia rather than to any of the fountains of Rome. An octagonal flight of six shallow steps of travertine leads to the platform upon which the octagon of the main basin stands. It is decorated at four of its angles with shell basins from which rise tall ribbed shapes (plate 20), the work of Carlo Fontana. They are extraordinarily effective and there is no other fountain decoration quite like them in Rome. From the centre of the basin rises a typical della Porta pedestal carrying a circular bowl pierced beneath the rim by four wolves' heads from whose mouths water curves in a graceful arc to Fontana's shells.

In these days I am more than ever attracted to Trastevere, which offers a comparatively peaceful retreat from the rush and noise of the other bank of the Tiber. The little piazza of S. Maria is sometimes deserted, and one can hear the fountain splashing and feel something of the spell which Rome cast over the travellers of the nineteenth century.

The fountain of S. Cecilia, in Trastevere (1929)

This church, dedicated to the patron saint of music, stands in the narrow lanes of Trastevere, surrounded by buildings of great antiquity. Those who come upon it suddenly and unexpectedly pause in delight before a gateway that leads into a garden planted with roses and clipped lemon trees. In the centre is a rectangular marble basin or tank full of running water which reflects the sky. Rising from the water upon a pedestal is an exquisite Greek *cantharus* of marble so fine and thin that it resembles alabaster. This immense vase, which must have come from a Roman bath, is, together with its plinth, perhaps eight or ten feet high. A thin jet of Acqua Paola is seen rising in the neck of the vessel and a stream of water pours from a small hole bored in the body of the *cantharus*.

This is the finest example to be seen anywhere of the early Christian atrium with its ablution tank filled with running water in which the worshipper dipped his hands in an act of ritual cleansing before he entered the church. The scene appears almost drowsy with antiquity and it is surprising to learn that it did not

A detail of the fountain in front of S. Maria in Traste

The *cantharus* fountain in the courtyard of S. Cecilia in Trastevere

exist until 1929, when the titular cardinal of S. Cecilia, Cardinal Bonaventura Cerretti, gave the *cantharus* and ordered the fountain to be designed. The inspired reconstruction has made it possible for us to see what the approach to a primitive Christian church was like. Only one other of the ancient churches of Rome, S. Clemente, has retained its *cantharus*, and in these two places only can we make a ritual ablution before we enter, as Christians did seventeen centuries ago. In this charming little garden in Trastevere one may sit upon the edge of the fountain and reflect how aesthetically superior the ancient *cantharus* was to the holy water stoup of the Middle Ages.

The Fountain of the Prisoner, in Trastevere (c. 1580)

Walking in Trastevere one day, I happened to stray into the Via Luciano Manara and was surprised to see, inset into a grassy embankment at the end of the street, a most unlikely fountain. Even at a distance I could see that it was not a native of Trastevere, and as I approached I recognized the characteristics of a fountain made by Domenico Fontana for Sixtus V and the Acqua Felice. What was it doing, I asked myself, in Trastevere, in the territory of the Acqua Paola?

It was one of Fontana's austere classical exercises: two fine pilasters, a heavy cornice, a charming apse-like interior, and a ribbed semi-dome above a beautiful lion's head which dripped water over the rocks of a grotto.

A passing stranger told me that it was called La Fontana del Prigione – the Fountain of the Prisoner. I asked why. He shrugged his shoulders. "Who can say?" Someone had scribbled on the wall in large letters the words *Fontana maladettaro.* . . . Why? Beside the fountain was a notice, *Acqua non potabile*, yet a passing workman, bending his head down to a jet, drank and departed. Altogether, I thought, a strange and unexpected fountain. It was some time before I discovered that the Prigione is the last surviving relic of the famous Villa Montalto which Sixtus V built, before he became Pope, upon the site of what is now the Central Railway Station in Rome. The gardens rambled all over the Viminal Hill and are said to have stretched almost as far as S. Maria Maggiore.

The Villa passed from the Montalto-Peretti family into the possession of the Savellis, then in 1696 it was bought by Cardinal Negroni and was one of the sights of Rome during the eighteenth century. It changed hands again at the end of the century when it became the property of Prince Massimo, in whose family it remained until 1870, when it was expropriated "for the needs of the City"; in other words, as the site for the railway terminus of Rome. Augustus Hare, writing in 1871, said that this killed the Prince Massimo of the time, and he died of a broken heart. An old book about the Villa Montalto mentions the odd fact that when the favourite horse of Sixtus V died the Pope had the animal stuffed, and this curious relic was still to be seen in the Villa at the time of its demolition. As one catches a train in Rome's Central Station, one may reflect that the maze of tracks and points covers the site of cypress avenues which for two hundred years were the whispering place of cardinals.

The destruction was complete. Terraces, cypress avenues, orange groves, fountains and fishponds all vanished beneath the picks of the railway engineers; and still one wonders why, of all the wonderful fountains of the Villa Massimo-Negroni, the Fountain of the Prisoner should have been selected to survive.

At first it was moved to the Via Genova, near the Via Nazionale, then it was taken to Trastevere.

I think probably the best contemporary account of the gardens of the Villa Montalto was written by an English traveller, Francis Mortoft, who went there with a party of friends in 1659. The first thing they noticed was the Neptune and Triton by Bernini, now in the Victoria and Albert Museum, London, which then adorned a fishpond. Mortoft, like other seventeenth century travellers, loved trick fountains and consequently enjoyed the "many devices to wash men unawares" with which the gardens were well supplied.

Near Neptune were two heads wearing wreaths which spouted water from the flowers and fruit; there was a water clock so arranged that anyone approaching to read the time received a jet of water "in a kind of an invisible manner", as Mortoft expressed it. There was a box of bowls which tempted the visitors to have a game, but the moment they went to pick up the bowls "we drew water in our faces, which made us have little desire to play at that tyme". As they were leaving, a gardener indicated a "cocke neare the doore", which, he whispered, if turned would wet others in the garden, but when Mortoft and his friends proceeded to do this they received a stream of water themselves, "so with much laughing at these mistakes, we tooke one sprinkling more and departed".

The Fountain of the Amphorae, in the Piazza dell'Emporio (1926)

That graceful two-handled vessel, the amphora, was the standard container for much of the produce of the ancient world. Ships' cargoes were packed in amphorae, and the amphora was the unit by which the capacity of a merchant ship was calculated. Wine, oil, honey, wax, caviare, dried fruit, olives and pitch are a few of the commodities shipped in amphorae, which were accordingly one of the most familiar objects in the commercial and domestic life of Rome. The amphora was also a measure of capacity, and any Roman who suspected that he was receiving short measure could consult the official amphora, the Amphora Capitolina, which was kept in the Temple of Jupiter on the Capitol, much as the English linear measurements are officially displayed in Trafalgar Square, London.

The wastage in amphorae was tremendous. Over the centuries a mountain of broken pottery accumulated upon a place set apart by the magistrates. This is some 120 feet high and covers an area of about sixteen acres, and one may walk over it and collect the handles of amphorae, some bearing the names of potters in Greek or Latin. Mount Testaccio, or Potsherd Mountain, as it is called, is a few steps from the Protestant Cemetery and the Porta S. Paolo and was in ancient times a convenient dumping ground near the docks and warehouses. No other artificial hill can be compared with it. It is built up of earthenware from all the countries of the Mediterranean, and is a striking monument to the use of the amphora in ancient commerce.

In the nineteen-twenties a competition was held for a fountain to be erected in the crowded Testaccio district, but the rules were forbidding and must have frightened off many an artist: the design, it was stipulated, must not incorporate statues, or groups of figures, bas-reliefs, bronze or marble. What then, one might ask, was left? These restrictions, however, did not deter the architect Lombardi, who won the competition with one of the most charming and imaginative modern fountains in Rome (plate 23). It was unveiled in 1926, and stands in the Piazza dell'Emporio opposite the Ponte Sublicio.

Steps lead up to a pile of amphorae perhaps twenty feet in height, placed one on top of the other, the graceful jars forming a group that must have been an everyday sight in a Roman warehouse or upon the deck of a galley. Water gently drips from the top of the pile, or oozes as honey might have oozed from a badly stoppered amphora from Hymettus. The Acqua Paola has stained the travertine an authentic terracotta colour so that one has the illusion that one might be looking at a pile of genuine amphorae. In any part of Rome this fountain would have been striking and unusual, but upon the banks of the Tiber, and on the outskirts of Testaccio, it stirs the imagination and one looks at it remembering the millions of those graceful jars which the Tiber brought to Rome from Greece and from Spain, from Mauretania, North Africa and Asia Minor.

There are many delightful modern fountains in Rome but, to my mind, this is the most memorable. With all its grace and dignity, it is essentially a homely monument, and exceptional in Rome where relics of the past are mainly from emperors and consuls, offering instead a marvellous vista of warehouses and shops, of kitchens and cellars. It may lead one to explore the great mountain of breakages which it commemorates, where one can roam over the brittle mound thinking not of Caesar but of slaves with shopping baskets, of careless maid-servants, of dockers and customs officers, and even of Roman rag-and-bone men whose contributions perhaps added to this phenomenal mound.

The fountain in the Piazza dei Quiriti (1928)

Few strangers ever visit the regions north of the Castel S. Angelo unless im-pelled by a morbid desire to see Roman suburbs of the nineteen-twenties. Here are wide avenues, rectangular streets, huge blocks of flats and business offices, and at least one marvellously "period" little park where nursemaids rock perambulators while seated between columns bound with fascist rods and inscribed with such words as "Honour" and "Imperium". Among much that is tasteless is the Piazza dei Quiriti and one of the best modern fountains in Rome (plate 22). The name of the piazza may puzzle some, but may remind others that the word Quirites denoted the ancient Romans in their civil character. When the Tenth Legion mutinied, Julius Caesar began his speech to them with the word "Quirites!", whereupon the men fell in shamefacedly and swore to be loyal soldiers. I suppose the English equivalent would be "Civilians!", with scornful implications if used by an angry general to his troops.

As I went to see this fountain I imagined that I should find some representation or symbol of Roman civic virtue, but it has nothing at all to do either with Rome or the Quirites. I thought it a most striking and puzzling fountain. Four naked female figures are seated above what might be an enormous lotus, or the cup of some huge flower, while they support with uplifted arms another, though smaller, lotus-like shape above them. From this a pine-cone gushes water that, overflowing from the small basin, partially veils the four caryatids as it falls into the larger basin, which in its turn overflows into the main pool at ground level.

The design is pleasing and balanced, but what remains in the memory is the puzzling expression upon the faces of the caryatids. They sit behind the veil of water as if performing some melancholy religious rite, yet no priestesses or sibyls have looked sadder. Are they perhaps slave girls who have been forced to hold the lotus shape above them and are on the point of rebellion? Two sit, their left knees raised and both arms lifted to support the burden, and the other two, with right knees raised, sit clasping their right ankles while supporting the lotus with one hand.

When the fountain was unveiled in 1928 there were angry newspaper protests against the nudity of the females, and the piazza became crowded for weeks with those who had come to see exactly how nude they were. (Incidentally, the ancient Romans could witness unmoved the disembowelling of men and beasts, but would recoil in horror from a nude sprinter.) The agitation soon died away, however, and the Fontana del Selva took its place among the finer fountains of Rome. It does not help to look up the word "Selva" in a dictionary in the hope of solving the enigma of the caryatids, since it is the name of Attilio Selva, the sculptor of the fountain.

X

THE FOUNTAINS OF ST PETER'S
AND THE VATICAN

THE VATICAN district, and the right bank of the Tiber generally, enjoyed a more generous supply of water in the first century than at any time until today. Two aqueducts terminated there, the Alsietina (2 B.C.) and the Trajana (A.D. 109); in addition water was piped across the bridges from the left bank, as we learn from Frontinus, who mentions that this had to be cut off when the bridges were being repaired. It is surprising to contrast such a supply with the drought conditions of the Middle Ages, which continued until Paul V brought the Acqua Paola to the Janiculum. Today the Vatican City receives two aqueducts, the Paola and the Pia Marcia. The Acqua Paola, which is seen in the twin fountains in front of St Peter's, is also the water displayed in all the fifty-nine fountains of the Vatican. Acqua Paola is used to water the gardens as well as for domestic purposes and for central heating. The drinking water is Acqua Pia Marcia, which was introduced after 1870. This is the water laid on to the private apartments of the Pope, and is the water used for baptism in St Peter's.

The most distinguished of the Vatican fountains is one which has not spouted water for untold centuries. It is the only fountain to have survived from the first century, a survival which it owes to its celebrity during the Middle Ages, when it became the most famous fountain in the Christian world. This is the colossal bronze pine-cone – La Pigna – which has bestowed its name upon the Giardino della Pigna of the Vatican Museum, where it is now to be seen.

La Pigna

There are few objects still standing in Rome upon which one could say the eyes of Augustus and his contemporaries had rested, but this might be said with tolerable certainty of La Pigna (plate 24). It is of first century date and was probably the central fountain in the Lake of Agrippa, in the Campus Martius, upon whose waters Tigellinus gave his master Nero the notorious orgy described by Tacitus. The guests assembled in a magnificent banqueting room built upon

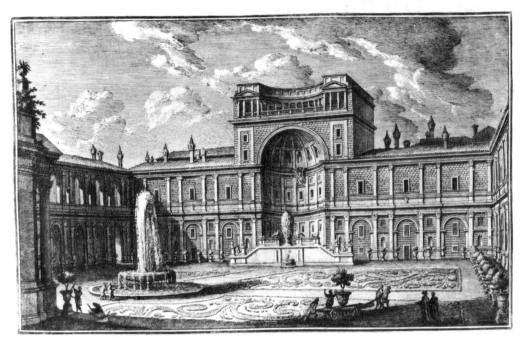

La Pigna in Bramante's courtyard in the Vatican; an eighteenth century engraving

a raft which was drawn round the lake by rowers seated in boats splendidly decorated with gold and ivory. Other theories about the Pigna have now been abandoned; among them that it had formed the summit of Hadrian's tomb or was a lid or stopper on the roof of the Pantheon. It is generally believed that it gave its name to that region of Rome where it was found, which is still called Pigna, a district which includes the Pantheon, the churches of the Minerva and the Gesù, as well as three of the largest palaces, the Palazzo Venezia, the Palazzo Doria, and the Palazzo Altieri.

La Pigna now stands in the semicircular niche at the far end of Bramante's courtyard of the Vatican Museum. Thousands who hurry along the corridors never give it a glance, though it is more interesting than many of the objects they will be shown in the museum. It is eleven feet high and was originally gilt. The water flowed from minute holes *per foramina nucum*, or from the base of the scales. In the last century a French archaeologist, M. Lacour-Gayet, discovered something which had eluded all previous investigators, the signature of the artist, which is engraved round the base of the cone: P . CINCIVS . P . L . CALVIVS . FECIT ("This is the work of Publius Cincius Calvius, freedman of Publius Cincius"). Though early records of the fountain may be few, the history

La Pigna in its medieval setting in the atrium of old St Peter's

The pine-cone fountain commissioned by Charlemagne for Aachen cathedral

of La Pigna after A.D. 500 is well known. In that period Pope Symmachus removed it, presumably from the Campus Martius, to the atrium of old St Peter's, where he devised a beautiful setting for it which inspired the wonder of future ages. Eight columns of red porphyry supported a dome of gilded bronze adorned with gilt peacocks and dolphins – both Christian symbols – and beneath this graceful canopy the Pine-Cone dripped water from every scale.

It was the first sight which caught the eye of the pilgrim who, having ascended upon his knees the thirty-five steps to the basilica, entered by one of three doors. He found himself not in the church but in the atrium, called the Paradisus, a wide paved space flanked by colonnades where food might be bought and where merchants had set up their souvenir stalls, the first *paternostrari*, whose modern descendants have migrated to the outer perimeter of the piazza. The Pigna rose above this crowded forecourt, and, as the modern pilgrim dips his finger in holy water, so the early Christian would dip his hands in the flowing fountain before he approached the church itself, which stood at the far end of the atrium. The immense bronze casting, shining with gold and rising above a marble pool, must have been an unforgettable sight. It seemed so to Charlemagne who, returning home after his coronation in A.D. 800, ordered a pine-cone fountain for his new cathedral at Aachen, where it can still be seen. Five hundred years later Dante was impressed by La Pigna; it was one of the three things he mentioned about Rome, the others being the Lateran and the Bridge of S. Angelo. He called it "the Pine of St Peter" and compared it to the face of a giant which he had seen in the last circle of hell.

Happily, this wonderful relic of first century Rome survived the Gothic sack of A.D. 410 and that of the Vandals in A.D. 455; it survived the incursion of the Saracens in A.D. 1046, when St Peter's was stripped of gold and silver; it emerged unscathed from the Norman sack of A.D. 1084 and the sack of 1527 by the armies of Charles of Bourbon. Probably its greatest danger was not from barbarian looters but from popes in search of bronze. It was one of the last celebrated features of old St Peter's to remain until the last moment during the rebuilding of the basilica. It was not moved until the beginning of the seventeenth century when, together with its gilded bronze shrine and the peacocks and dolphins, it was taken down and removed to a courtyard of the Vatican. There, perhaps, its greatest peril awaited it. In 1613 Paul V, looking for metal to cast the statue of the Madonna which stands on top of the column outside the main entrance to S. Maria Maggiore, melted down the bronze dome, two of the peacocks and other decorations, but stopped short at La Pigna itself, either because he had found sufficient metal for his purpose or because of the reverence the fountain had inspired for eleven centuries. La Pigna now stands in Bramante's niche as nobly as it did in ancient and mediaeval Rome; and on each side of it is a bronze peacock, two of its ancient companions.

The fountains of St Peter's

The twin fountains in front of St Peter's (plate 25) are probably the most celebrated in the world. Though they were erected centuries before the fountains in the Place de la Concorde and Trafalgar Square, and other famous fountains in Europe and America, no others have ever challenged their supremacy.

When Queen Christina of Sweden saw them for the first time, during her official welcome to Rome, she thought they were a display specially devised in her honour, and suggested, with royal consideration, that, as she had seen them, the water might be turned down. When told that the fountains played at full pressure day and night, she was incredulous, and perhaps when she knew Rome better she may have been astonished to reflect that all through the night hundreds of other fountains, with no one to admire them, were thundering, gushing, splashing and tinkling away in the darkness all over the city.

The fountains of St Peter's are particularly impressive in the small hours of the morning, as I know well, having seen them at that time and at sunrise. Years ago, during a hot summer, when I was staying a few minutes' walk from St Peter's, I would sometimes, if unable to sleep, go out at night and walk round the piazza. It was a strange experience to be the only person in that mighty reassembly of the marble and travertine of ancient Rome. To stand there at three o'clock in the morning in the light of the lamps round the obelisk, with two arcs of reflected light curving right and left from the colonnades, was to experience a sense of solitude which went beyond loneliness. Fortunately the fountains, cheerfully shooting their shafts of Acqua Paola into the night, link the piazza with normality; and the darkness resounds with the reassuring splashing of Lake Bracciano.

The basilicas of Constantine faced the east, as the pagan temples did, thus the first light of a summer morning strikes the dome of St Peter's and descends over the east front until the terrace and the steps are bathed in sunlight. The first fountain to be sunlit is that on the right as you face the church; its companion on the left must wait in the shadow of the southern colonnade until the sun has risen higher in the sky. Now, with returning light, the fountains are seen in all their splendour, enlivening the scene with sound and movement, whipping sudden showers of thin spray to the pavement at the slightest touch of wind. Members of the Sanpietrini, who generation after generation have repaired the church, swept it, and attended to its many needs, appear upon the terrace with brooms. Across the early shadows of the piazza, their own shadows carried before them, hurry priests from all parts of the world who, having put their names down on the rota for an altar, are about to experience the fulfilment of the visiting priest's dearest wish in Rome, to say Mass in St Peter's.

In order to appreciate how much the architectural scene owes to the fountains, one should go there on a day when they are being cleaned or repaired. One is immediately aware that something is not as it should be. The piazza seems dead. It is extraordinary that the absence of two showers of water should make so much difference, and one longs for the moment when they will spring into life again.

Though they are alike in design, the two fountains are of different ages. That on the right, near the Vatican Palace, has a long history; its companion is of more recent date and was added for reasons of symmetry. Before Bernini designed the present piazza, the old basilica presided over a small, irregular open space in which, in the early Middle Ages, there was a fountain fed probably from local sources; but the first fountain in approximately the position of the right-hand fountain of today was built in 1490 by Innocent VIII. The construction was

Plate 30. The mask fountain in the Park of the Orange ⸤

recorded by Johann Burchard, Papal Master of Ceremonies from 1484 until 1506, who commented that he did not think another like it would be found in Italy.

It was a large fountain of a design which was to become familiar in Rome in the course of the following century: a granite basin with a smaller one above which received water from a jet. Several drawings of the fountain have survived, including more than one by Martin van Heemskerck, a Dutch artist who worked in Rome from 1533 to 1536; a print of 1600 seems to show that the water spouted down from slits cut under the rim of the upper bowl, as in the fountain of S. Maria in Trastevere.

Innocent died before the fountain was completed, and the finishing touches were added by his successor, the Borgia Pope, Alexander VI (1492-1503). Though Alexander's character may resist biographical whitewash, it can be made to appear several shades lighter by remembering, not his bad points, which are only too well known, but his interest in architecture and his services to learning. In Rome, Alexander finished the roof of S. Maria Maggiore, decorated (like so many other churches) with the first gold from America; he fortified the Castel S. Angelo and restored a number of churches, as well as the fountain of S. Maria in Trastevere. His contribution to the completion of the fountain in front of St Peter's was the addition of four gilded bulls, the Borgia emblem, which gave to the fountain its romantic name, the Fountain of the Golden Bulls. These were removed after his death and replaced by four stone figures of naked cherubs, a form of decoration which, as I have mentioned in connection with the fountain in the Piazza d'Ara Coeli, was to be employed eighty years later by Jacopo della Porta.

The fountain remained unchanged for more than a century until, with the arrival of the Acqua Paola in 1612, Paul V thought it unworthy of his new water supply. Maderno accordingly provided a larger fountain (frontispiece), but at the same time retained the shape of the older one. For the first time a designer was able to use a powerful jet of water with the height and pressure of the Vatican Hill behind it. Maderno, therefore, instead of designing a small bowl for a low-pressure jet to fill, reversed the bowl and made it a splashing place for the descending stream of water, a feature which gives the fountains of the piazza their distinctive character.

Maderno's fountain was one of the sights of Rome for more than forty years as it sent up its magnificent shower of Acqua Paola and shared the piazza with the obelisk. When Evelyn visited St Peter's in 1644 he admired the fountain

31. La Terrina

32. The Fountain of the Sea-Horses in the Borghese Gardens

A drawing by Martin van Heemskerck showing the Vatican and the façade of old St Peter's. The fountain in the foreground is the old Borgian Fountain of the Golden Bulls, demolished by Maderno in 1614

"out of which gushes a river rather than a stream which, ascending a good height, breaks upon a round emboss of marble into millions of pearls that fall into the subjacent basin with great noise; I esteem this one of the goodliest fountains I ever saw". Fifteen years later Francis Mortoft stood in the same spot and wrote, "out of this Fountaine the water rises in such a vehement manner that it is enough to strike astonishment to a man that at first beholds it"; and in 1670 Lassels added that "it throweth up such a quantity of water that it maketh a mist always about it, and oftentimes a rainbow – when the Sun strikes obliquely upon it".

By that time, however, Bernini had completed the piazza and the colonnades, and already the lonely fountain on the right, as the visitor approached the basilica, began to look distinctly odd. The credit for balancing the square with a second fountain on the other side is due to Clement X (1670–76) who is said never to have walked in the piazza without being worried by the lack of symmetry. He ordered Carlo Fontana, a nephew of Maderno, to copy his kinsman's fountain in every detail and to erect it in a corresponding position to the south: and this was done in 1675, the year before Clement died.

The two fountains are now so much eroded by the Acqua Paola that it is not easy to make out in the worn, mossy stone the papal coats of arms with which they are decorated. The old fountain bears the Borghese eagle and dragon of Paul V, while its companion, which actually appears more ancient and weathered, bears the Altieri stars of Clement X. One reason why the more recent fountain

The piazza of St Peter's in 1600; in the foreground is the Fountain of the Golden Bulls

looks the more ancient of the two is because it receives the full force of the Tramontana, the north wind, from which Maderno's fountain is partially protected by the northern wing of the colonnade.

The Gardens of the Vatican

The Gardens of the Vatican, which cover less than a hundred acres, are greatly inferior in size and layout to the gardens of many princes and most Renaissance and post-Renaissance cardinals. Those portions which have not been built upon are, nevertheless, interesting as a part of the old Mons Vaticanus and as the "prison", from 1870 until 1929, of five popes.

There are no other gardens like them. At every turn the dome of St Peter's presents itself in a rural setting, sometimes beyond a screen of chestnut leaves or at the end of an ilex avenue, and once fantastically framed by the archway of a rose garden. It is also a garden from which youth and womanhood – save briefly during the Renaissance – have been excluded. It is an old man's garden, or rather the garden of a succession of old men. With the cares of the world upon their shoulders and so much to do in a short time, one cannot expect to find that many popes have been gardeners; there have been one or two, but no more, conse- quently the Vatican Gardens have continued century after century unaffected by that restless passion for alteration which afflicts most gardeners and their gardens. This does not mean that the Vatican Gardens are neglected or archaic, but it does mean that you could find your way about them with the plan which Giovanni Battista Falda made in the seventeenth century. There are a few addi- tions, however, which would have puzzled Falda. For example, there is the Vatican Radio Station, in a charming setting on the highest part of the hill, and the white marble railway station, a station with no ticket office, no bookstall or left-luggage office, but a place for a choir to sing hymns to the pope should he depart or arrive by train, an event which has not yet occurred.

The Gardens are dedicated to the leisure of popes. Here they walked under shady avenues during summer days; in the seventeenth century they drove over the hilly paths in coaches of red lacquer and gilt; here they might have been seen dismounting from their white mules to sit for a moment beside a fountain, or to hold an informal meeting under a chestnut tree. Pius IV (1559–65) loved to receive friends in the exquisite garden-house which Pirro Ligorio built for him, where centuries later Pius VIII and Gregory XVI sometimes gave audiences. The cardinals would be seated on the oval sweep of stone seats, a sight which must have recalled a meeting of the Roman Senate. Gregory XVI, who could be stern and remote in public, relaxed in the Gardens and sometimes unexpectedly exhibited a schoolboy delight in secretly turning a water-tap and drenching his cardinals, a trick which Pius IX also, though less surprisingly, enjoyed playing. I have, however, searched the Vatican Gardens in vain for trick fountains, which if they still exist, must long since have become unworkable.

Curiosity is aroused by thought of the papal fountains. What kind of fountains did those greatest of all fountain-makers create for their own pleasure? The answer is that they spent all the money and skill on public fountains; their own fountains, save for two or three exceptions – the Galleon of Jan van Santen, Bernini's Bee fountain, and perhaps Maderno's mighty fountain in the Court of the Belvedere – are nothing out of the ordinary. Water was, of course, precious in the Vatican until Paul V brought the Acqua Paola there in 1612, and early fountains are hard to find.

The most beautiful pre-Pauline fountain is to be seen (if you can ever locate the man with the key) in the courtyard of Pirro Ligorio's glorious reconstruction of a classical country house, which is known as the Villa Pia or the Casina of Pius IV (plates 27 and 28). Ligorio, who also built the Villa d'Este at Tivoli, never designed anything more beautiful than the poetic little jewel of the Vatican Gardens. The Pope gave his permission to take as much marble as he needed from Domitian's stadium in the Piazza Navona, so this elegant architectural translation follows the usual Roman course of metamorphosis or resurrection, though here at least there is no need to mourn the loss of a classical ruin, for Ligorio created from the ancient marble something more beautiful than any stadium.

The fountain stands in the centre of an oval courtyard. It takes the form of two infants, seated upon two wide-mouthed dolphins, who face each other across the length of a marble basin which is full of clear blue water. There is a trickle from the mouths of the dolphins and a quiet bubbling movement from the central jet, and upon a hot summer's day this tinkling Arabian restraint is more cooling than the sound of a waterfall. The villa is a two-storey classical building of pale biscuit colour balanced on the opposite curve of the oval by another matching pavilion which is not, as the first is, a house where the pope could live, but a delightful summerhouse from whose shade you look down to the Gardens and to a lily pool immediately below, presided over by a statue of Cybele. In the vestibule of the villa itself there is a life-sized figure of the many-breasted Diana of the Ephesians worked in shells, while the exterior walls of villa and summerhouse carry bas-reliefs showing the ancient world in its most austere and attractive aspects.

One can imagine how the long, thin nose of S. Charles Borromeo must have lifted in disdain when his uncle, Pius IV, summoned him to this lovely and un-christian garden, as he often did, we are told, to discuss the sins of the world. It is curious how frequently one reads that Leo X loved to discuss artistic and literary matters there, since the villa had not been built in his time, which is a pity, for, of all the popes of the sixteenth century, he almost certainly would have enjoyed it most. The mistake is an inspired one, for the villa ought to have been built in 1460 instead of in 1560: it is an expression of the Renaissance in its first purity and, as one sits there enjoying it, one thinks of Brunelleschi's Pazzi Chapel and Alberti's "Temple" at Rimini, to which period the villa would seem to belong.

The Eagle fountain in the Vatican Gardens; Maderno's triton is at the right-hand side of the picture

Unfortunately the Villa Pia began to fall upon evil days when Leo XIII declared it to be unhealthy, and perhaps the lily pool did breed a few mosquitoes. The result was that the Pope, who loved summerhouses, built himself another one – now part of the Vatican Radio Station – in a higher part of the Gardens. He used it frequently in July and August. After saying his morning Mass, he would go to the summerhouse, attended by the Swiss Guard, and would spend the day there.

The Gardens still bear evidence of the enthusiasm of Paul V for his Acqua Paola, which reached the Vatican Hill directly from the Janiculum in 1612, and three fountains date from this period. The water which enters the Gardens on the north displays itself for the first time in a large and unattractive fountain called the Eagle, from a battered Borghese bird upon its summit. It is an attempt at a group of rustic grottoes, but the rock used is too small and the general effect is one of artificiality. Among the stone figures placed in the water at the mouth of the grottoes is one of a triton, by Stefano Maderno, seated upon a monster fish and holding a shell to his mouth, the well-known attitude of Bernini's master-piece. Anyone unaware of the date of this figure might think it a copy of the more famous Triton, but when the Eagle fountain was made Bernini was a schoolboy, and something like thirty years were to pass before he was to make the Triton in the Piazza Barberini. Signor Cesare d'Onofrio has traced the derivation, and one may imagine the young Bernini contemplating the commonplace fountain and selecting, with the eye of genius, the one feature which could be transformed into something greater. I have wondered whether the indifferent rocks of the grottoes may also have inspired Bernini's famous Grotto of the Four Rivers.

The second of the Pauline fountains is the unusual Fountain of the Sacrament, in which a central, jet-like wheel of water represents a monstrance while rising jets which flank it on each side are the altar candles. The third is a superb fountain which would be one of the most popular sights of Rome were it in a public place. This is a beautiful scale model of a seventeenth century, three-masted warship fifteen feet long, whose mainmast is about twelve feet high. It was made by the Flemish artist Jan van Santen about 1620. The galley is of lead, the sails are of brass, and the rigging of copper. Cannon protrude from the gun-deck and send out a constant broadside of water, while jets rise from the yards and, shooting into the air, curve and descend upon the deck in spray, which admirably simulates the smoke of battle. The ship floats upon a generous basin of water and is the most striking fountain in the Vatican; and indeed one of the most unusual fountains in Rome (plate 26). It is a delicate fountain and requires frequent attention. It was restored under Clement IX and Pius VI and, at the moment of writing, is in perfect order.

The most important contemporary fountain of the Acqua Paola is to be found in the courtyard of the Belvedere, where Maderno designed a massive and impressive fountain of the traditional bowl and basin shape, which is not unlike the two fountains in the piazza, save that the top bowl has not been reversed and the jet is a modest one. A touch of originality are the four jets which rise from ground level and curve up to fall into a huge granite basin which came from the Thermae of Titus. Not far away, near the old papal coach-house, now the garage, a most interesting fountain was to be seen until recently, an early Bee fountain by Bernini, and evidently his first attempt at that difficult design. It is now to be found in a more public position in the wall of the Via Pellegrini, not far from the Porta S. Anna.

Bernini was only twenty-seven when he carved this, his first fountain and also his first attempt to model the Barberini bees which in later life he was to send swarming over so many Roman monuments. Since the age of sixteen he had been a prodigy, and by the time he was twenty-seven he was established in the Vatican by his patron Urban VIII, who had been pope for two years. There is a story that Bernini had a workshop near the place where the Bee fountain was originally sited, and that one day the Pope went there to see his favourite and was so pleased with the fountain that he wrote the Latin words which may still be read above it:

Quid miraris apem quae mel de floribus haurit
Si tibi militam gutture fundit aquam?
Why stand amazed at the bee who draws from the flowers the honey
When from his throat he supplies honey-sweet water for you?

The fountain is a carved wall panel of foliage and rocks where five bees stand in a semicircle facing the water. As originally designed, a thin spurt of water curved from the mouth of each bee, but they no longer expel water but appear instead to be taking it in. The idea of a bee fountain evidently lay maturing in Bernini's mind for another nine years, when he carved the famous Bee fountain now at the bottom of the Via Vittorio Veneto.

The only pope, after Paul V, who took a serious interest in the Vatican Gardens and its fountains was Benedict XV (1914–22), who had several avenues made through the neglected *Boschereccio*, the "woodland", and brought water there. Three of his fountains still play, and it is delightful upon a hot day to come upon them well sited in patches of sunlight amid the surrounding trees and shrubberies. One small rustic fountain was a particular favourite with the Pope. From a central stream eight thin jets of water curve down to the basin of the fountain, and during his daily walks, if one of the jets was clogged, Benedict would not move until it had been cleared. Another is a modest basin fountain of the kind one sees in a hundred Italian gardens. It is enlivened by four jets which spring from the lower pool and fall back upon themselves. The third fountain is a large and massive circular colonnade which rises from a pool and supplies a granite basin with its jet. It is a singular design and is said to recall the old Castigliana of S. Pietro in Montorio, which no longer exists.

The enthusiasm which Benedict XV was able to expend upon the Vatican Gardens was continued by his successor, Pius XI (1922–39), who for the first seven years of his reign was the last "Prisoner of the Vatican". He transformed thirty acres by planting new flower beds and shrubberies and brought the Gardens within range of irrigators, installing many miles of water pipes and hundreds of sprinklers. That is the reason why the Vatican lawns are now green when elsewhere in Rome the grass has vanished in the heat of summer.

With the settlement of the "Roman Question" in 1929, in the seventh year of his reign Pius XI found himself at liberty, if he wished, to leave the Vatican Gardens. They were no longer the only place where the Pope could enjoy the shade of trees and the sparkle and murmur of fountains.

Plate 33. Detail of Pope Julius III's fountain on the Via Flam
Overleaf Plate 34. Grotesque head from the Piazza Navona, now in the Borghese Gardens. Plate 35. T
from the Piazza Navona, now in the Borghese Gar

XI

THE ACQUA PIA ANTICA MARCIA
AND ITS FOUNTAINS

SEVERAL INVENTIONS that were commonplace in other countries invaded
the Papal States in the forties and fifties of the nineteenth century; among
them were the telegraph, railways, and gas-lighting. The introduction of
such novelties was the work of enterprising foreigners who, unaware that the
Papal States were about to expire, eagerly signed ninety-nine-year leases with a
government that had only a few more years to live. In a moment charged with
irony, Pius IX, reversing the belief of his predecessor, Gregory XVI, that steam
locomotion was an invention of Satan, accepted the gift of a pontifical train,
made in France, shortly before renouncing travel and becoming the "Prisoner of
the Vatican". His flamboyant coaches, mounted upon rails in the Palazzo
Braschi, are now among the sights of Rome.

Among England's contributions to the modernization of the Papal States was
a cast-iron aqueduct, the Acqua Pia Marcia. Enthusiasts had discussed for a long
time the possibility of reviving the famous aqueduct which had been built a
hundred and forty years before Christ by Quintus Martius Rex, of whom little
is known save that his *imperium* as praetor was extended for twelve months to
enable him to complete, and bestow his name upon, this construction. It was
Rome's first high-level aqueduct, and for taste, purity and temperature, its water
rivalled, perhaps even exceeded, that of the Aqua Virgo. The Aqua Marcia
terminated upon the Capitoline Hill, from which pipes were soon laid to the
Caelian, the Aventine, and the Quirinal hills, and in later times this was the water
used in the Baths of Caracalla and Diocletian.

The engineers of 1840, who had surveyed the sources of the old Aqua Marcia
some sixty miles east of Rome, proclaimed them to be in perfect condition, and
as no aqueduct had been built since Paul V constructed the Acqua Paola two and
a half centuries previously, it was considered time to revive this ancient source.
The Pontifical Government held back, deterred by the difficulties and the cost of
such a venture, and nothing was done until two English engineers, James Shep-

herd and George Henry Fawcett, formed the Anglo-Roman Water Company with a capital of £200,000, and were granted a lease of ninety-nine years, dating from 8 November 1865. The early records of the company contain many English names: Henry Robert Woolbert, James Teare, Richard Ward, Edwin Dinning Cole, Henry Frederick Ward, and Francis George Whitham (curiously transformed in some documents into "Francesco Giorgio Whitwham"). In two years' time the company was reconstructed and the name was changed to the Società Anonima dell'Acqua Marcia.

The water flowed into Rome in the late summer of 1870 at a point a few hundred yards nearer the Central Railway Station than the present *mostra* in the Piazza della Repubblica. On 10 September it was officially welcomed by Pius IX in the last public ceremony to be held by a pontiff as sovereign of the Papal States. The Pope was cheered by large crowds who cried "Long live Pius! King, King, King!", unaware that they were seeing the last regal pontiff, and also the last pope who would be seen outside the Vatican for more than half a century. Pius appeared in cheerful spirits. He drank a glass of Acqua Pia Marcia and praised its freshness and purity, then he returned to the Vatican. Ten days later – the famous "Venti Settembre" – Rome was in the hands of Victor Emmanuel, and Pius was the first "Prisoner of the Vatican".

The arrival of the Acqua Pia Marcia and the end of the temporal power inspired a last cruel pasquinade. One morning the maimed old statue outside the Palazzo Braschi was seen to bear a paper upon which was written "Bevi, e . . . Marcia!" – "Drink, and . . . march off!"

Like many who have worked in Rome for brief periods, I have always found so much to employ and interest me that I have rarely had the time to leave the city, except for a day at Ostia or a visit to the Alban Hills or Tivoli. When I saw that the source of the Acqua Pia Marcia would take me beyond Tivoli into the Sabine Mountains, I looked forward to seeing a region which, although only sixty miles away, was entirely unknown to me.

The road to Tivoli is not interesting, and rather more than half way is haunted by a pungent outbreak of sulphuretted hydrogen (a whiff of home to anyone from Harrogate!) which announces the presence of Bagni Aquae Albulae, where the Emperor Augustus once took a cure, some say, for neurasthenia; then the road continues, and almost before I had ceased to marvel that the nose can adjust itself to such smells, I was climbing up to ghostly Tivoli.

This lovely place poised upon its gorge has been immortalized by many

Pope Pius IX (1846–78)

artists, and even the sound of Tivoli has been preserved whenever nimble fingers race over the keyboard in a cascade of treble notes. But Liszt is the least demanding of the ghosts, and the Villa d'Este the most obvious of memories. Old inhabitants will take you to a vast terraced ruin on the Carciano road which they say was the Villa of Maecenas, and they will show you another opposite the great waterfall which a long tradition claims to be the Villa of Horace. The building, now a private house, has had the good fortune to be owned by an appreciative English family since 1879 when it was bought by F. A. Searle, who spent his last years there in works of loving restoration. He was followed by his son-in-law, C. H. Hallam, a classics master from Harrow, who convinced contemporary Latinists that the building really was the Villa of Horace. Now it is owned by his great-great-granddaughter, the Vicomtesse d'Ailhaud de Brisis and her husband. Somewhere nearby is the Villa of Cynthia, who used to throw wine cups at Propertius then make it up and cover him with kisses; though only popular legend identifies these sites, upon which one broods, hoping them to be genuine, since the Augustans were more like ourselves than anyone until the Renaissance. Indeed, it is perhaps a little too easy to fancy that we might have slipped unnoticed into a place at a supper party given by Maecenas.

The Romans loved Tivoli, or Tibur, for its beauty, and as a refuge from the plague. It also enjoyed the odd reputation of being the only place in which ivory was not discoloured by exposure or time; consequently the vaults of the temple of Hercules were stacked with tusks. The atmosphere was believed to be equally kind to the human skin, and many fashionable Roman women went there to improve their complexions.

Those who have read much Latin verse, and have translated Horace into colloquial English, are able to make the life of the villas of Tibur during the Augustan Age resemble a fashionable country-house party in Edwardian England; and though the ascetic Augustus, dipping dry bread in water and eating a lettuce or a green apple for dinner, scarcely recalls King Edward VII, on the other hand the assembly of bankers, colonial administrators, imperial conquerors, fashionable literary men and the Roman equivalent of the Jersey Lily, do, one must admit, lend a certain similitude to the scene. Among those who had villas there, and probably enlivened dinner parties with stories of strange lands, was P. Sulpicius Quirinus who, as mentioned by St Luke, was Governor of Syria "when there went out a decree from Caesar Augustus, that all the world should be enrolled".

I left Tivoli with regret and followed the road eastward through the beautiful wooded valley of the Aniene. Turning a corner suddenly, I surprised one of those delightful groups which have no real period in time, belonging, as they do, to time itself. A number of peasants were loading sacks upon five or six donkeys, and one of the animals, alarmed by the abrupt appearance of my car, moved suddenly and discharged a cascade of chestnuts over the road. When we had gathered them up and had reassured the donkey, I asked where they found a market for their chestnuts. They replied, of course, Rome. And I went on, remembering that the time of year was approaching when, as darkness falls, an ancient, warm and pagan smell steals through the most sophisticated streets of the capital, and, should you trace it to its source, you would come upon a figure seated against the wall of a church or palace, crouched above a brazier, its face touched by a red glow of charcoal, its fingers slowly turning the chestnuts with the air of a sorcerer reading the future.

I came to Vicovaro, a little hill town clasped by ancient walls, which Horace knew as Varia. Six miles north into the lovely valley of the Licenza (which the poet called Digentia) is the site of the famous Sabine Farm where Horace, having shaken the dust of Rome from his toga, enjoyed the delights of a country life. A lane shaded by trees winds its way up to a grassy platform among the hills where the ground-plan of Horace's retreat, a villa of about twelve rooms, is marked out by foot-high walls capped with cement to keep them waterproof, the neat work, I believe, of the American Academy at Rome. For years the noise of battle echoed round the hills as scholars aimed books and articles at one another, some claiming that the villa was not that of Horace, others that it was, but now at last one can sit with confidence under the chestnut trees and believe that this was the place where the little poet – for Horace was small, tubby, and prematurely grey – lent a hand with the harvest (a soft, writer's hand, one feels sure) and, much more important, wrote some of the poems which are full of an appeal that has kept them alive through all the storms and changes of time. In the eighteenth century, when the villa was first located, so many English travellers climbed the hill to see it that the local people believed Horace to have been a celebrated Englishman: and indeed he is so, by adoption, and a person nearer, dearer, and more comprehensible, than many of our contemporaries.

His Sabine Farm was a small rural estate managed by a bailiff who had lived in the city and was swept from time to time by moods of boredom with the country. At such moments he longed for the taverns and the music-halls and was apt to neglect the oxen and forget to shut the sluices.

There were five tenant farmers, who paid rent to Horace either in money or in kind, and were important enough to take part in the municipal life of Varia, and eight slaves. As poet-farmers go, Horace had quite enough on his hands. I wondered in which of the rooms outlined on the grass he had offered those rustic meals of pork and beans, and his own rough wine, to millionaires like Maecenas; and how interesting it would be to know if Augustus had ever sat there, perhaps nibbling a dry biscuit or sampling the poet's grapes.

Having regained the main road, I continued my journey to Agosta, still in the valley of the Aniene. The road and the countryside were deserted. Mountains rose on every side and each foothill was capped with a small white town. Every mile took me deeper into a landscape which reminded me of a wilder, sadder Tuscany. It seemed to me astonishing that this bleak Sabine land of mountains could exist upon the doorstep of Rome. Friends had often spoken to me of the wildness of the Abruzzi and Calabria, and had urged me to go there before new roads had transformed the ancient life of those regions; yet sixty miles from Rome are hundreds of mountain villages and hill towns which are as remote as if they were still in the Middle Ages; indeed my map showed innumerable roads that encircled mountains and expired at two thousand feet with nothing beyond but trackless wastes. I found Agosta to be a small hill town, not as high as some, nevertheless the road petered out some way below and I left the car to walk the remaining way up to the town by a mule track.

The houses, built one above the other on shelves of rock, rose on each side of narrow alleys, dark and sunless even at mid-day, and the doorsteps of some buildings were level with the roofs of others. The town terminated in a look-out that could hardly be termed a piazza, about which were grouped the church, the village pump, and a café. A radio was playing in the café and an old man, its only occupant, sat morosely at an empty table. When I spoke to him he was relieved, I felt, to find that I was a foreigner and not an agent or an official, and he gladly accepted my offer of a drink. He asked for a glass of hot vermouth. I have never been fond of vermouth and had never heard of anyone heating it, but in the hope that this might improve it, I ordered two and was rewarded with a rich, aromatic drink, scented with herbs and spices, the kind of cordial with which sybaritic monks might have cheered themselves in snowbound monasteries. The old man was uncommunicative, and when I told him that I had come from Rome to see the source of the Acqua Pia Marcia he looked at me as if I were insane. As we sat sipping hot vermouth, I remembered a story which a Roman friend had told me about a town like Agosta. It was that his mother, when travelling in some remote part of Italy, had been attracted by the peace of a small hill town and upon the impulse of the moment decided to retire for a few weeks to escape from the worries of her family. As near as I can remember them, these were his words.

My mother is extremely *simpatica*, and as long as I can recollect the members of our family, my cousins, nephews and nieces, even my uncles and aunts, confessed their troubles to her and begged for her advice. But when her own family grew up and brought their troubles to her, she became distressed. For example, she did not approve of the girl I wished to marry; my brother and his wife did not get on together and my sister was a constant anxiety; and when my mother saw this old town, she said to herself that she would escape from all of us for a few weeks and gather strength to return and listen to our woes.

Her arrival in such a small place was a sensation. No one could understand why she had come to live there. However, in a few days she had the whole town at her feet. The priest, who because of some dispute with his superiors had been rusticated to that remote place, began to preach his sermons to her alone, saying how good it was to have someone at last who could understand him. This she found distinctly embarrassing, as he leaned from the pulpit and talked only to her, at the same time castigating members of his flock, who were, of course, present, as ignorant dolts, liars and hen-stealers.

Then, one by one, the women began to bring their anxieties to my mother, who was appalled to find that the troubles of this Arcady were the same as those from which she was trying to escape: husband trouble, wife trouble, family feuds and hatreds. However, as everyone knows, the problems of others are easier to bear than one's own, and my mother cheerfully accepted her role as general confidante until one day the Mother Superior told her that a novice had fallen in love with the priest! That determined her to retreat from her retreat. Hastily arranging a transfer for the novice to a convent near Rome, my mother came back enthusiastically to her own troubles!

Climbing down the streets, observed by impassive faces, I regained my car, wondering what emotions seethed beneath the apparent peace of that ancient place.

I found the springs of the Pia Marcia about a mile from Agosta, grouped beside the road and, like the other sources I had seen, covered with protective buildings. I was told that the water was rain that had fallen twelve months previously in the Sabine Mountains and had come, fresh, clear and filtered, through miles of volcanic rock. There are seven principal springs, and some have names, such as Rosoline, Serena, S. Lucia, and, in particular, one called Mola di Agosta whose water was described to me as "rich and very pure". Who but a Spaniard or an Italian would dream of calling water "rich"? The Pia Marcia is the most technically complex and interesting of the aqueducts, but, being neither a hydrographer nor an engineer, I was more concerned to see the kind of country in which these Marcian springs are gathered.

I thought it a remote, melancholy countryside, romantic and withdrawn, and lacking in the friendly warmth of Tuscany which, though the Sabine landscape is wilder and on a larger scale, it so greatly resembles. It was a mellow autumn day but there was no harvest bustle, the lean vineyards, empty of workers, ridged the hills and no farm carts came lumbering along the lanes; and looking at the land, I saw how thin and rocky it was. On my way back to Rome I noticed a town called Anticoli Corrado, standing high on its hill, and I could not remember why the name was familiar to me. I saw from the map that a side road ran up to it through a valley and then expired upon a mountainside, and, perhaps reluctant to leave those enigmatic mountains, and curious also to see another of the hill towns, I turned aside and went there. On the way up I recalled why I had heard the name of the town: it was famous in the nineteenth century as the home of many of the artists' models who used to haunt the Spanish Steps. They were well described by Dickens, who recognized among them characters seen regularly at exhibitions of the Royal Academy, and also by W. W. Story, who mentioned them in his *Roba di Roma*, and noted in particular an old man known as Padre Eterno because of his studio life as the Deity. Most writers of the time were delighted by the picturesque and delightful group at the foot of the Steps, the white teeth, the sunny Italian smiles, the pretty girls in red or blue skirts, wearing head-dresses of folded linen, the young men in blue jackets and goatskin breeches. Among the older generation was a venerable character called Old Felice, who played the bagpipes and was said to have walked to Paris and back.

The road circled up to a picturesque old town built round a large, irregularly shaped piazza, in fact the top of the mountain. There was a pleasant fountain in the centre around which a number of men were gathered, elaborately pretending to be disinterested in the arrival of a stranger. A profound peace lay upon the scene. I asked the way to the town hall and was directed to a hilly little street and an old mansion just off the piazza. Standing in front of this building, leaning on a staff, a survival, it seemed, from the models of the Spanish Steps of long ago, was an old shepherd who wore shapeless grey cloth stockings and peculiar sandals of skin.

The mayor had gone to Rome for the day, but I was courteously received by a deputy in a small room full of canvases, broken clay models, statuettes, and the usual jetsam of a studio, tokens of Anticoli Corrado's association with the arts. It was true, I was told, that the great-grandfathers and grandmothers of the present inhabitants had been immortalized in the work of the nineteenth century painters, and a citizen of the town could hardly go into any gallery in which such pictures were to be seen without recognizing an ancestor.

A chance remark brought the surprising information that the models who sat for the sculptor Mario Rutelli for the figures on the *mostra* of the Acqua Pia Marcia, in the Piazza della Repubblica in Rome, were both from Anticoli Corrado. I was told that the gigantic male figure, Glaucus, who wrestles with a huge fish, was a fine-looking fellow named Francesco Toppi, and the model for the four water nymphs – for they are all the same woman – was Vittoria Placidi. Both are no longer living, but several old people in the town still remember

The figure of Glaucus from the Fountain of the Na

them and whenever they go to Rome and pass the Fountain of the Naiads they think of them and are proud that, though the world at large may not know it, those famous figures were their own folk. I was told that Vittoria Placidi died while still young and still in possession of that beauty which shines through the spray of the fountain, but Francesco Toppi lived to be an old man and had two daughters who, as far as my informant knew, were still alive and in Rome. What an odd experience it must be to cross the Piazza della Repubblica and see one's father, greatly magnified and in bronze, in perpetual conflict with a fish.

Among the prominent features of the surrounding landscape is a mountain nearly three thousand feet high and crowned, of course, with a white town. A similar wavering road winds up to it as to Anticoli Corrado and also expires upon the mountain-top. The name of this town is Saracinesco.

A century ago it was also famous for artists' models, for flashing dark girls and swarthy young men, but it was also notable for an even more interesting reason. It is said that during the Saracen raids of the ninth century a party of marauders became cut off in the Sabine Mountains from the main body and, taking refuge on one of the highest peaks, founded a town that has been known as Saracinesco ever since. Lanciani, after discussing the incursion of A.D. 846 in *The Destruction of Ancient Rome*, writes: "There is no doubt that a foraging party, having been cut off from the main body, and finding a retreat impossible, took shelter among these rocky precipices, and that afterwards they were allowed to form a settlement and live in peace by substituting the cross for the crescent. Some of the inhabitants, who come to Rome every winter clad in their picturesque costumes as painters' models, have preserved their Arabic names, like El-Mansour (Almansorre). Elmansour is also the name of a cave in the neighbourhood of the village. From this point of view, therefore, our valley of the Anio forms a counterpart of the Saas-Thal in the Valaisan Alps, the villages and peaks of which still preserve their Saracenic names (Monte Moro, Allalin, Mischabel, Alphubel, Almagell, Belferin, etc.), from the invasion of 927."

Though it was later than I could have wished, and the sun had clouded over and a cold wind was blowing, I was unable to pass the turning to Saracinesco, so, leaving the main road once more, I began the long climb up the mountain. Arriving at the end of the road, I was again obliged to leave the car and walk the rest of the way. Narrow lanes led to groups of houses built on different levels, and the highest part of the town was a long wide platform covered with grass and shrubs and containing no buildings. The view downward was like that from an aeroplane.

The town appeared to be deserted and many of the houses seemed to be un-inhabited. The silence was so oppressive that, rather absurdly, I called "Is there anybody about?", as if I were in an empty house. At length a window opened above me, and a middle-aged woman wrapped in a black shawl asked what I wanted. After a few words, she came down and told me that my assumption was correct: Saracinesco was practically deserted; there were only a hundred and eighty people left in it. I was surprised to hear there were so many. There was no work for them locally, and most of the inhabitants had moved to Rome where they sold flowers at street corners. She said that the people were proud of their descent from the Saracens. The flat space in which the town ended was known as the Castle; and I wondered whether excavation would reveal an Arab *kasr*.

I arrived back in Rome as the lights were being lit. I passed the *mostra* of the Acqua Pia Marcia in the Piazza della Repubblica and watched the rush of water with a new interest. I could imagine the wild Sabine land of its origin, and I could fancy it sweeping underground past Tivoli and across the Campagna on its way to Rome. I admired Glaucus and the naiads beneath their mighty shower-bath, glad to know their family history; and I wondered whether the young man who was selling carnations was a descendant of the Saracens. Such reflections are not unusual after a day spent in the countryside near Rome.

The fountains of the Acqua Pia Marcia, which are many, are mostly the adopted children of the aqueduct, since the great age of fountains had ended when it was built. Many ancient fountains, however, which were originally fed by the older aqueducts were for technical reasons taken over by the Pia Marcia, so that one has the anomaly that a water supply which came to Rome only in 1870 pours from many fountains erected in the sixteenth and seventeenth centuries. Though the Pia Marcia nourishes many fountains in all parts of Rome, no great fountain, except the *mostra* of the aqueduct, the Fountain of the Naiads, displays this valuable and prized drinking water.

Among the most interesting Marcian fountains are:

La Terrina, in the Piazza della Chiesa Nuova

The fountains of the Villa Giulia

Bernini's Bee fountain, in the Piazza Barberini

The Fountain of the Lateran, in the Piazza di S. Giovanni

The fountains of the Borghese Gardens, in particular the Fontana dei Cavalli Marini

The two lions at the foot of the Cordonata on the Capitol

Two details of the Fountain of the Naiads. *Above* The Nymph of Subterranean Waters. *Right* The Nymph of the Lakes.

The Fountain of the Naiads (1870–1911)

A fountain that created protest and indignation when it was first seen in 1901 is the *mostra* of the Acqua Pia Marcia, the Fountain of the Naiads (plate 29), at the top of the Via Nazionale. The four bronze nymphs, who disport themselves beneath powerful jets of water, appear innocent enough today, but contemporary critics compared them to drunken peasants, a comparison which puzzles a modern onlooker, to whose eyes they resemble sophisticated types of nineteenth century womanhood. Whatever charm they possess is perhaps due to this period atmosphere, which recalls the lost world of Maxim's and the Moulin Rouge, of the Gibson girl, of spas frequented by weary royalty and eccentric grand dukes, a world of Cliquot, feather boas, tight waists, and a sound which will probably never be heard again, known to contemporaries as "frou-frou". What distinguishes the nymphs from earlier nude figures on public view in Rome is perhaps that they appear to be not naked and unashamed, but coyly undressed.

When Pius IX welcomed the Acqua Pia Marcia to Rome on 10 September 1870, the terminal *mostra* was not in the position of the present fountain, but several hundred yards or so nearer to what is now the Central Railway Station. Neither the station nor the Via Nazionale had been built then, and the first *mostra* was approximately where the Dogali monument now stands in the small garden between the present fountain and the station. Prints of the time show a simple but effective fountain: a tall central jet towering above a circular basin round whose edges a diadem of smaller jets played inwards.

In the same year the Via Nazionale was made, leading from the Baths of Diocletian to the Forum, and two years later the railway station was constructed, completely altering the appearance of that part of Rome. It was then decided to demolish the fountain and to rebuild it on a more splendid scale at the top of the Via Nazionale. The architect entrusted with the design was Alessandro Guerrieri, who, though he wished to create something unusual, produced what in general effect is an improved version of the original fountain. It is still a large circular basin with a powerful central jet, but the inward jets are not mounted on the rim of the main basin but beneath a second, smaller basin into which they deliver their water. A new feature, however, was an architectural structure rising from the main basin with four plinths for statues. When the fountain was first erected in 1888 there were no statues, and the architect suggested that four marble lions might be suitable occupants of the plinths. This, however, did not appeal to the authorities who thought, and rightly, that four reclining water nymphs would be a more original and attractive adornment.

While the discussion was in progress, the year 1888 brought an exalted visitor to Rome, the twenty-nine-years-old German Emperor, William II, who had recently ascended the throne. In order that the imperial eye might not alight upon an incomplete public monument, four plaster lions were hurriedly placed on the four vacant platforms on the *mostra*, and an early photograph shows them in position nine years later. Legislators and artists continued to argue, and eventually, in 1897, a Commission approved the design of the sculptor Mario Rutelli of Palermo for four reclining nymphs: the Nymph of the Ocean with a sea-horse, the Nymph of the Lakes with a swan, the Nymph of the Rivers with a water-snake, and the Nymph of Subterranean Waters with a reptile.

Rutelli employed Vittoria Placidi of Anticoli Corrado as his model, and the four nymphs represented her in four slightly different attitudes. Instead of casting the bronzes in Rome, Rutelli returned to his native Palermo where he con-structed a foundry for the purpose. Aware, perhaps, that Rome keeps few secrets, he wished to spring a surprise upon her, and were this so, his wish came true. In January 1901, a stout hoarding concealed the fountain from view, and in its shelter the sculptor assembled his gigantic water maidens. Someone may have peeped through the hoarding to be dismayed by the sight of them, for a meeting of the Council on the Capitol spread the news that Rutelli's figures were an affront to the morals of Rome. The Mayor was requested to order their removal from the fountain and their banishment to an unfrequented part of the Borghese Gardens. The debates, which have been recalled by Signor Cesare d'Onofrio in his *Fontane di Roma*, followed, with appeals to decency, fears for the young and innocent, and references to morality and civilization. Some speakers deplored the fact that the Council's request for reclining nymphs should have been so erotically interpreted. "The sculptor has taken four divans," said one speaker, "which vary from the sea-horse to a marine monster, upon which he has spread out his nymphs, not nymphs with elegant forms like those which abound in the art of the eighteenth century but nymphs elevated not with the purity of water but with cheap wine like peasants of the Campagna."

The Liberals, who on principle took the opposing view, while demanding the unveiling of the fountain, reminded the critics that similar outbreaks in the past by outraged moralists had resulted in the absurdity of adding trousers to the nudes of Michelangelo and metal kilts and chemises to several statues in St Peter's. Roused by the debates and by comments in the newspapers, the public gathered expectantly round the hoarding, anxious to put their morals to the test. On Sunday, 10 February, the hoarding was scaled and eventually pulled down, and the Fountain of the Naiads was revealed by the crowd. The newspaper, *La Capitale*, commented in the morning that the statues had made no one blush and did not even interest the choirboys who "honoured the peculiar unveiling with their presence". The comment of *Il Popolo Romano* was that on the whole it was agreed that the fountain was a fine work of art and that the Capitol had been unduly alarmed. Only the *Osservatore Romano* insisted that the nymphs were artistically disreputable and an abomination.

Since then the fountain has taken its place among the great *mostre* of Rome, and it has the distinction of being one of the most spectacular fountains after dark when floodlighting lends added dignity and importance to it. The central figure of the sea-god, Glaucus, was not added until 1911. Rutelli was again the sculptor and his model was, as I have said, another inhabitant of Anticoli Corrado, a young man named Francesco Toppi. He holds a fish which expels a jet of water more powerful than any except those of the twin fountains in front of St Peter's.

La Terrina (1580–90)

The many fountains of the Acqua Pia Marcia are the adopted children of this aqueduct since, with the nineteenth century, and with water laid on to houses, street fountains were no longer necessary. Many ancient fountains once fed by the Vergine, the Felice and the Paola were for technical reasons taken over by the Pia Marcia, which nourishes lost children of other aqueducts all over Rome.

An odd-looking fountain lies sunk into the pavement of the Piazza della Chiesa Nuova, just off the Corso Vittorio Emanuele II. It is known as La Terrina – the Tureen (plate 31) – and it is one of a number of diverse sights all, in the characteristic Roman manner, within a pace of each other. Behind the fountain is a statue of Pietro Trapassi, better known as Metastasio, who began life as a poor boy reciting in the streets and ended as the most celebrated composer of operatic *libretti* of the eighteenth century. The "Chiesa Nuova" nearby is S. Maria in Vallicelli, which was built in 1575 by S. Philip Neri for his Society of the Oratory, a church whose vocal and instrumental services gave the word "oratorio" to the vocabulary of music. The sacristan will show you the rooms in which S. Philip Neri lived, also his tomb, and, near the altar, two groups of saints painted, surprisingly, by Rubens.

The "Tureen" is a worthy member of this varied group. It is the only covered fountain in Rome, though no one apparently knows why the travertine lid was added to it. It resembles a huge turtle that has burrowed into the pavement, and Signor d'Onofrio has called it a *piccolo mostro architettonico*, as indeed it is. But it

Plate 38. The fountain in the Via della Ciste

Overleaf Plate 39. A fountain in the gardens of the Villa Sciarra. Plate 40. A courty
fountain in the Palazzo del G

• ACQVA NON POTABILE •

is a pleasant, harmless monster and there is much that is beguiling in its ugliness. Its history is singular. It vanished for thirty-five years and re-appeared in the Piazza della Chiesa Nuova only in 1924. Its original piazza, where it was erected, perhaps by Jacopo della Porta between 1580 and 1590, was the Campo dei Fiori, an open-air market which is still as picturesque today as it was in former centuries.

Early prints show the fountain to have been originally without a lid. It was a delicate marble basin, oval in shape with elongated sides, an authentic design which della Porta repeated in the lower bowl of the fountain in the Piazza d'Ara Coeli. Owing to the low pressure of the Vergine, it was inset in the pavement and approached by a short flight of steps. The centre of the bowl was occupied by four bronze dolphins which are thought to have been four of the eight originally cast for the Fontana delle Tartarughe, only four of which were used in that fountain.

The Campo dei Fiori was the place of execution during the sixteenth and seventeenth centuries, and also the place where the Inquisition held its parades and burnt heretics at the stake. It was also the scene of horse and cattle markets and was often packed with crowds. Possibly a sunken fountain with the merest trickle of water was frequently fouled by refuse and on occasions was used as a grandstand (the gallows were in line with it), and it is easy to understand why it was covered in.

It has been assumed by some who have studied such matters that the lid was placed in position as early as 1622, a date suggested by a faint inscription beneath the ball or knob of the lid. It reads: "Love God and do not fail; do good and let them talk. 1622." However, this date cannot be accepted since Evelyn in his *Diary*, under the date 18 February 1645, mentions that he passed through the Campo dei Fiori and saw the fountain "casting out water of a dolphin", which he could not have seen had the fountain been covered. As Evelyn mentioned only one dolphin, perhaps the other three had been destroyed or stolen, and already, when he saw it, the fountain was in poor repair and due for reconstruction. I suggest, therefore, that the lid was added not at the beginning but at the end of the seventeenth century, and that possibly the inscription with its early date applies to another monument of which the stone of the lid formed part. In any event, the cover was firmly in place by 1753 when Giuseppe Vasi printed an etching of the Campo dei Fiori in his *Magnificenze di Roma*, published in that year. The two most prominent features in the square are the gallows and, nearby, La Terrina. The horsemen and other rustic figures in the Campo appear to be wearing clothes of an earlier period than 1753 and, of course, the artist may have sketched the square years before his book was published: it is also a fact that in past centuries rural fashions were decades behind those of the court and the aristocracy. At a guess, I should date the addition of the lid to the years between 1645 and 1700.

In 1889 various anti-clerical factions decided to affront the Vatican by erecting a monument to the Dominican philosopher, Giordano Bruno, near the spot where he was burnt for heresy in the year 1600. The old fountain was removed to make way for the statue and La Terrina vanished for thirty-five years. The statue of Bruno, the nearest thing in Rome to a Protestant memorial, now rises above the market-place, commemorating a man who is of singular interest to Englishmen for his visit to England in 1583, in the course of which he lectured at Oxford, eulogized Elizabeth Tudor, and was friendly with Sir Philip Sidney, to whom he dedicated his *Last Tromp*, which was printed in London by Thomas Vautrollier. While visiting his publisher in Blackfriars, Bruno, by a curious and intriguing tradition, is said to have met an unknown young man of nineteen or twenty named Shakespeare.

However, to return to La Terrina. During the nineteen-twenties the dismantled fountain was discovered in the cellars of a Roman museum, and it was decided that it should be restored to public life. A place was excavated in which it could burrow in the Piazza della Chiesa Nuova where, in 1924, an older generation, which could still remember La Terrina in its original position in the Campo dei Fiori, gave the returned fountain the warmest of welcomes.

The Villa Giulia (1550-55)

The most distinguished of the many adopted children of the Acqua Pia Marcia are the two road fountains on the Via Flaminia, on each side of the Via di Villa Giulia, and the Nymphaeum - beautiful even in its restored condition - of the Villa itself. In 1550 all three fountains were fed by the Acqua Vergine and it was suspected that the Pope, Julius III (1550-55), had actually committed the offence of tapping the aqueduct to provide his fountains with water, though he called the process gathering the "leakage waters".

Julius was called by Petrucelli the Heliogabalus of the Church, though he might also have been termed its Kubla Khan, since during the five years of his pontificate he cared for nothing but his "pleasure dome" on the northern slope of the Pincian Hill. His election took place at a moment when presumably the Divine attention was withdrawn from the Conclave, and Ranke says that as a

The wall fountains of Pope Julius III on the Via Flaminia, an eighteenth century engraving

group of cardinals was one day assembled round the altar in the Sistine Chapel, discussing the difficulties of the election, Cardinal Ciocchi del Monte, as he then was, approached them and said jokingly, "Take me, and the next day I will choose you for my favourites and intimates." He was an unlikely choice, and a writer of the day said that "few bets would be taken on his chance": nevertheless, in the political complexity of the election he was made Pope. He had once been chamberlain to Julius II, and in memory of that association he took the name of Julius III. Unlikely candidate though he may have been, he was at least filled with self-assurance. Vasari relates that when he met the cardinal in Florence on his way to the Conclave, he said, "I am going to Rome and shall assuredly be Pope. Get ahead with what you have in hand and as soon as you hear the news, set out for Rome at once, without waiting for a summons." Vasari obeyed the command with such alacrity that he was present at the coronation.

Almost at once Julius decided to disregard the cloudy skies of the Reformation and to live as though the blue heaven of the Renaissance stretched above him. His pontificate coincided, in England, with the reigns of Edward VI and Mary I, with the execution of Lady Jane Grey, and the marriage of Mary with Philip of Spain; in France, Henry II (and Diane de Poitiers) were on the throne. Leaving

The Nymphaeum of the Villa Giulia, a seventeenth century print

all serious matters in the hands of his advisors, Julius decided to enjoy himself and, as he suffered from gout and loved rich food, he forbade anyone to tell him any bad news in case it gave him indigestion.

His five years as Pope represented a triumphant flight from reality; the monument to his pontificate was the exquisite Villa Giulia, which, like the Casina of Pius IV in the Vatican Gardens, brought the springtime of the Renaissance into the middle years of the sixteenth century. Vasari claimed to have been responsible for its design, together with Ammanati and Vignola, while Michelangelo, then seventy-five, acted as advisor. Julius loved to travel by barge from the Castel S. Angelo up the Tiber to a point near the modern Ponte del Risorgimento, where a landing-stage had been arranged for him. Minstrels played as the decorated and garlanded barge was rowed upstream, and crystal lanterns were in readiness for a return after dark through the summer night. A pergola covered the short distance across the fields to the Via Flaminia, which the Pope crossed before he climbed a flight of steps to the Villa. At this point on the public highway he erected a fountain and horse trough, the work of

The Nymphaeum of the Villa Giulia today

Ammanati, which still stands there. Vasari mentions how he often visited the Villa Giulia in company with Michelangelo to see how the work was progressing; and on one occasion they found the Pope there with several cardinals, and Julius made way on the seat for Michelangelo to sit beside him, though the master declined the honour. But the villa was never completed: the Pope was too restless and changeable. His moods defeated even Vasari, who wrote, "he understands little of design and disliked in the evening what had pleased him in the morning".

Today the Villa Giulia, after many vicissitudes, is the Etruscan Museum, and the old wall fountain on the Via Flaminia, at the corner of the Via di Villa Giulia, is still in action, though few bestow a glance upon it as they dash past. It is difficult to reconcile the busy road today, crowded with cars and lorries, with the leafy and idyllic scene pictured in sixteenth century prints. The fountain too has changed. Ammanati's simple classical screen has been given an upper storey which has changed its character. The granite basin into which the water falls is the same, though the head of Apollo, which originally flowed with Acqua Vergine, has been replaced by a bearded mask (plate 33) flanked by two monster fishes and now dispenses the Acqua Pia Marcia. This, before its conversion to the modern aqueduct, was the earliest of all the Vergine fountains, and in date a good thirty years before Gregory XIII decided to take the Acqua Vergine to the Piazza del Popolo and other public squares in Rome.

Those who visit the Etruscan Museum find themselves in the superb semi-circular courtyard of the Villa Giulia which led to the Nymphaeum, the only surviving example in Rome of that Hellenistic type of fountain. As Pope Julius knew it, the courtyard was filled with some of the finest statues of antiquity. In the centre stood the spectacular porphyry basin, now in the Vatican Museum, which some think came from Nero's Golden House, while every niche was occupied by a notable work of art. Ammanati wrote a letter to Messer Marco Bonavides, describing the statues of the courtyard, which reads like the catalogue of a museum: there was a Hercules leaning on his club with three apples in his right hand; a naked Pan with bagpipes; a statue of Lavinia, daughter of King Latinus; a Bacchus leaning on a faun; indeed, the courtyard was a *Who's Who* of Olympus. After the Pope's death, when the Villa was confiscated by the Apostolic Chamber to defray his debts, a hundred and sixty bargeloads of statues were removed to the Vatican.

What chiefly interested me were the beautifully restored remains of the Nymphaeum, a revival of classical design which, with Pirro Ligorio's summer-house of Pius IV in the Vatican Gardens, is unique as the Renaissance idea of a Roman country house. A stone balustrade surrounds a sunken lily pool, a portion of the terrace rests upon the heads of marble caryatids, and various mysterious-looking doors lead to windowless chambers, the Renaissance (and ancient Roman) substitute for air-conditioning, where the owner of such a villa and his friends might enjoy a siesta in the hottest days of summer in cave-like gloom, soothed by the drip of water through the moss-covered rocks of a grotto.

After the death of Julius III, no one seemed to care for the Villa or to know what to do with it. Suffering from insomnia, Sixtus V once believed he could find sleep there, but his doctors forbade him to do so because of the *mal aria* encouraged by the number of fountains and the damp vegetation. There was a time when the Vatican housed distinguished guests there for the night before their official entry into Rome, but by the eighteenth century the place was abandoned and was evidently considered sufficiently remote to be the scene of exalted crime. When Nathaniel Wraxall was in Naples the first Lady Hamilton told him a macabre story about the Villa Giulia, which he reprinted in his *Memoirs* in her own words:

About the year 1743 (she said), a person of the name of Ogilvie, an Irishman by birth, who practised surgery with great reputation at Rome, and who resided not far from the Piazza di Spagna in that city, being in bed, was called up to attend to some strangers who demanded his professional assistance. They stopped before his house in a coach, and on his going to the door, he found two masked men, by whom he was desired to accompany them immediately, as the occasion which brought them admitted of no delay, and, in particular, not to omit taking with him his lancets. He complied, and got into the coach, but no sooner had they quitted the street in which he resided than they informed him that he must submit to have his eyes bandaged, the person to whom they were about to conduct him being a lady of rank, whose name and place of abode it was indispensable to conceal. To this requisition he likewise submitted; and, after driving through a number of streets, apparently with a view to prevent his forming any accurate idea of the part of the city to which he was conducted, the carriage at length stopped. The two gentlemen his companions then alighting, and each taking him by the arm, conducted him into a house. Ascending a narrow staircase, they entered an apartment, where he was released from the bandage tied over his eyes. One of them next acquainted him that it being necessary to deprive of life a lady who had dishonoured her family, they had chosen him to perform the office, knowing his professional skill; that he would find her in the adjoining chamber prepared to submit to her fate, and that he must open her veins with as much expedition as possible, a service for the execution of which he should receive a liberal recompense.

Ogilvie at first peremptorily refused to commit an act so highly repugnant to his feelings. But the two strangers assured him, with solemn denunciations of vengeance, that his refusal could only prove fatal to himself without affording the slightest assistance to the object of his compassion; that her doom was irrevocable, and that unless he chose to participate a similar fate, he must submit to execute the office imposed on him. Thus situated, and finding all entreaty or remonstrance vain, he entered the room, where he found a lady of a most interesting figure and appearance, apparently in the bloom of youth. She was habited in a loose undress, and immediately afterwards a female attendant placed before her a large tub filled with warm water, in which she immersed her legs. Far from opposing any impediment to the act which she knew he was sent to perform, the lady assured him of her perfect resignation, entreating him to put the sentence passed on her into execution with the least possible delay. She added that she was well aware no pardon could be expected from those who had devoted her to death, which alone could expiate her trespass, felicitating herself that his humanity would abbreviate her sufferings and soon terminate their duration.

After a short conflict with his own mind, perceiving no means of extrication or of escape either for the lady or for himself, being moreover urged to expedite his work by the two persons without, who, impatient at his reluctance, threatened to exercise violence on him if he delayed. Ogilvie took out his lancet, opened her veins, and bled her to death in a short time. The gentlemen having carefully examined the body in order to ascertain that she was no more, after expressing their satisfaction, offered him a purse of Zechins as a remuneration, but he declined all recompense, only requesting to be conveyed from a scene on which he could not reflect without horror. With this entreaty they complied, and having again applied a bandage to his eyes, they led him down the same staircase to the carriage. But it being narrow, in descending the steps he contrived to leave on one or both of the walls, unperceived by his conductors, the marks of his fingers which were stained with blood. After observing precautions similar to those used in bringing him thither from his own house, he was conducted home, and at parting the two masks charged him, if he valued his life, never to divulge, and if possible never to think on, the past transaction. They added, that if he should embrace any measures with a view to render it public or to set on foot any inquiry into it, he should be infallibly immolated to their revenge. Having finally dismissed him at his own door, they drove off, leaving him to his reflections.

In the morning the doctor reported his adventure to the papal authorities, who gave him a police guard and asked him to try and reconstruct his mysterious journey. This he was eventually able to do, and upon the walls of the Villa Giulia he recognized his blood-stained fingermarks and also the room in which he had been forced to bleed the young woman to death. It turned out that the murderers were the Duke of Bracciano and his brother who had put their sister to death for defaming the family honour, and the story ends with the plausible anticlimax that, instead of being brought to justice, the murderers, through influence, escaped with a heavy fine.

The Fountain of the Bees (1644)

Pope Urban VIII and Napoleon were devoted heraldically to bees. Three bees displayed on an azure field were the armorial bearings of the Barberini family to which Urban VIII belonged, and it is believed that Napoleon designed his bees from the three hundred golden bees found in the tomb of the Frankish king, Childeric, who died in A.D. 481. Urban's bees have proved more permanent and are to be found in Rome wherever Bernini erected a monument to his great patron. Had Urban continued to reign beyond the twenty years allotted to him, no doubt those insects would have been as numerous in Rome as lions in Venice. Apiarists may be interested to know that the finest, the most decorative and the most numerous swarm are to be seen inside St Peter's, upon Bernini's canopy above the high altar.

The idea of a bee fountain occurred to Bernini when he was in his twenties, and Urban's obvious delight with it (the Vatican wall fountain) inspired the artist to develop the idea and to design a more ambitious version some twenty years later. This is the unusual little fountain at the corner of the Via Vittorio Veneto and the Via S. Basilio. It has been in that position only since 1919.

Plate 42. Detail of a fountain in the Palazzo Ve

Plate 43. Detail of the fountain in the courtyard of the Institute of Biblical St

The original site was at the corner of the Via Sistina on the opposite side of the Piazza Barberini, where it was set against the wall of a house but impinged so much upon the roadway that many a coach must have driven into it in the dark. It was, however, allowed to remain until 1887 when the Piazza Barberini, no longer a countrified square, became crowded with coaches and carriages, and the fountain was then removed either because it was an obstacle to traffic, or in order to preserve it. It disappeared for forty-two years, which exceeded the retirement of La Terrina in similar circumstances. In 1919, however, it reappeared in the characteristic manner of vanished Roman monuments, and was connected with the Acqua Pia Marcia. (The Triton fountain, only a few yards away, in the centre of the piazza, casts up Acqua Felice.)

Bernini has placed the three Barberini bees on the edge of the pool, where they are expelling the water in three thin jets which fall into the basin beneath them. They have settled in the hinge of a huge fan-shaped shell which carries a pontifical inscription to the effect that the fountain was erected in 1644, the year, as it happened, of Urban's death. Thus Bernini's work for this pope began and ended with a bee fountain.

Many people think this fountain is one of the most charming in Rome, but it has never been one of my favourites; I dislike the sight of enlarged insects, and bees the size of pigeons are not (to me) at all attractive. As a composition, however, it is a masterly exercise in the execution of what many sculptors would think an impossible, even a ludicrous, theme.

Possibly the least known of Bernini's three bee fountains is to be seen nearby in the courtyard of the Barberini Palace. It is the traditional fountain of two basins, with an octagonal base containing the main pool almost at pavement level. The three bees are not at first obvious. They are to be found clustered together at the top of the fountain, in the act of drinking from the jet.

The Park of the Orange Trees

A small public park on the Aventine is known by several names, the Parco dell'Aventino, the Parco Savello, the Parco di Santa Sabina, and – best of all – the Parco degli Aranci, from the rows of orange trees planted there. Its attraction is the view it affords across the Tiber to the west of St Peter's, but, to me, it is one of those places which are becoming few and precious where the peace of the last century appears to linger.

The time to go there is at eight o'clock on a summer's morning, when you will probably find no one but a group of priests standing on the platform of the

44. The staircase fountain in the Villa Corsini

boundary wall, gazing across the river and identifying the domes and towers, and a young nursemaid rocking an infant in a perambulator. Then the bells of S. Sabina nearby begin to ring, and other bells join in; but the Aventine infant, accustomed to these morning sounds, sleeps soundly on.

Passing beneath an archway, one enters the charming little Piazza Pietro d'Illyria; at one end is a huge mask fountain (plate 30) like that of the Via Giulia, though much larger, and at the other is the church of S. Sabina, the most perfect fifth century basilica in Rome. A few steps more, and one has the impression of stepping upon a stage set ready for a romantic comedy, or perhaps an opera. This is the Piazza dei Cavalieri di Malta, which is celebrated for the gateway of the Priory of the Knights of Malta, with its keyhole peep of the distant dome of St Peter's framed in an avenue of cypress trees.

But to return to the Park of the Orange Trees. An unusual fountain stands in the shadow of the pines and the orange trees, gently arching four thin streams of Acqua Marcia into a marble basin. It is one of the migratory fountains of the sixteenth century and stood in its distant youth in the centre of the Piazza Montanara, near the Theatre of Marcellus, a picturesque square which no longer exists. Farm workers and country folk used to gather there to be hired, as they still do in the Piazza del Pantheon. With the care and good taste which Italians always bestow upon works of restoration, the old fountain, and even the small bricks on which it stood, have been moved and set up under the pines and oranges, every detail as it was in the Piazza Montanara.

Another migratory fountain is to be seen in the garden. It is a wall fountain in the form of a rockery from which the winged head of a cherub spouts a stream of Acqua Pia Marcia into a marble basin that rests upon the extended wings of a large bird. The bird, in its turn, spouts water from its beak into a basin at ground level which is lined with scraps of antique green marble. An inscription states that the fountain came from the Palazzo Accoramboni in the Piazza Rusticucci when the palace was demolished in 1927. This provokes two memories. The name Accoramboni recalls one of the great scandals and crimes of the sixteenth century, and the Piazza Rusticucci was the name of a beautiful, casual little piazza on the edge of the piazza of St Peter's until the construction of the ugly but well-meaning Via della Conciliazione swept it out of existence in the nineteen-twenties.

Should other Roman fountains become displaced in future years, no place could be found for their retirement more dignified or more enchanted than that beneath the orange trees of the Aventine.

The obelisk and fountain of St John Lateran, a seventeenth century print

The Fountain of S. Giovanni in Laterano (1603–7)

Rome can show no better example of a fountain's subjection to an obelisk than the modest basin which crouches in the shadow of the Lateran obelisk in the Piazza di S. Giovanni in Laterano. No fountain, of course, could assert itself in competition with the world's tallest obelisk, and even Bernini would no doubt have been unable to reconcile the fountain with its uncompromising neighbour, as he was able to do so brilliantly, but with a more reasonable monolith, in the Piazza Navona.

The obelisk, which was discovered buried in the Circus Maximus in the reign of Sixtus V, was moved to the Lateran by Domenico Fontana in 1586. That is probably the reason why some writers have attributed the fountain to him. But he was not the designer. He merely erected the obelisk as the Pope commanded. Views of the piazza drawn after Fontana's departure from Rome show the obelisk but no fountain.

The fountain was erected at the foot of the obelisk in 1603–7 at the expense of the Canons of the Lateran, a short period which nevertheless embraced the reigns of three pontiffs, all of whose arms at one time appeared upon the monument. Clement VIII, who died in 1605 while the fountain was still unfinished, is represented by an Aldobrandini bar of continuous Maltese crosses which can still be made out on the frieze; two large Florentine lilies no longer in position once commemorated the learned Leo XI, who caught a chill and died twenty-seven days after his election; and a much battered Borghese eagle recalls Paul V (1605-21) in whose pontificate the fountain was finished. In the last century when the lilies of Leo XI vanished, a large statue of St John, seated and reading a book, was also removed, and the flow of water, which was originally expelled from the beak of the Borghese eagle, was changed to two fine Borghese griffins which now spout arcs of water into the upper basin.

The fountain is not a successful one, neither could it hope to be in such over-powering surroundings; nevertheless it is interesting as one of the original children of the Acqua Felice, for its splendid lower melon-shaped bowl of marble, also as a practical demonstration that only obelisks of moderate size are compatible with fountains.

The fountain has been separated in recent times from its original aqueduct and is now fed by the Acqua Pia Marcia.

The Borghese Gardens

The Borghese Gardens were laid out during the eighteenth century by Prince Marcantonio Borghese, the father of Prince Camillo Borghese, who married Pauline Bonaparte. He selected an Edinburgh man, Jacob More – "More of Rome", as he was called – to design the gardens in the English style, though now in their maturity they appear typically Italian. Nevertheless, Romans will some-times point to people sitting on the grass or rowing on the lake, or to children watching the puppet show on Sunday, and say how English it is and that one might be in Hyde Park; though an English eye, moving over gigantic magnolias and myrtle hedges twenty feet high, might fail to recognize a resemblance.

There are several attractive fountains in the Borghese Gardens, the best being the Fountain of the Sea-Horses (plate 32) in the green oval known as the Piazza di Siena. This is a fountain often fathered on Bernini, though it was designed in the eighteenth century in the style of Bernini, by Christopher Unterberger. Four prancing sea-horses support a beautiful marble basin from which springs a graceful, flower-like marble stem that bubbles with Acqua Pia Marcia. The fountain is urban and possibly might look even finer in a Roman piazza. It was greatly admired in former days, so say diarists of the last century, by those who stopped their carriages at the Piazza di Siena during their evening drives and, descending, walked up to admire the lively hippocampi.

A few steps nearer the lake, and one comes to a place of intersecting gravel

The central jet of the Fountain of the Sea-Horses in the Borghese Gar

The water clock and the fountain of Moses in the bulrushes, in the Pincian Gardens

pathways where the trees part to allow the sun to descend upon a peculiar and reminiscent fountain. Rising from a pool of water are the four grotesque heads (plate 34) from the northern fountain of the Piazza Navona, and nearby upon a gravel path the four tritons (plate 35) blow their horns towards the ilex trees. Many may have wondered why these figures should have been copied, as it seems, and erected in the Borghese Gardens, but the truth is that these are the originals by Jacopo della Porta, carved in 1575, and removed here from the Piazza Navona in 1874 for reasons which are possibly concealed in the dark mysteries of patronage, since they were replaced by modern copies. Of all the migratory or exiled fountains, and fountain figures, these are the most surprising, and perhaps it is not imaginative to fancy them superior to their substitutes.

The Gardens contain a pleasant Venus fountain, and a copy of the ancient Silenus fountain in the Capitoline Museum. This shows a bearded Silenus

tail of the Fountain of the Sea-Horses

kneeling with a wineskin upon his shoulders from which a powerful jet of water escapes.

The Gardens merge almost imperceptibly into the Pincio with its hedged walks with their busts of celebrated Italians, its obelisks and its fountains and, above all, the terrace which commands what has been called the most interesting view in the world: the vista, described by so many writers, westward to St Peter's. Before the year 1870, anyone who went to the terrace to watch the sunset might have seen two or three gilt coaches drawn by black horses toiling up the slope of the Pincian Hill, and from one would step the Pope, and from the others, cardinals; after strolling up and down, they would re-enter their coaches and vanish down the ilex avenues. The most memorable fountain shows Pharaoh's daughter discovering the infant Moses in the bulrushes, and distinction is given to it by the skilful use of water plants. I have never discovered any bulrushes, probably they were out of season, but the little stone Moses is cradled in a dense assortment of aquatic vegetation.

Every small boy is fascinated by the Clepsydra, or water clock, a tall and massive grandfather in shape, which stands on the edge of a pool and has the status of a fountain. It is recorded that when the maker, a certain Father Embriaco, died, no one could be found who understood the clock, which remained motionless for years, until a watchmaker mastered the system of activating the pendulum by directing alternate jets of water upon two small metal leaves which communicated movement to the whole mechanism.

The Cordonata lions

The two fine basalt lions at the foot of the stairway to the Capitol were among the first fountains in this part of the city to flow with Acqua Felice in 1588-9. They became the two most popular lions in Rome during public rejoicings in the seventeenth century when they often ran with wine, one with red and the other with white. Joshua Reynolds, describing the sights of the Capitol in one of his notebooks, wrote: "You must by no means neglect to look at the two lions of Egyptian marble who spout water out of their mouths. They screw up their mouths for that purpose, as a man does when he whistles, among the best antiques of their kind in Rome."

So good, in fact, that in 1880 they were taken away and placed inside a museum, and two lions of white marble were substituted. These were removed only in 1955 and the original lions brought back to their old places and connected, no longer with the Acqua Felice, but with the Acqua Pia Marcia.

XII
THE ACQUA PESCHIERA

THE TOWN of Rieti, partly encircled by walls of the thirteenth century, stands in the mountains above the Velino valley, sixty miles to the north of Rome. It is proud of its geographical position as *Umbilicus Italiae*, a distinction which is proclaimed in eighteen languages upon a stone in the pavement of the piazza. It is strange to know that Rieti was celebrated for its oculists during the Middle Ages. Responding to a suggestion from his friend and protector, Cardinal Ugolini Conti, afterwards Gregory IX (1227-41), St Francis, when troubled by his eyes, travelled to the mountain town to see a specialist, which appears to have been no mean ordeal. "And so they cauterized his head in several places, cut open his veins, put on plasters and applied eye-washes, but he made no progress and was almost continuously getting worse."

This land of mountains is the birthplace of Rome's most recent aqueduct, the Acqua Peschiera, whose source lies a few miles from Rieti, beyond the small town of Cittaducale where, it is said, more water is to be found in wells and springs than in any other part of Italy. The ancient spa of Cutiliae - now Terme di Cotilla - is still in existence, the place where the Emperor Vespasian, who was born in the district, died while taking the waters: it was the moment of his celebrated remark, "An Emperor should die standing", when, being helped to his feet, he expired in the arms of his attendants.

The scene is one of great natural beauty. Mount Nuria itself is the source of the Peschiera and has been, as it were, mined for water. The aqueduct begins in a series of complex tunnels in the heart of the mountain and the overflow slides from beneath Mount Nuria and ripples away over clear stones.

The first sight that catches the eye as one approaches the entrance tunnel is a striking memorial, dramatic even in Italy, in the form of a group of miners in bronze, steel helmeted, with picks and shovels, at work upon the tunnels of the aqueduct; beneath are the names of forty men who died during its construction. One enters the mountain by a gallery which leads to subterranean electrical

The *mostra* of the Acqua Peschiera

stations. As in most modern factories, it is a rare experience to catch sight of the product, though one can hear it booming away inside the mountain. Mount Nuria acts as an outlet for the mountain rainfall for miles around, and the water takes six months to reach the source, so that in August Rome receives water that fell upon the Central Apennines during the previous February.

During the excavations the engineers discovered a cave full of water in the heart of the mountain, which has been preserved and is now a sight that compensates the visitor for endless tramps along clammy tunnels. One enters a cave that is a rival to the Blue Grotto in Capri. Lights sunk in the rock turn the water a brilliant green. It comes gushing from the dark depths of the mountain and immediately it falls into the grotto is transformed into liquid emerald. Another notable sight is a tunnel with the direction board, "A Roma, Kg. 86"; the place where in 1940 Mussolini swung over an electric switch and sent the first flood of Acqua Peschiera on its way to the capital.

A few miles from the source the aqueduct divides into two sections at the electrical power station of Salisano. One section, the Peschiera Sinistro, approaches Rome from the east; the Peschiera Destro takes a westward route, crossing the Tiber at Poggio Mireto Scalo, about thirty miles north of Rome, at a point where the Rome–Florence railway runs beside the river for some miles. The right-hand arm of the aqueduct is considered the main branch, at any rate it has been given the distinction of providing the public display of Acqua Peschiera in the *mostra* of the Piazzale degli Eroi, not far from the Vatican City.

The *mostra* was hastily constructed of concrete and was erected without the usual *concorso*. Someday, perhaps, a more worthy terminal will be devised for an aqueduct whose origins in the depths of a mountain would have appealed so much to the imagination of ancient Rome. Though a few fountains are fed by the Peschiera, this is entirely a matter of mechanical convenience.

XIII

THE FOUNTAINS OF THE RIONI

AMONG THE most original and charming, but, at the same time, most deceptive, of Rome's fountains are those of the *rioni*, the ancient regions, or
wards of the city. The regions fluctuated in number during the Middle
Ages but were often twelve and might, with some reservations, be called a
survival of the fourteen administrative districts into which Augustus divided
Rome in 10 B.C.

Throughout the waterless Middle Ages, and well into the Renaissance, some
of the once populous regions on the hills became uninhabited and were merely
names, but with the growth of Rome in later centuries the old regions were
revived and subdivided and now number twenty-one. All lie within the Aurelian
Walls. The new modern districts which stretch round Rome in all directions are
not called *rioni* but *quartieri*, of which there are thirty-five.

Though the ancient *rioni* no longer possess any administrative significance,
they have a sentimental appeal. The link is not with classical but with mediaeval
Rome when each region was commanded by an elected captain who commanded
a militia called, from the distinctive banners of the regions, *banderesi*. The fierce
local rivalry of the *rioni* and the heraldic splendour of their appearance when they
took to arms and marched with banners flying to the sound of the alarm bell of
the Capitol, is perpetuated today in Siena when the *contrade* of that city compete
in the race for the Palio.

Among those who have been attracted by the romance of the *rioni* was
Benedict XIV (1740–58), who ordered that the ancient emblems which distinguished them, and were pictured upon their banners, should be engraved in
stone and displayed at street corners in the various districts. These memorial
tablets bearing such symbols as a half moon, three swords, a lion's head, a stag,
an angel, often puzzle those who wander through the ancient streets of Rome;
some possibly believe them to be the heraldic achievements of the families whose
old palaces stand nearby. With the arrival of the papal aqueducts in the sixteenth

261

century, each region had its own fountain, though these had long since vanished when, in the year 1927, Professor Tommaso Bencivenga, Director of the Department of History and Art, suggested to the Governor of Rome that the regional fountains should be revived.

The idea was adopted by the Municipality, which held the usual competition, asking artists and architects to submit designs for ten of the most ancient and interesting of the regions, each fountain to be an expression of the history of the district. The contest was won by Professor Pietro Lombardi who the year before had delighted Rome with his striking Fountain of the Amphorae, now in the Piazza dell'Emporio. He designed ten wall fountains so mediaeval in spirit that one comes upon them today, only forty years afterwards, scarcely able to believe them to be modern. For that reason, as I have said, they are deceptive, and, as they are also among the most patronized of fountains, they have become well chipped and knocked about in the course of forty years, which adds still further to their venerable air. As a group, and as the creation of one man, they are unique, and, in admiring them, one must pay tribute to the genius of Professor Lombardi who has contributed more than any living architect to the beauty and the originality of the fountains of Rome.

A notable feature of the group is that all ten fountains were designed, and nine of them were in position, in 1927; the tenth was delayed by street reconstructions but was unveiled a year or so later. Each fountain is a composition in which first thought has been given to the history of the region. They are as follows:

The Rione Campo Marzo. This fountain is to be found in the Via Margutta, near the Piazza di Spagna, in the heart of the artists' quarter. It represents three sculptor's stools and two easels surmounted by a vase full of paint brushes. The water pours from the mouths of two satyr masks which stand on the easels.

The Rione Pigna. This delightful marble pine-cone fountain is almost opposite the south side of the Vittorio Emanuele Monument on the edge of a small green lawn in the Piazza di S. Marco. It resembles in miniature the famous bronze Pine-Cone of the Vatican from which the *Rione* takes its name. The water does not ooze or spurt from the base of the spines, as in the original Pigna, but flows in two drinking taps near the base of the cone.

The Rione Monti. This charming fountain stands in the Via di S. Vito not far from S. Maria Maggiore and near the Arch of Gallienus. Three heraldic hills, each one decorated with a star, represent three of the original Seven Hills of Rome which fall within the *Rione.* The water descends from the central points of the stars into three marble basins.

The Rione Tiburtina. This fountain, near the Verano cemetery, was destroyed during an air raid in the last war. It was not unlike the fountain of the Rione Monti: three hills from which water descended into marble basins.

The Rione Ripa. This fountain is built into the walls of the old S. Michele Institute, a large building in Trastevere which was founded as a home for vagabond children by Cardinal Odescalchi in 1863. Its design is that of a mariner's wheel carved in marble, a reference to the papal port, the Ripetta, which was swept away when the Tiber embankment was made in the last century. The water falls from the centre of the wheel, and also from two mooring rings which are sculptured on each side of the fountain. Strangely isolated in Trastevere, this fountain is a charming memorial to a vanished scene whose picturesque Venetian bustle may be reconstructed from Piranesi's engraving of the Port of Ripetta as he saw it in the eighteenth century. Barges loaded with hay and casks of oil and wine, lighters, fishing boats and gondola-like craft with small arched cabins of reeds amidships, are seen pressing forward to a majestic flight of steps and a stately quayside, the creation of Clement XI in 1707. The superb steps recall those in the Piazza di Spagna which they preceded by some twenty years and whose design they possibly influenced. The fountain of Clement XI, which stood on the balustrade above the steps, has fortunately been preserved and is to be seen not far from its original site on the embankment near the Ponte Cavour.

The Rione of Trastevere. Many will think this the most original of the regional fountains. It is in the Via della Cisterna in Trastevere and, in tune with the convivial character of the district, shows a barrel, a vat and two wine measures (plate 38). When the fountain was unveiled in 1927 wine flowed instead of water and a great *festa* was held.

The Rione of the Borgo. This large district, which includes St Peter's and the Vatican, had no fewer than three of Lombardi's fountains. One, which stood in the Piazza Scossa Cavalli, disappeared when the piazza was demolished during the construction of the Via della Conciliazione. The second is one of the most charming of all the regional fountains, the Fountain of the Four Tiaras (plate 37). It is at the Porta Angelica just behind the eastern arm of Bernini's colonnade and shows three papal tiaras connected with the keys of St Peter, surmounted by a fourth tiara. From the handle of each of six keys a spout of water falls into three melon-shaped basins of marble. Perhaps the most unusual of the Borgo fountains is the Cannon-ball fountain near the Castel S. Angelo (plate 36). The inspiration of this fountain was obviously the *Cortile delle Palle* – the Court of the Balls – in the fortress. Beneath a stone and brick arch stands a pyramid of cannon-balls.

Three of the regional fountains. *Above left* The Rione Pigna. *Above right* The fountain in the Piazza della Cancelleria. *Below* The Rione Ripa

One is carved in the shape of a mask from whose mouth the water pours, and on the sides of the arch two cannon-balls embedded in the stone pour streams into two side basins. This is a pleasing and evocative fountain. One remembers the cannon-ball which Benvenuto Cellini claimed to have shot from the nearby castle which slew the Constable of Bourbon during the siege of Rome in 1527, and also the cannon-ball said to have been fired from the same place by Christina of Sweden which ended near the Villa Medici.

The Rione of S. Eustachio. This, the tenth, and last, of Lombardi's regional fountains, is in a short street called the Via dei Staderari which leads from the Piazza Navona to the church of St Eustace and the Pantheon. It is the most puzzling and, to me, the most original of the group. Within an archway, decorated with five stone balls, are four ancient folios, two on each side, upon whose bindings are carved squares, compasses and other architectural implements. The water pours from the books into the bowl of the fountain. Suspended between the books in the centre of the fountain is the pelt of a stag hanging head down. This is a fountain puzzle which no one could interpret without some knowledge of the street changes in this part of Rome.

The name Via dei Staderari has been given to the street only in recent times to commemorate the "Staderari", the scale and weighing-machine makers who in ancient times had their shops and workshops in the locality. The old name of the street was Via dell'Università because it led from the Piazza Navona to the old University, the "Sapienza", now no longer there. The four books symbolize the University, the five stone balls are the Medici *palle* in honour of Leo X, who is considered to have been the second founder, and the skin of the stag is the emblem of the *Rione*, and also of St Eustace.

The diligent explorer may perhaps discover an eleventh regional fountain, which, though it is not the work of Professor Lombardi, is a worthy companion to his group of fountains. It is inset into the wall of a building in the Piazza della Cancelleria, which lies within the region of Parione. It is a work of unusual design: a cardinal's hat with its many pendant tassels forms the background for an oval shield upon which are carved a winged dragon, or griffin, the emblem of Parione, and what to an English eye is a Tudor rose from whose centre water curves into a sarcophagus below. The fountain commemorates not only Parione and its griffin but also its celebrated resident, Cardinal Raffaello Riario, nephew of Sixtus IV, who built the Palazzo della Cancelleria at the close of the fifteenth century. The rose was the heraldic badge of the Riario family. This delightful little fountain was the creation of the late Professor Publio Morbiducci.

XIV
OBELISKS AND FOUNTAINS

THIRTEEN LARGE obelisks survive in Rome from a much larger number, while London, Paris and New York have only one each. Six of the obelisks re-erected by the popes form architectural adornments for fountains; these are, in the order of their re-erection:

> The Vatican obelisk (83 ft), 1586
> The Lateran obelisk (105 ft), 1588
> The obelisk of the Piazza del Popolo (79 ft), 1589
> The obelisk of the Piazza Navona (54 ft), 1651
> The obelisk of the Piazza del Pantheon (20 ft), 1711
> The obelisk of Monte Cavallo (50 ft), 1786

These heights refer to the shafts and do not include plinths and pediments.

The Vatican obelisk

The obelisk now in front of St Peter's was the only one in Rome to remain upright from the time of its erection in the first century until its removal to its present position by Sixtus V in the sixteenth century.

It was brought to Rome by the Emperor Caligula (A.D. 37–41) in a ship specially built in Egypt for the purpose, which was described by Pliny as "nearly as long as the left side of the port of Ostia". Some idea of its size may be gained from the fact that it carried not only the obelisk, which weighed 331 tons, but also 1,000 tons of lentils as ballast. It remained for years as one of the sights of Italy until Claudius decided to use it as the foundation of a new breakwater at Ostia, loading the vessel with concrete until it sank in the required position. The breakwater eventually supported a lighthouse 200 feet in height.

The obelisk was erected in a country racecourse in the Vatican district known as the Circus of Nero, the property of the imperial family, where a sporting young emperor might practice in private the art of driving a four-horsed racing chariot. Side by side with the racecourse, indeed its northern boundary, was a

Plate 45. The Venus fountain in the Villa Doria-Pan

roadside cemetery on the slopes of the Vatican Hill. Ancient tradition has always maintained that St Peter was martyred at the foot of the obelisk in Nero's Circus and that he was buried in the adjacent cemetery.

Two and a half centuries later, Constantine's architects levelled an enormous shelf or platform on the hill and built St Peter's in such a way that the high altar was immediately above the Apostle's tomb; on the south the basilica took in the northern side of the racecourse, whose obelisk, still in its original position, now rose on the south side of the church. Until 1940 archaeologists stated confidently that the south wall of old St Peter's rested upon the northern walls of the racecourse; but in that year excavations under the basilica, authorized by Pius XII, revealed a succession of graves beneath the nave but no sign of the circus wall. Thus the old position of the obelisk became puzzling unless, of course, the spectators in Nero's Circus sat, not on stone seats, but on the grass banks of the Vatican hillside, as in many a country racecourse.

The proposal to move the obelisk to the front of the church was discussed as early as the pontificate of Nicholas V, though nothing was done for a hundred and thirty years. The problem of moving an obelisk that weighed over three hundred tons was one that no engineers had tackled since ancient times. However, this did not deter Sixtus V, who, the moment he was elected, appointed a committee to make plans for its removal and re-erection. The committee of cardinals and bishops, though well out of its depth, did find out that the obelisk, firm as a rock, was leaning seventeen inches from the perpendicular. It was decided in the time-honoured Italian way to hold a competition, and engineers were requested to suggest plans for the task. The beginning of a pontificate was a good moment to hold such a contest since Rome was then full of artists, architects, inventors, also cranks of every description, who had come from many parts of the country in the hope of catching the eye of the new pontiff. No fewer than five hundred are said to have entered the competition.

The winner, perhaps not surprisingly, was the Pope's friend and favourite, Domenico Fontana, who produced a scale model of the obelisk made of lead together with a complicated scaffolding, which became known as "Fontana's Castle". By pulling a string, the miniature obelisk was made to rise from its plinth and then to be lowered to a horizontal position: another pull of the string, and it rose from the horizontal to the vertical. Fourteen years afterwards, in 1590, the year his friend and patron died, Fontana published *Della Trasportatione dell'Obelisco Vaticano*, which is full of fascinating plates depicting the removal and re-erection of the obelisk; one shows the obelisk standing in its old position near the Sacristy while round about are grouped a crowd of competitors with their fantastic machines and scale models.

The night before the task of lifting and moving the obelisk took place Fontana received the blessing of the Pope, and on the following morning, 30 April 1586, the architect, with all who were associated in the work, attended early Mass and communicated. Everything went smoothly. Fontana's calculations were faultless: the obelisk was lifted and lowered to the ground as smoothly and as gently as in his scale model.

Preparations for moving the Vatican obelisk from the south side of St Peter's. The unfinished dome is shown on the left of the picture; below is a portrait of Domenico Fontana

When the obelisk was on the ground, the mediaeval tradition that the bronze ball on the top contained the ashes of Julius Caesar was proved to be without foundation. The ball is now in the Hall of Bronzes in the Museum of the Palazzo dei Conservatori on the Capitol, bearing traces of having been used as a target by the imperial ruffians during the sack of Rome in 1527.

It took five months to erect "Fontana's Castle" in the piazza of St Peter's, preparing the new foundations and drawing the obelisk there. At last, upon 10 September 1586, everything was ready for the re-erection. Large crowds

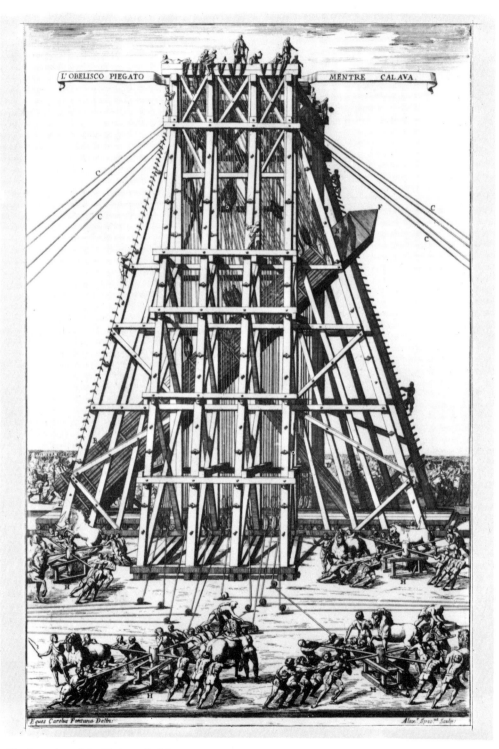

The lowering of the Vatican obelisk

The consecration of the obelisk in the piazza of St Pe

stood behind barriers; absolute silence was commanded under pain of severe punishment. The motive power was that of nine hundred men and a hundred and forty horses harnessed to windlasses. The carpenters who worked on and under "Fontana's Castle" wore iron crash-helmets; commands were given by trumpet while a bell ordered the windlasses to stop. At one moment during the lifting of the obelisk the strain on the cables heated them dangerously and the silence was broken by the voice of a seaman from Bordighera, named Bresca, shouting "Put water on the ropes!" Instead of punishment, he and his descendants were given the right to provide the palms used in St Peter's on Palm Sunday.

The obelisk was raised into its position without any further incident. Later in the month it was exorcised as a pagan monument; as a cross containing a relic was fixed to the summit, the Swiss Guard fired their arquebuses. Unlike all the other obelisks in Rome, it has no hieroglyphs and it is impossible to date it. Instead, it bears a Latin inscription of the first century in which Caligula consecrated it to his predecessors, Augustus and Tiberius. The four sides of the plinth carry inscriptions by Sixtus V. On the north side the obelisk is dedicated to the invincible Cross; the inscription on the south records that Sixtus V removed the monument, which had been dedicated to the wicked cult of heathen gods, with great toil and labour into the precincts of the Apostles; the eastern inscription calls upon all hostile to the Cross to fly, for the Lion of Judah conquers; and on the west Christ's victory and rule are proclaimed, and He is asked to protect His people from all evil. Thus the Pope's inscriptions explain why he was interested in digging up obelisks and re-erecting them in prominent parts of the city: he thought of them as symbols of paganism which it was his duty to exorcise and Christianize.

The obelisk was not at first associated in any way with the fountains. At the time of its erection only the predecessor of the earlier fountain was in existence, and it was not until the end of the seventeenth century and the arrival of the second fountain that the obelisk became part of the best known fountain-obelisk composition in the world (plate 25).

Sixtus V proclaimed an indulgence of ten years for all who, while passing beneath the obelisk, adored the cross upon its summit and said a paternoster. Upon a sunny day in November in 1786 two men were walking up and down in the piazza. One was Goethe, the other was the painter, Johann Tischbein. Goethe noted in his diary that they "walked up and down in the shade of the great obelisk, which is full wide enough for two abreast, eating grapes which we purchased in the neighbourhood".

The Lateran obelisk

In February 1587, an obelisk broken into three portions was discovered at a depth of twenty-four feet below the Circus Maximus. Fontana put five hundred men to dig it out, and three hundred of these were kept busy day and night in holding back water that flowed into the excavation, probably from the Aqua Crabra, one of the most famous of Rome's ancient streams. Sixtus V, having rewarded the finder, ordered Fontana to repeat his success of the year before by removing the new obelisk to the Lateran Square. This was done in 1588 after Fontana had joined the three pieces together and had sawn three feet from the base to make the shaft stand upright.

The Lateran obelisk is the tallest standing obelisk in the world – 105 feet, as compared with 69 feet and 68 feet for the obelisks in New York and London and 74 feet for that in the Place de la Concorde, Paris. These measurements are of the shafts and do not include the plinths. It is not only the most interesting obelisk in Rome; it is also the only obelisk, as the Egyptian inscription states, which was not one of a pair.

It was cut for the Pharaoh Thothmes III (1501 B.C.) who wished it to stand in one of the courts of the temple of Karnak, but he died before it was erected. It was left to his grandson Thothmes IV to erect it in Karnak and add the inscription which states that his grandfather had made it as a monument to the god Amen-Ra and that it was the first instance of the erection of a single obelisk in Thebes. It stood in the temple for more than a thousand years.

In A.D. 330 Constantine the Great decided to remove it to his new city of Constantinople, but it got no further than Alexandria. There it was seen, some twenty-seven years later, by Constantine's successor, Constantius, who had an immense barge made for it on which the stone, which weighed 460 tons, was towed across the Mediterranean by a trireme manned with a crew of three hundred rowers. It was landed on the banks of the Tiber, three miles from Rome, to which it was drawn in a cradle upon rollers, entering the city by the Ostian Gate. Its erection in the Circus Maximus was described by Ammianus Marcellinus, who says that after it had been lifted above its plinth it hung suspended there with "many thousands of men turning it round and round like a millstone, till at last it was placed in the middle of the square".

Exactly when and how this enormous shaft fell is unknown. A contemporary of Fontana's, Michele Mercati, who wrote *Degli obelischi di Roma* in 1589, made a study of all the obelisks which were dug up and re-erected in his time, and he believed that they were not thrown down by earthquakes or by any natural cause, but by man. He said that every obelisk he had seen dug out of the ground was broken in three parts, the lower part showing evidence of fire and holes drilled for the insertion of levers.

The Lateran obelisk is the most ancient monument in Rome.

The obelisk of the Piazza del Popolo

The obelisk which stands in the centre of this square was the first to be seen in ancient Rome. It had been standing in Egypt for approximately thirteen centuries when Augustus saw it after the defeat of Antony and Cleopatra in 31 B.C., and decided to transport it to Italy. He may have intended it to be a symbol of the conquest of Egypt, possibly also a tribute to Apollo, to whom he believed his success to be due. It was consequently twice dedicated to the sun: the first dedication had been to Ra, in the City of the Sun, Heliopolis, thirteen centuries before Augustus dedicated it in Latin. The ship which brought the obelisk to Rome was the first of its kind ever seen by the Romans. The stone weighs about 235 tons.

The obelisk was erected in the Circus Maximus, perhaps about 10 B.C., where it remained throughout the splendours of imperial Rome and during the city's decline and fall. The inscription is unusually interesting, because an Egyptian priest named Hermapion translated the hieroglyphics into Greek, and his version was preserved by the historian Ammianus Marcellinus. All four sides are inscribed with invocations to the sun.

The obelisk was discovered in the ruins of the Circus shortly after the discovery of the Lateran obelisk, thus becoming the third of Fontana's annual obelisks. Sixtus ordered its immediate erection in the Piazza del Popolo where, as I have said, a fountain of the Acqua Vergine had been in existence since 1572. The obelisk joined it in 1589, and together they were the first objects seen by those who entered Rome by the Porta del Popolo until they were parted in the nineteenth century, when the present square was designed. Valadier's reconstruction of the piazza, the most splendid architectural scheme since Michelangelo's design of the Capitol, while it banished the old fountain, gave even greater importance to the obelisk, which now stands in spectacular isolation escorted by four Egyptian lions which still spout Acqua Vergine.

The obelisk of the Piazza Navona

This obelisk, which forms the central feature of Bernini's Fountain of the Four Rivers, would have been shipped to England had the Earl of Arundel found it easily portable, states John Evelyn in his *Diary*. Evelyn saw it in the year

Plate 47. The Fountain of the Dragons at the Villa d'

1645 when it was lying broken in five pieces near the tomb of Cecilia Metella on the Appian Way. The shaft was quarried at Syene in Egypt, by order of the Emperor Domitian (A.D. 82–96) and, having been transported to Rome, was possibly erected outside the temple of Isis and Serapis in the Campus Martius, which that emperor restored after it had been burnt down. The strange thing about the obelisk is that while the stonework is exemplary the hieroglyphics are in Babu Egyptian, and, as Sir E. A. Wallis Budge wrote, "no Egyptian ever cut the inscriptions on it". It is unique among Roman obelisks as one upon which a Roman emperor is seen dressed as an ancient Egyptian pharaoh in the act of offering bread, wine and incense to an Egyptian god. The inscription also mentions, in hieroglyphics, Domitian's father, the Emperor Vespasian, and his brother, Titus.

The obelisk was removed to the Appian Way about A.D. 309 and erected in the circus which the Emperor Maxentius had built in memory of his deceased son, Romulus, whose tomb was nearby. No one knows when it fell down and became lost amid the ruins of the circus. It is known, however, that it was suggested to Sixtus V that it might be dug up and erected outside the church of S. Sebastiano, which, with its catacombs, is not far away; but for some reason the Pope never carried this out. In 1651 Innocent X ordered the five pieces of granite to be brought to the Piazza Navona to be put together by Bernini and incorporated by him in his design for the central Fountain of the Four Rivers. Thus it was the curious fate of a monument, first erected by Domitian, to return after centuries of oblivion and neglect to occupy the place of honour in a piazza which had been originally designed as an amphitheatre by the same emperor. Many will think Bernini's Four Rivers the most successful, certainly the most dramatic, combination of obelisk and fountain in Rome (plate 15).

The obelisk of the Piazza del Pantheon

This, the smallest of the fountain obelisks (plate 3), was thought by the Italian archaeologist, Antonio Nibby, to be a Roman imitation, though Sir E. A. Wallis Budge believed it to be genuine and suggested that it had once stood outside the Temple of the Sun in Heliopolis. It bears the name and titles of Rameses II. It is not known when it was brought to Rome or when and by whom it was erected in the forecourt of the temple of Isis and Serapis, for, like the column in the Piazza Navona, it is said to have been discovered in that rich mine of ancient Egyptian sculpture. This obelisk has a twin in the public park, once the Villa Mattei. Both obelisks were discovered in the fourteenth century.

The sanctuary of Isis occupied a site on the line of the present Via del Collegio Romano; Lanciani said that whatever may be left of that great structure is concealed by the buildings of the Via di S. Ignazio and the Via di S. Stefano del Cacco. The Egyptian priests with their shaven skulls and white linen garments were a familiar sight in ancient Rome, and many fashionable women were numbered among their converts. During the morality drive in the reign of Tiberius, mentioned by Tacitus, among others, an incident occurred in the temple of Isis, reported by Josephus, which gave Tiberius cause to expel the Egyptians and close the temple. After casually mentioning the crucifixion of Christ, Josephus says that about the same time a shameful event occurred in the Iseum at Rome. He tells the following story.

A wealthy young Roman named Decius Mundus fell in love with a young married woman named Paulina, who was a model of virtue and modesty; her husband, Saturninus, was said also to have been an admirable character. When Mundus found that Paulina rejected his advances, he announced that he would starve himself to death. The members of his household included a freedwoman named Ide, a female "skilful in all sorts of mischief", who managed to convince her employer that, given sufficient gold, she could entrap the object of his passion. He readily gave her the money. Ide knew that Paulina was a devout follower of Isis. She went to the temple and offered to give the gold to the high priest if Paulina could be beguiled. The priest accordingly went to see Paulina and told her that the god Anubis had revealed that he had fallen in love with her and wished her to go to him in the temple that night. Paulina told her husband that she had received a summons to go and sup and spend the night with the god Anubis, to which Saturninus, convinced of his wife's virtue, amiably gave his consent.

> Accordingly, she went to the temple [wrote Josephus], and after she had supped there, and it was the hour to go to sleep, the priest shut the doors of the temple; when, in the holy part of it, the lights were also put out. Then did Mundus leap out (for he was hidden therein) and did not fail of enjoying her, who was at his service all the night long, as supposing he was the god; and when he was gone away, which was before those priests who knew nothing of this stratagem were stirring, Paulina came early to her husband and told him how the god Anubis had appeared to her.

Three days afterwards, Mundus, meeting Paulina in the street, confessed the plot to her. Horrified, she went to her husband and begged him to help her. He went at once to the Emperor and told the story. The result was that an enquiry was held, the temple was closed, the priests were crucified and the statue of Isis was thrown into the Tiber. Ide, the freedwoman, was also put to death, and Mundus was exiled.

But the cult of Isis had enormous vitality. The temple was thriving again in the reign of Titus (A.D. 79–82), when a fire in A.D. 80, that lasted for three days, destroyed it, together with the Pantheon and the Baths of Agrippa. The damage in the district was so great that it took years to repair and the rebuilding extended over the reigns of Domitian, Nerva, Trajan, and Hadrian. One of the earliest buildings to be restored was the temple of Isis, which Domitian rebuilt with great lavishness, bringing over from Egypt the stones of an ancient sanctuary and re-erecting them in the Campus Martius.

The two fountain obelisks I have mentioned are not the only ones which are said to have come from the temple of Isis. In all, these number no fewer than five: the Pantheon obelisk; the obelisk of the Fountain of the Four Rivers in the Piazza Navona; the obelisk of the former Villa Mattei; the small obelisk which Bernini mounted on the back of an elephant in the Piazza della Minerva; and the obelisk discovered in 1883 near S. Maria sopra Minerva (the twin of the Pantheon obelisk), now incorporated in the Dogali Monument near the Central Railway Station.

Even remote provincial towns had their temples of Isis. The London Museum, in Kensington, possesses a jug found in Southwark on which some Londoner of the first century had scratched the words, *Londini, ad fanum Isidis,* "London, at the temple of Isis".

The obelisk of Monte Cavallo

The obelisk that stands between the Dioscuri on Monte Cavallo is one of a pair found at different periods near the tomb of Augustus. The first to be discovered, in 1587, during the pontificate of Sixtus V, was erected by Fontana outside S. Maria Maggiore, where it still stands. The second was not unearthed until 1786, when Pope Pius VI ordered it to be incorporated with the Quirinal fountain.

Both these obelisks were quarried in Egypt and some believe that they were shipped to Rome by Domitian. There is little to be said about them save that they do not appear to have been set up near the Mausoleum of Augustus until a late period, and are probably the two obelisks referred to by Ammianus Marcellinus – *Duo in Augusti monumento erecti sunt.*

To some, the Monte Cavallo obelisk is the happiest conjunction of obelisk and fountain in Rome.

XV

COURTYARD AND
VILLA FOUNTAINS

THOUGH fountains in courtyards and villas are beyond the scope of this book, they are only technically private and anyone sufficiently interested can easily see them. Every palace courtyard has its fountain, often elaborate like the baroque vitality of the courtyard of the Palazzo del Grillo (plate 40), but sometimes as simple as an ancient sarcophagus into which water slowly drips through a bed of fern and moss.

The monstrous traffic of Rome has within recent years overflowed even into the once peaceful courtyards of the palaces, which now have become parking places for those with flats or offices in the buildings. A few courtyards are, however, still inviolate. Having descended the ramp from the Capitol, it is worth while to cross the road to the palace almost immediately opposite, the Palazzo Massimi all'Ara Coeli, and ask the caretaker's permission to enter the courtyard where, in semi-darkness, a triton seated in water (a family connection obviously of Bernini's Triton) receives, from what appears to be centuries of duckweed-green moss, streams of water upon his worn shoulders.

A few steps from the Corso Vittorio Emanuele II, the fountain connoisseur should trespass for a moment in the courtyard of the Palazzo Massimo alle Colonne, whose semicircular portico supported by Doric columns cannot be missed. Here, again in semi-darkness, a charming Venus stands in an architectural alcove while several thin streams of water curve upwards towards her (plate 41). This fountain is entirely classical in spirit and might indeed have survived from the time of Hadrian.

A different type of courtyard fountain is to be seen in the garden of the Palazzo Venezia where, within a circle of palm trees known as "the oasis", a large statuesque composition by Carlo Monaldi dates from 1730. It depicts Venice most strangely in the guise of a young female Doge in the act of casting the ring of the Serenissima into the water, while round about four cherubic infants symbolize the Venetian conquests of Cyprus, Dalmatia, the Morea and Candia.

The fountain in the courtyard of the Institute of Biblical Studies

It is an eccentric product of Venetian decadence, and though it might be rash to say that it is the only example in sculpture of the Republic as a good-looking young female, I can think of no other.

The fountains of the villas were naturally among the most elaborate in Rome and many of these are still in working order. The public fountains of the Borghese Gardens are well known, so are those of the Villa Sciarra on the Janiculum (plate 39). Also upon the slopes of the Janiculum are the gardens of the Villa Corsini, where a delightful water staircase is still in working order (plate 44). The fountains of the Villa Medici enliven what is one of the finest Renaissance gardens left in Rome.

Less accessible, and less known, is the park of the Villa Doria-Pamphilj which is some six miles in area and carries the Acqua Paola into Rome upon its boundary wall. Among its fountains is a grotto in which a statue of Venus holds a marble shell at waist level (plate 45), but the most interesting of the fountains is Bernini's Fountain of the Snail (plate 46), now strangely isolated in an English-looking park and sometimes surrounded by grazing sheep. It is believed that Bernini designed this fountain for the Piazza Navona but Innocent X thought it too small

Detail of a fountain in the Villa Pamphilj   The sarcophagus fountain in the Via Bocca di Leone

and insignificant for such a site. It is also said that the Pope's imperious sister-in-law, Donna Olimpia, liked it and lost no time in claiming it for the Villa Doria-Pamphilj.

Many unknown fountains are to be discovered in villas and palaces, such as that in the courtyard of the Institute of Biblical Studies in the Via della Pilotta, which some think was designed in the reign of Sixtus V. It is remarkable for a new kind of aquatic creature, half lion and half fish, an unsatisfactory freak which shows how sensible fountain designers were to stick to dolphins (plate 43).

Fountains which are in a category of their own are the innumerable ancient sarcophagi used as horse troughs which are to be seen all over Renaissance Rome. Some are pagan, many are Christian, and most of them came from the tombs of distinguished citizens of ancient Rome. A typical example is the richly carved sarcophagus in the Via Bocca di Leone, near the Piazza di Spagna, which receives a spout of water from a bearded mask.

XVI
THE VILLA D'ESTE

THE FOUNTAINS of the Villa d'Este at Tivoli twenty miles from Rome have been numbered among the sights of Italy for four hundred years, and they may be seen more easily and to better advantage today than at any time since the sixteenth century. After dark they are romantically illuminated in a manner that would have delighted their creator, Cardinal Ippolito d'Este II, as well as those whose names have been associated with the Villa in later times, such as Fragonard and Liszt.

Cardinal Ippolito was the son of Lucrezia Borgia and Alfonso d'Este, Duke of Ferrara. He was born in 1508 and educated in France. While still in his thirties, he became the richest and the most aristocratic cardinal of the time. He was an art collector, a supporter of the d'Este alliance with France, and a builder of palaces whose halls were filled with a princely household of two hundred and fifty gentlemen and servants. When he was Papal Nuncio in France, his relations with Francis I were those of a fellow monarch rather than those of a churchman, and the bond between them was strengthened by Ippolito's connoisseurship.

He was the "Cardinal of Ferrara", so frequently mentioned by Benvenuto Cellini in his *Life*, who managed to release the artist from the dungeons of the Castel S. Angelo into which he had been flung on a charge of stealing jewels from the papal tiara during the Siege of Rome. Once Cellini had been freed, the Cardinal arranged for him to work in Paris as goldsmith to Francis I, where he made the famous salt-cellar now in the Kunsthistorisches Museum, Vienna. At first Cellini admired and revered the Cardinal but later characteristically turned against him, embittered possibly by imaginary grievances.

Returning to Italy, Cardinal Ippolito swayed the French faction in favour of the election of Pope Julius III (1550-55), and was rewarded with the Governorship of Tivoli. Both Pope and Cardinal were characters from the golden days of the Renaissance who were obliged to move on the chillier and more restricted stage of the Counter-Reformation. Both were great builders and both erected famous villas: the Pope built the Villa Giulia on the Pincian Hill, the Cardinal built the Villa d'Este at Tivoli. Julius commanded the services of Vignola and Vasari with Michelangelo as adviser; Ippolito sought the help of an extra-ordinary genius, Pirro Ligorio, who has yet to find his biographer.

Ligorio, too, was a Renaissance character. He had arrived in Rome from Naples about 1540 and had made a name as archaeologist, architect, epigraphist and topographer. There was scarcely an excavation on any classical site from 1540 to 1568 that Ligorio did not conduct, or examine and describe. His energy was prodigious. There are twenty-two of his folio volumes illustrated with thousands of pen and ink sketches in the archives of Turin, ten more volumes in Naples, one in the Bodleian, at Oxford, and two in the Vatican Library. Unfortunately the great man had one unforgivable and unforgettable sin: he could not, it seems, help falsifying evidence. Sometimes he did this so clumsily that no one could have been deceived, at others so brilliantly that the greatest experts were taken in.

The Villa d'Este, a print of 1581. Among the fountains shown are the Fountain of the Dragons (23), the Avenue of the Hundred Fountains (13), the Oval fountain (17), the Fountain of Rome (21), and the Owl fountain (22)

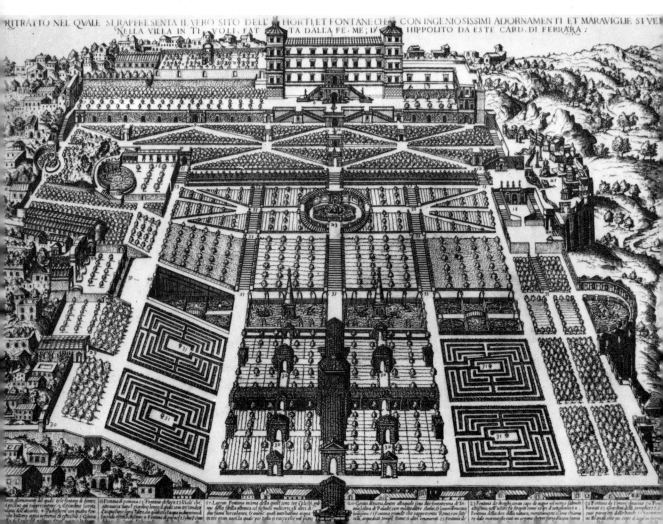

The Owl fountain at the Villa d'Este, showing trick fountain jets spurting up from the pavement. The owl can be seen standing on the rim of the upper bowl of the fountain

His has been called "the blackest name in the calendar of Renaissance forgers". But it is impossible to dislike Ligorio. He made nothing out of his misdeeds or, if he did, he was never able to save anything. Perhaps the day may come when someone who admires the summerhouse of Pius IV in the Vatican Gardens and the Villa and gardens at Tivoli – two of his best essays in perfection – will tell the story of his life, and place him against the background of Renaissance forgery; perhaps, after all, a branch of art rather than of crime.

The Villa d'Este was conceived by Cardinal Ippolito, and planned by Ligorio, soon after 1550, but years of hard work in terracing the ground and in engineering the water supply from the river Anio were necessary before anything could be seen. Most of the fountains were, however, functioning by the sixties of the century when the first pontiff to admire them was Pius V (1566–72); in 1572 Gregory XIII visited the gardens in the first year of his pontificate and was so fascinated by the water organ that he insisted on encores and asked to meet the inventor. Thus the fountains of the Villa d'Este are earlier by a decade than the fountains of the Acqua Vergine, and contemporary with such famous creations as the Neptune fountain in Bologna and the Neptune of Stoldi Lorenzi, who was already lifting a dripping trident upon his rock in the Boboli Gardens lake in Florence. One can imagine what an inspiration the Tivoli fountains must have been to those like Domenico Fontana, Flaminio Vacca and the two della Portas who in the years to come were to fill the squares of Rome with the whisper and rustle of the Acqua Vergine.

It may appear remarkable to anyone who knows how easily a garden can be altered at the whim of the owner, to see how closely the gardens of the Villa d'Este, four centuries after their construction, resemble the earliest plans and engravings. The reason is, of course, that they are constructed upon an elaborate system of underground canals, culverts, water mains and pipes, and to change them would have involved an engineering feat of some magnitude. The marvel is not that they should have remained unchanged but that they should still exist. The intractable element which endows them with their beauty and their fame might easily have deserted them, and indeed the neglect into which the gardens fell in the eighteenth and nineteenth centuries nearly brought this about.

As we walk beneath the giant cypresses and admire the Avenue of the Hundred Fountains (plate 48), with the Oval Fountain at one end and Rometta, or Little Rome, at the other; as we see the Fountain of the Dragons (plate 47), of the Owl, of Proserpine, of Diana, and the Rotunda of the Cypresses, which so delighted Liszt, all of them, though sadly eroded, much as they were seen by men of the sixteenth century, we may reflect with sorrow that the owner of such peace and beauty received small consolation from his creation. The irony which sometimes presides over the last years of millionaires decreed that Cardinal Ippolito should not have been a happy man. Suffering from gout and allied ailments, his political life ruined by the enmity of France and the hostility of Paul IV and Pius V, his hopes of the papal tiara finally frustrated, his infrequent visits to his villa were rarely carefree, poisoned, as they were, by the hatred of the citizens of Tivoli to whom opposition to their governor was almost a tradition. He died in Rome aged sixty-four and was buried in S. Maria Maggiore in Tivoli.

After his death the Villa was owned by one Este cardinal after another until eventually it passed to the dukes of Ferrara. It was shamefully neglected during the sixteenth and seventeenth centuries and became a wilderness during the eighteenth and nineteenth. The vegetation, nourished by so much water, became riotous. At one period in the eighteenth century, in 1743, the Villa was offered for sale, but there were no buyers. Still, to artists and poets the gardens had never been more enchanting. Fragonard found there the inspiration that was to form and influence his style. As a young *pensionnaire* of the French Academy at the Villa

The Fountain of the Dragons at the Villa d'E

Medici he spent a summer at the Villa d'Este in 1760 with the Abbé de Saint-Non, who wrote: "Fragonard is all on fire; his drawings are very numerous; one cannot wait for another; they enchant me. I find in them some sort of sorcery." A lovely memory of that visit is his *Gardens of the Villa d'Este* in the Wallace Collection, London, which shows the Eagle fountain with the balustrade above and two statues embowered in enormous trees.

When the male line of the Estensi came to an end in 1803, the Villa d'Este was inherited by Maria Beatrice d'Este who had married the Archduke Ferdinand of Austria; and under Habsburg ownership the Villa sank still further into decay. There was only one bright period, from 1850 to 1896, when a young German priest, Monsignor Gustav Adolf von Hohenlohe, brother of Prince Hohenlohe, fell in love with it and longed to see it once again a centre of art and learning. He obtained from the Austrian crown the lease for life without rent on the under-standing that he kept the buildings and gardens in repair. Hohenlohe had a rapid and successful ecclesiastical career. In 1865, the year before he became a cardinal, he received his friend, the musician Liszt, into the Church, an event which pro-vided some amusement for the Roman cynics who said that Liszt had retreated into the priesthood to avoid marriage with the Princess Wittgenstein, whose divorce had come through at that moment; a suggestion, however, that was unjust. But Liszt never received more than the first four of the seven degrees of priesthood, which left him free to return to a layman's life, if he wished, and even to marry, but it admitted him to the numerous company of those in Rome at the time who, enjoying the odour of sanctity without responsibility, were entitled to wear clerical gowns and shovel hats and to use the title of Abbé.

Liszt was the most distinguished of the artists, musicians and men of letters who were invited by Cardinal Hohenlohe to stay at the Villa d'Este. For many years he arrived in September and spent two or three months there enjoying the tranquillity of the gardens and composing music. He also presumably enjoyed immunity from the women who continued to pursue him, though he was then in his fifties. He composed there the third volume of the *Années de Pèlerinage*, which includes "Les jeux d'eaux à la Villa d'Este" and the two threnodies, "Cyprès de la Villa d'Este", in which one can hear the tinkle and rush of the fountains and envisage the gloom of the cypress trees.

The transformation of Liszt into the silver-haired Abbé, as odd a metamor-phosis as Byron in holy orders (if such a thought were possible), did not interfere with his emotional life, indeed the Abbé's gown was perhaps an added induce-ment to those admirers who were always assaulting a citadel that was only too

detail of the Avenue of the Hundred Fountains at the Villa d'Este willing to capitulate. Consequently, it is not surprising that the Villa d'Este was to witness an unusual incident during one of Liszt's visits there. This was the pursuit of the ageing *maestro* by a violent Russian girl of nineteen, Olga Janina. She was, of course, a countess. In the words of his biographer, Ernest Newman, Liszt "collected princesses and countesses as other men collect rare butterflies, or Japanese prints, or first editions" (or should one say that they collected Liszt?).

Olga Janina had married, when fifteen, a husband whom she had horse-whipped during the honeymoon and left, to become a mother at sixteen. She had musical inclinations and, arriving in Rome, persuaded Liszt to take her as a pupil. When her efforts became not entirely musical Liszt took fright and fled to the Villa d'Este. This did not deter his admirer. Dressing herself as a gardener's boy, and holding a bunch of flowers, she was admitted to the gardens and was not long in discovering her victim. Liszt put up a token struggle but soon surrendered. When the affair ended with Olga's attempt to kill her lover and herself (she appeared ready for all contingencies with a pistol and poison), she retired to Paris and described the love-affair under the guise of fiction. She confessed that in the morning, as she waited for her lover to awaken, she was grasping a dagger with the intention of killing him should his first words be remorseful, but, happily for Liszt, they were affectionate.

When, with the death of Cardinal Hohenlohe in 1896, the ownership of the Villa d'Este reverted to the Austrian crown, neglect once more choked and tangled the gardens. The Villa was once again merely a costly encumbrance. Nevertheless, a frequent visitor of that time was the Archduke Franz Ferdinand whose assassination at Sarajevo was the prelude to the first world war. With Italy's declaration of war against Austria the Villa was confiscated and has remained ever since the property of the Italian Government. Thanks to the care and restoration carried out by the *Direzione Generale delle Antichità e Belle Arti*, the Villa d'Este and its foundations have been restored to life. Happily they survived a threat to their existence in 1944 when, during the second world war, an air raid on Tivoli destroyed a portion of the Villa and damaged the water pipes so badly that for the first time for centuries the fountains ceased to flow.

Now, however, restored once more, the white lances are tossed into the sky and the rivers rush over the ancient stones; and as one sees the blown mist, like smoke, above the Cascade, and as one stands beneath the Oval Fountain in a cool cavern whose walls are falling water, one may remember Fragonard and Liszt, or perhaps reflect that these noble fountains were the forerunners of the fountains of Rome.

BIBLIOGRAPHY

Acqua e luce per Roma, Azienda Comunale Elettricità ed Acque, Rome, 1958.

Ashby, Thomas, *The Aqueducts of Ancient Rome*, Oxford, 1935.

Beckett, Walter, *Liszt*, Master Musicians series, London and New York, 1956.

Budge, E. A. Wallis, *Cleopatra's Needles and other Egyptian Obelisks*, London, 1926.

Coffin, David R., *The Villa d'Este at Tivoli*, Princeton, N. J., 1960.

Corsetti, G., *Acquedotti di Roma*, Rome, 1937.

Creighton, M., *A History of the Papacy during the period of the Reformation*, London, 1897.

D'Onofrio, Cesare, *Le Fontane di Roma*, Rome, 1957.

Engelbach, R., *The Problem of the Obelisks*, London, 1923.

Farnell, L. R., *The Cults of the Greek States*, five vols, Oxford, 1896-1909.

Fermor, Patrick Leigh, *Mani, Travels in the Southern Peloponnese*, London, 1958.

Frontinus, Sextus Julius, *The Stratagems and the Aqueducts of Rome*, Loeb Classical Library, London and New York, 1925.

Gaddo, B. di, *Le Fontane di Roma*, Genoa, 1964.

Gregorovius, F., *History of the City of Rome in the Middle Ages*, six vols, London, 1894-8.

Herschel, Clemens, *The two books* [of Frontinus] *on the Water Supply of the City of Rome*, Boston, 1899, London, 1913.

Lanciani, Rodolfo, *I commentarii di Frontino le acque e gli acquedotti*, 1880; *The Destruction of Ancient Rome*, London, 1899; *The Ruins and Excavations of Ancient Rome*, London, 1897.

Lawson, John Cuthbert, *Modern Greek Folklore and Ancient Greek Religion: a study in survivals*, Cambridge, 1910.

Masson, Georgina, *Italian Gardens*, London, 1961; *Italian Villas and Palaces*, London, 1959.

Mastrigli, F., *Acque, Acquedotti e Fontane di Roma*, Rome, 1928.

Middleton, J. H., *The Remains of Ancient Rome*, London, 1892.

Pausanias's Description of Greece, translated with a commentary by J. G. Frazer, six vols, London, 1898.

Pecchiai, P., *Acquedotti e fontane di Roma nel cinquecento*, Rome, 1944.

Rodd (James Rennell), Baron Rennell, *The Customs and Lore of Modern Greece*, London, 1892.

Scherer, Margaret R., *Marvels of Ancient Rome*, London, 1955.

Van Deman, Esther, *The Building of the Roman Aqueducts*, Washington, 1934.

Vitruvius Pollio, Marcus, *On Architecture*, Loeb Classical Library, two vols, London and New York, 1931-4.

Winslow, E. M., *A Libation to the Gods*, London, 1963.

INDEX

The figures in *italic type* indicate illustrations.

294